THE BIBLE
AND THE
HISTORIAN

THE BIBLE
AND THE
HISTORIAN

*Breaking the Silence About God
in Biblical Studies*

PAUL S. MINEAR

ABINGDON PRESS
NASHVILLE

THE BIBLE AND THE HISTORIAN
BREAKING THE SILENCE ABOUT GOD IN BIBLICAL STUDIES

Copyright © 2002 by Abingdon Press

This book is printed on elemental-chlorine-free paper.

Library of Congress Cataloging-in-Publication Data

Minear, Paul Sevier, 1906–
    The Bible and the historian : breaking the silence about God in
biblical studies / Paul S. Minear.
        p.   cm.
Includes index.
    ISBN 0-687-03043-9 (Bdg.: pbk.: alk. paper)
        1. Bible—Theology.   2. Bible. N.T.—Criticism, interpretation, etc.
I. Title.
    BS543 .M56 2002
    225.6'7—dc21   2002008839

A form of chapter 1 first appeared as "J.S. Bach and J. A. Ernesti" by Paul Minear, from OUR COMMON HISTORY AS CHRISTIANS, edited by Leroy Howe, copyright © 1975 by Oxford University Press, Inc. Used by permission of Oxford University Press, Inc.

A form of chapter 2 first appeared as a lecture presented by invitation to the 23rd Convention of the Catholic Theological Society in Washington, D.C. June, 1968, published as "The Transcendence of God and Biblical Hermeneutics" in the *Proceedings* of that Society (Yonkers: St. Joseph's Seminary), 23:1-19.

A form of chapter 3 first appeared as "Christian Eschatology and Historical Methodology," *Neutestamentliche Studien für Rudolf Bultmann*, ed., W. Eltester (Berlin: Alfred Töpelmann, 1954); Beihefte 21, *Zeitschrift für die neutestamentliche Wissenschaft*.

A form of chapter 4 first appeared as a presidential address at the annual meeting of the Society of New Testament Studies, published as "Ontology and Ecclesiology in the Apocalypse," *New Testament Studies*, 12 (1966): 89-105. Reprinted with the permission of Cambridge University Press.

A form of chapter 5 originally appeared in the Dudleian Lecture at Harvard University (April 27, 1954), published as "Revelation and the Church's Knowledge of God," *Harvard Divinity School Bulletin* 20 (1954): 19-37.

A form of chapter 6 first appeared as an address to a conference of priests of the Church of Sweden in 1947, published in 1950 as Supplement 13 in the *Svensk Exegetisk Arsbok*, and later reprinted as "The Interpreter and the Nativity Stories," *Theology Today* 7 (1950): 358-75.

A form of chapter 7 first appeared as "On Seeing the Good News," *Theology Today* 55 (1998), 163-74. It also appeared as Supplement 2 in my book, *The Good News According to Matthew: A Training Manual for Prophets* (St. Louis: Chalice Press, 2000), 137-48.

A form of chapter 8 first appeared as one of the Laidlaw Lectures delivered at Knox College in the University of Toronto, published in revised form as "Some Glimpses of Luke's Sacramental Theology," *Worship* 44 (1970): 322-31.

A form of chapter 9 first appeared as Paul S. Minear, "Logos Affiliations in Johannine Thought," in *Christology in Dialogue*, Robert F. Berkey and Sarah A. Edwards (Cleveland: The Pilgrim Press, 1993), 142-56. Copyright © 1993. Used by permission.

A form of chapter 10 first appeared as "The Promise of Life in the Gospel of John," *Theology Today* 49 (1993): 485-99.

A form of chapter 11 first appeared as "The Family" *The Poetics of Faith*, ed. W. A. Beardslee (Missoula: Society of Biblical Literature, 1978), 201-13.

A form of chapter 12 first appeared as "The Cosmology of the Apocalypse," *Current Issues in New Testament Interpretation*, ed. W. Klassen and G. F. Snyder (New York: Harper, 1962), 23-37. Used by permission of HarperCollins Publishers.

A form of chapter 13 first appeared as "Some Pauline Thoughts on Dying," *From Faith to Faith*, ed. D. Y. Hadidian (Pittsburgh: Pickwick, 1979), 91-106.

A form of chapter 14 first appeared as one in a series of lectures delivered at Boston University, published as "Peace in the New Testament," *Celebrating Peace*, ed. L. S. Rouner (South Bend: University of Notre Dame, 1990), 118-31.

A form of chapter 15 first appeared as "Theology—Vocation or Profession?" *Doing Theology Today*, ed. Choan-Seng Song (Madras: Christian Literature Society, 1976), 1-16.

A form of chapter 16 first appeared as a lecture at Duquesne University, published in *Unterwegs zur Einheit*, eds. J. Brantschen and P. Selvatico (Freiburg: Herder, 1980), 791-802.

A form of chapter 17 first appeared as "The Crucified World, The Enigma of Galatians 6:14," *Theologia Crucis, Signum Crucis*, ed. C. Andresen and G. Klein (Tübingen: J. C. B. Mohr, 1979), 395-408.

A form of chapter 18 first appeared as "To Ask and To Receive: Some Clues to Johannine Ontology," *Intergerini Parietis Septum*, ed. D. Y. Hadidian (Pittsburgh: Pickwick, 1981), 227-50.

A form of chapter 19 first appeared as "Thanksgiving as a Synthesis of the Temporal and the Eternal," *Anglican Theological Review* 38 (1956): 4-14; and then in *A Kierkegaard Critique*, ed. H. A. Johnson & N. Thulstrup (New York: Harper, 1962), 292-308. Used by permission of HarperCollins Publishers.

A form of chapter 20 first appeared as "Gratitude and Mission in the Epistle to the Romans," *Basileia*, ed. J. Hermelink and H. J. Margull (Stuttgart: Evangelische Missionsverlag, 1959), 42-48.

A form of chapter 21 was originally published in *The Conversation Continues: Studies in Paul and John*, edited by Robert Fortna and Beverly Gaventa © 1990 Abingdon Press. Used by permission.

02 03 04 05 06 07 08 09 10 11—10 9 8 7 6 5 4 3 2 1

MANUFACTURED IN THE UNITED STATES OF AMERICA

To
Richard Hoffman Minear
whose expert help has made this book possible

CONTENTS

FOREWORD

It was the biblical scholar Johann Albrecht Bengel who coined the saying,

> Apply yourself wholly to the text;
> apply the text wholly to yourself.

As Bengel worded it, this maxim is an exhortation with considerable value. Generations of church members have heeded its prompting, whether they knew of Bengel or not; and in doing so they have contributed to periods of remarkable church health. But what would we make of Bengel's maxim if we altered its second line, changing it to read,

> Apply yourself wholly to the text;
> and the text will apply itself wholly to you!

Clearly that would wake us up. For what Bengel composed as a hortatory rule would now become a promissory declaration, describing what actually happens—what will continue to happen—when we read the Bible with care. In such reading, the Bible ceases to be a mere object; it takes hold of us.

As a partial analogy we may think of our experience with the arts of music and painting. After a concert—say one centered in Brahms's *Requiem*—we sometimes comment that we were carried away, not by our choice, but by the combined power of music and word.* And the same can happen in the viewing of a painting. We cannot truly look at

---

* On the Requiem of Brahms note especially Minear's *Death Set to Music* (Atlanta: John Knox Press, 1987). On Bach's cantatas, and on the venues in which such music was and is performed, see the first chapter in the present volume; also C. Wright, *Listening to Music* (St. Paul: West, 1996), 133.

Vermeer's "Head of a Young Girl," for example, without sensing that she was looking at us before we turned our glance to her: "to meet this girl's gaze is to be *implicated* in its urgency."* We are similarly implicated when we immerse ourselves in the biblical traditions, even when—perhaps especially when—we find them strange to our ears.

It is first of all here that revered Yale professor and ecumenical pioneer Paul Minear proves to be a truly extraordinary guide. For well over half a century he has been directing his attention to the text of the Bible, especially that of the New Testament, while being keenly aware that, all the while, that text has been directing its attention to him. And he has written honestly and engagingly about the fruit that ripens precisely along the interpretive path that bears traffic in both directions. We bring our questions to the writers of the New Testament, and they in turn question us. To read the Bible with care is to find more than what we normally call "meaning"; it is to be implicated in a textual *event*.

Why is Bible reading an event? Because of God! As the subtitle of this book declares, *the* subject of the Bible is inextricably God. This God continues day by day to speak to us by means of the Bible. And in his speaking he proves to be the persistently gracious hound of heaven who, caring infinitely about us, will not leave us to our own devices. In the Bible God is known, in fact, as the One Who Comes. There is, then, no neutral reading of this ancient text. When, as Christians, we turn to the New Testament, when, that is, we are addressed by early Christian traditions, we are inevitably immersed in the doing of *theology* in the presence of God.

We are, however, addressed by other traditions as well, notably those that have developed since the eighteenth-century Enlightenment, and these humanistic traditions often arrest us with their own extraordinary power. We read the Bible not only as children of Abraham—literally and/or spiritually—but also as children of Isaac Newton, John Locke, Adam Smith, Immanuel Kant, and others. Referring to descent through traditions, then, we may say that Christians have two parents, the traditions of the Bible and the traditions and disciplines of scientific modernity. And this dual parentage presents its own issues.

Do we detect, for example, consistent harmony and mutual reinforcement between our two tradition-parents? And if so, do we then find it relatively simple to read the Bible as children of the Enlightenment? One might think so, for in the West a large part of biblical studies moves right

---

* E. Snow, *A Study of Vermeer* (Berkeley: University of California Press, 1994), 3 (emphasis added).

along on a simple assumption: As the "important" biblical traditions played their own part in leading to the Enlightenment, so the interpretive traditions developed from that base convey us without great difficulty back to the Bible. It is vis-à-vis this assumption that Paul Minear calls us sharply to attention.

To be sure, in many regards there is familial harmony between our two lines of tradition, causing us to be greatly enriched by both. As numerous Western philosophers and statesmen have seen, both lines place great weight, for instance, on liberty, even if they do not use the word in precisely the same way. There are junctures, however, at which one or the other of our tradition-parents threatens to marginalize the other. Much to our detriment, for example, a literalistic reading of scripture can shove aside the traditions of the Enlightenment.

It is, however, the opposite threat that claims the principal attention of Paul Minear, namely the degree to which a simple and single-minded devotion to scientific historiography can severely attenuate our ability to hear the strange word of scripture. Minear himself can lead us to give thanks for the Enlightenment's liberation from the dead letter of dead doctrine. His chief concern, however, is to wake us up to the numerous ways in which, pursued by itself—and thus virtually canonized—scientific interpretation can blind our eyes to God's revelation and stop our ears to God's Word.

> There are more things in heaven and earth, Horatio,
> Than are dreamt of in your philosophy.*

With his colleagues in the biblical guild, then, Minear works as a critical, historical exegete discovering riches old and new as he interprets text after text. But precisely as he listens—precisely *because* he listens—he often hears an unfamiliar voice addressing him, one that challenges some of the presuppositions of the method by which he learned to discern that voice. It is as though a well-trained archaeologist successfully unearthed a mummy, only to have the mummy sit up and pose questions about the very method by which it had been discovered! That may seem a rather bizarre analogy, but metaphorically applied to our author, it has the virtue of reminding us that, without abandoning the best of biblical scholarship, he is ready to be questioned by the strange Word of God, and in *all* regards. He is thus a paradigm of the biblical scholar who stands *under* the Word, following it where it leads.

Think of the various settings in which we read the Bible. We sometimes open it in solitude, thirsty for a word that speaks to us individually.

---

* Shakespeare, *Hamlet*, 1.5.

We read it in our families. We study it in the classroom, knowing that a paper will shortly come due. Finally we read it aloud and indeed sing it in our worship communities. The last two of these are of paramount importance, and in this volume they are given special attention in their relationship to each other.

For when we listen intently in our classrooms in order *to prepare* ourselves to listen faithfully and effectively in our churches, we hear these texts much as did those who heard them originally. Patiently leading us by the hand, then, Minear transports us into the vibrant worship services of the first-century churches. Here we do not silence our critical faculties, but we do find that in that scene, text and worship flow into each other. We not only read the Bible; we also give thanks for it. For, with our early Christian ancestors we listen to scripture in a setting punctuated by prayers of thanksgiving to God, by confessions of faith, by the singing of hymns, by utterances under the inspiration of God's Spirit. Opening the text as we sit at table with the first Christians, even while we sit at table with our contemporaries, we praise God. We are also repeatedly surprised.

I offer a single example, knowing that others will emerge as the reader turns to Minear's pages themselves. Consider the age-old question of faith and reason. That is a matter often posed and constructively discussed as an abstract philosophical issue. Without denying the important philosophical dimensions, would we not be wise, however, to make our initial approach by rereading passages of scripture in the company of our earliest Christian ancestors. Accepting Minear's invitation to visit their communities, that is, we listen to New Testament authors again and again, and in that listening we encounter early Christians for whom the issue of faith and reason received its Christian shape in the transformation of memory.

A new perspective emerged, that is, when Jesus Christ was remembered by those who, in the act of remembrance, knew the one remembered to be present and active among them as their risen Lord.[*] This remembered and present Messiah was discerned by them—and can be discerned by us—neither by reason on its own nor by faith that is divorced from reason. As noted above, he is discerned in the singing of a hymn, in prayers uttered in his name, in attending to the word of scripture, in the communal breaking of bread, or when the Spirit leads us to stay with a paraplegic colleague as the tower collapses, sensing in this frail human being on earth the risen Messiah himself (cf. Matt. 25:40).

---

[*] See especially parts 2 and 3 of this volume; and cf. L. E. Keck, *Who Is Jesus? History in Perfect Tense* (Columbia: University of South Carolina Press, 2000).

Here, listening to scripture in the corporate context of Christ's church, we expand our vocabulary, learning and relearning our own Christian tongue, not least by noting that to a large extent God has chosen to speak to us in metaphors.* With Minear as our guide, we begin to sense, for example, that the terms "heaven" and "earth" are resurrected in our own speech when we in the modern church learn to listen to the ways in which New Testament churches actually used those words. We even find common terms taking on surprising dimensions. We thought we were well acquainted with such words as "family," "peace," "hope," "liberation," and "mission." Now, tutored by Paul Minear, we discover in these terms far more than we expected, especially when we learn to use them in connection with such startling expressions as "new creation." Listening with first-century ears, we sense that *in reality* the curtain between the invisible and the visible is far more porous than we had assumed. And it is in sensing both the invisible and the visible that we begin to see the *world* as it actually is.

I return, then, to the reworded saying of Bengel. What happens when, as children of the Enlightenment, we apply ourselves to the ancient text of the New Testament? And what transpires when, as children of the Bible, we find that ancient text applying itself to us? In an age much given to "cool reason" and thus ill-practiced at dreaming; in an age undernourished in exegesis that is highly disciplined, richly imaginative, and theologically powerful, we turn to the present volume. Then, from it we turn to our own Bibles, and in reading and rereading we are reminded of the poet's eye that

> in a fine frenzy rolling,
> Doth glance from heaven to earth, from earth to heaven;
> And as imagination bodies forth
> The forms of things unknown, the poet's pen
> Turns them to shapes and gives to airy nothing
> A local habitation and a name.*

For us that local habitation is the church of heaven and earth, and that name is the name above every name. We are thus put in mind not only

---

* Compare the contribution of one of Minear's colleagues in the ecumenical movement: George Lindbeck, *The Nature of Doctrine: Religion and Theology in a Postliberal Age* (Philadelphia: Westminster, 1984).

* Shakespeare, *A Midsummer Night's Dream*, 5.1.

of the poetry of the Bard, but also of the perceptive exegetical writings of Paul Minear. For, sitting with him at worship in an early Christian church, we learn many things, chiefly how to read the book that has its own way of reading us.

J. Louis Martyn

PREFACE

Readers of the New Testament quickly discover contrasts, both potential and actual, between the perspectives of the New Testament authors and the perspectives of modern historians. These contrasting perspectives provide the focus of the essays selected for this book. My own teaching has compelled me to explore these contrasts. Trained in college, seminary, and graduate school, I have been assigned a double task: to apply current methods of historical research to the New Testament and, at the same time and in the same classroom, to train ministers and priests in their responsible use of the Bible as God's self-disclosure to his people. For more than sixty-five years, in carrying out this double assignment, I have been baffled and challenged by the contrasts between the perspectives of modern historians and those of biblical authors.

The writer of the Gospel of Matthew provides a prime example of these contrasting perspectives. Early in his Gospel, Matthew tells a story that anticipates and underlies everything that happens thereafter. Until readers understand this story they will not grasp Matthew's understanding of what follows. The story begins with a man named Jesus, who comes to the prophet John to be baptized (Matt. 3:13-17). The heavens open. A voice from heaven identifies Jesus as a beloved Son. God's Spirit then leads Jesus into a wilderness, where he is subjected to a triple trial by the devil, a trial lasting forty days. Jesus succeeds in unmasking and repelling the devil, and is fed by the angels. To Matthew, and presumably to his first readers, all of this is simply *what happened*.

But to a modern historian only four of the story's details are possibly

17

factual: John (though not as God's messenger), Jesus (though not as God's Son), the wilderness (though Matthew's map was not the same), and the forty days (though on a different calendar). The most that a historian may venture about the story is that Matthew, and presumably some of those who preserved the Gospel, believed it to be true. Matthew's chief actors—God, the devil, the Spirit, the heavens, the Son, the angels—remain a veritable "black hole" in the skies of the historian. But to Matthew, only the presence of those actors made the story worth telling, and in this respect, the world revealed in the story is the invisible but real world recognized as such by the entire New Testament. How different from the world of the academic historian!

The essays that follow examine the disparities between the worlds of the biblical author and the modern historian without trying to minimize or eliminate them. Part 1 explores ways in which modern historical methods have muted the biblical witness to revelation and transcendence, and the resulting differences in perspective between biblical authors and modern biblical scholars regarding eschatology, ontology, and cosmology. These essays deal with the New Testament as a whole. Part 2 examines the memories of the Messiah as recorded in the four Gospels and selects specific narratives to illustrate the exegete's dilemmas precisely where modern historians and theologians are most likely to disagree about the significance of the Gospel texts. Part 3 extends this analysis to the Epistles. I examine especially the confidence of these letter writers that the Messiah continued to be present in and with the churches. In part 4 we listen to the voices of the churches, rejoicing in their citizenship in heaven and expressing their gratitude for many gifts from the Messiah.

These essays can truly be called "fugitive" essays because they originally appeared in widely separated times (five decades) and places (seven countries), in at least eight journals and eleven *Festschriften* in honor of colleagues in many different schools. They represent a discipline called biblical theology, whose death has been announced on many occasions. Whether or not the discipline is dead, the perplexities persist and merit more penetrating analysis than they have received. This will remain true, I think, as long as a gulf separates the scriptures of the church from the best of contemporary scholarship.

Each essay's original appearance is specified on the copyright page. The essays survive in this rebirth with some changes to enhance the coherence of the work. There have been some deletions from the original essays of materials unrelated to the concerns of this collection, additions to explain some terms that may bewilder contemporary students, and changes to reflect concern for more inclusive language. The deletions include many scholarly citations, omitted to save space and to focus attention on the biblical texts themselves. I trust that this book will give ample evidence of two major personal convictions: first, the massive debt owed by biblical interpreters to modern scholars since Ernesti; second, the potential contributions of the New Testament itself to all the disciplines that are devoted to recovering its multiple messages.

Finally, I want to express deep gratitude to J. Louis Martyn for his contribution of the foreword, to other former students who have kept me in touch with the field during my retirement, to the friends and colleagues whose *Festschriften* furnished the stimulus for writing these essays, and to my family who insisted that I undertake this project and who helped at every turn.

Paul S. Minear

PART I

Divine Revelation and Historical Research

Introduction to
PART I

These five chapters introduce the difficulties faced by biblical scholars in dealing with biblical responses to divine revelation. The first chapter traces the emergence of these difficulties some two and a half centuries ago in the work of the German rector in a school in Leipzig: J. A. Ernesti. In 1761 he wrote a small book that was translated into English by the American biblical scholar Moses Stuart. During my graduate studies at Yale in 1930–32, I read that book as part of my orientation in the historical method for interpreting scripture. I did not consult that book again until I was examining the origins of J. S. Bach's *The Passion According to Saint Matthew*. Then I found to my surprise that these two men had been teachers at the same school in Leipzig, where they engaged over many years in a bitter contest that involved, among many other things, the role of music in the interpretation of scripture. I have called this contest an early storm warning because it anticipated so many later debates. The inheritance that modern scholars have received from this contest is a troubled one. Ernesti's descendants have become increasingly skeptical, as he was not, of all claims to divine revelation for biblical authors. Does God disclose his presence and will to a people of his own choosing? Is that people able to discern such disclosures? What knowledge of God results?

The second chapter extends the conflicting modes of biblical interpretation from Bach and Ernesti to writers more contemporaneous and influential for our own work. I deal first with Rudolf Bultmann, whose voice remains strong within the profession, especially in areas of literary and historical criticism. He limits the authentic transcendence of God to the gospel, the proclamation of Jesus' resurrection, which evokes the moment of faith. Several of his successors limit such transcendence to the "language-event" of preaching, removing it further still from nature and history. Such a language-event now becomes the responsibility of the theologian and the preacher, not of the historian. Against such a drastic limitation, of course, the New Testament everywhere issues a vigorous protest.

It is this protest that provides the central concern of the third chapter. Several ecumenical assignments prompted scholars to raise this protest, and it is their contributions that I report in a *Festschrift* for Bultmann himself. Here the central concern is with modern methods of dealing with scriptural eschatology and with the earliest Christian understanding of the kingdom of God. Interest comes to a focus on the attitudes toward time that were inherent in the early accounts of the death and resurrection of Jesus and the realities of a new creation.

These apostolic and prophetic attitudes toward time become the central concern in the fourth chapter, where I analyze the challenges presented to the historian by specific texts in the book of Revelation. The category of history does not appear in these texts and it becomes quite misleading when the texts are forced into conformity to the modern category. By contrast the category of the heavens, so absent from modern historical discussion, is assumed to be the ultimate reality. Historians are primarily concerned with placing all events within earthly time and the temporal process; biblical writers are essentially concerned with the eternal purposes and time-transcending activity of the creator of the heavens and the earth. Moreover, in sharp contrast to modern thought, which tends to reduce the heavens and the earth to spatial measurement, biblical writers assume the basic and continual interpenetration of the two realms, with the heavens providing the creative source, the daily sustenance, and the final goal of everything earthly. Because the categories of space and time are no longer of use in measuring heavenly realities, biblical thought makes dubious the modern scholars' reliance on those categories.

The fifth chapter summarizes the knowledge of God conveyed to the churches through God's self-revelation according to the entire New Testament.

——— 1 ———
The Musician Versus the Grammarian: An Early Storm Warning

Almost three centuries ago a contest emerged within the faculty of St. Thomas School in Leipzig, a contest that has never been fully resolved but still marks a schism in the soul of the modern Christian. It was the struggle between the now famous cantor, Johann Sebastian Bach, and the once famous rector, Johann August Ernesti—the one a musical genius and the other a pioneer in the historical criticism of the Bible. Both were gifted interpreters of the New Testament, although the media of interpretation they utilized were very different.

When we ask the source of enmity between rector and cantor it may appear at first that the struggle arose out of nothing more than personality conflicts and professional jealousies—factors not unknown in other faculties. In this case, however, that is hardly an adequate explanation, as we shall see. In 1723, at the age of thirty-eight, Bach was appointed musical director of two churches in Leipzig and cantor of St. Thomas School. Each Sunday he directed the choirs, alternating between St. Thomas and St. Nicholas churches. Each year he composed some sixty cantatas to be performed by choirs and orchestras in either church. Members of the choirs and orchestras were drawn from students in St. Thomas School where Bach was instructor in music, Latin grammar, and the Latin catechism.

It is evident from this roster of duties that Bach needed help. He secured it, as his predecessors had done, from several prefects. These were "senior pupils who took over much of the cantor's duties and whose satisfactory work was of vital importance to a smoothly running musical organization."[1] They directed the choirs in the churches, in the streets during public festivals, and at the weddings and funerals of prominent families.

In 1734 the Leipzig Council chose as new rector of the school a young philologist, Johann August Ernesti. He began his new post at the age of twenty-seven, when he was more than two decades Bach's junior. He wanted to make St. Thomas an outstanding center of humanistic studies, and in his judgment this required a definite break with tradition. The school had been designed to combine scholastic and musical purposes, and admission had been restricted to boys with both scholastic and musical capacities. At his appointment, approximately one-fifth of the students' time was occupied with theology and one-fifth with music.[2] Ernesti believed that higher scholastic excellence could be attained only by reducing the time and status given to music. He "hated to see his charges waste so much time by singing in the streets, attending funerals or weddings, and rehearsing for performances."[3] In his judgment, students were there to study and not to sing. Accordingly, a basic objective of the school was abandoned: "to guide the students through the euphony of music to the contemplation of the divine."[4]

It was inevitable, then, that rector and cantor should differ strongly. The occasion for overt conflict arose in 1736 over the question who should have authority to appoint, and therefore to discipline, the student prefects. On one occasion, in singing at a wedding, the boy choristers had been guilty of unseemly behavior, provoking some stern disciplinary action on the part of the first prefect, one Gottlieb Theodor Krause. The rector had defended the choristers and had punished the prefect by ordering a public flogging for him. Because of this disgrace, this prefect and surrogate of Bach's had withdrawn from school.[5] Thereupon the rector had appointed a new prefect, Johann Gottlieb Krause, an act by which he openly challenged Bach's authority. In retaliation Bach demoted the new appointee to the rank of third prefect and replaced him with another student whose musical gifts he claimed to be superior. The rector demanded the higher post for his appointee. The cantor refused. The rector then instructed the choristers not to obey any Bach appointee. Bach in return refused to allow the Ernesti appointee to participate in any service. And so it went.

At issue in the conflict between cantor and rector were other and far more important matters. As one interpreter says, we may see here "the tragic conflict between the last and most mighty musical representative

of the age of faith and one of the younger protagonists of the age of reason and science."[6] Two epochs, two cultures, two philosophies of education were at stake. Should secondary education continue to be grounded
in Christian theology? If so, should music be given a central place in such
training in theology?

Two Approaches to the Bible

At issue were two differing approaches to the Bible, both of which
have since demonstrated their efficacy. Bach was a devout, zealous
Lutheran who continued the spirit, ethos, and biblical understandings of
the seventeenth century. Ernesti was a child of eighteenth-century
rationalism, with its antipathy toward aesthetic, allegorical, and analogical interpretations of the Bible. He wished to ground exegesis on philological evidence, literal meanings, and rational deductions.

For knowledge of Ernesti's exegetical work we rely here upon a single,
slight volume published by him in 1761: *Institutio Interpretis*. Both in
Germany and in America the appearance of Ernesti's book constituted a
landmark in biblical studies. The following quotations, taken from the
fourth English edition of *Elementary Principles of Interpretation* (1842),
indicate the author's emphasis:

> [Interpretation is] the skill which enables us to attach to another's lan-
> guage the same meaning that the author himself attached to it. (p. 14)
> The interpreter must beware lest he seek for diversity of meaning where
> none really exists. (p. 38)
> Nothing can be more pernicious in exegesis than uncertainty. (p. 20)
> There can be no certainty unless a kind of necessity compels us to affix
> a particular sense to a word, which sense must be one. (p. 22)
> The literal meaning is not to be deserted without evident reason or neces-
> sity. (p. 82)
> Language can be properly understood only in a philological way. (p. 27)
> Greater weight in exegesis should be attributed to grammatical considera-
> tions than to doctrinal ones. (p. 31)
> The design of the Holy Spirit can be understood only so far as he himself
> has explained it, and afforded obvious grounds for explanation. (p. 24)

I need not spell out here either the novelty of these attitudes in the
eighteenth century or their profound impact upon later biblical studies. It

was not, however, so much the scientific goal that motivated Ernesti as it was the desire to conform biblical studies to the standards of classical studies. Perhaps his most decisive and influential axiom was this: "The Scriptures are to be investigated by the same rules as other books" (p. 27).

It would be wrong to picture Bach's position as wholly antithetical to Ernesti's. For example, the cantor had no less respect for the primacy of the biblical text than did Ernesti. For instance, in the *St. Matthew Passion* the text of the Gospel provides the structure of the oratorio without abbreviation or amendment. Moreover, the goal of Bach's music is determined by the verbal text. But at one point there is a decisive contrast between cantor and rector. The cantor believed that the biblical text was designed to release within the reader an intense kind of spiritual activity. He must therefore help the text produce in his own audience an emotional action appropriate to the text at hand. He should give priority not to the axis between the Gospel and other ancient books, nor between each successive sentence and the biblical author's conscious and literal intent, but to that between the events narrated and the contemporary audience whose members are called on to respond to those events in unqualified immediacy and with their whole being. Music should function in such a way as to bring the

> stories told in the Gospel out of remoteness into a highly actual relation to the audience, comparable to Nathan's address to David, "Thou art the man" (2 Sam. 12:7 [KJV]). . . . The decisive task of the cantatas consists not in narration or dramatic presentation of the events, but in an always new relation of this event to . . . the present.[7]

The Bible is unlike other books in that through it God speaks. And since God's purpose is sovereign and invasive, the Bible becomes the most purpose-filled book. The Bible aroused in Bach "the most purposive music, which invades the mind and being in such a way that the listener has no rest."[8]

Other contrasts between cantor and rector are related to this basic one. Concentration on the human author's literal meaning leads to the philological accent; concentration on the human responses to God's presence leads to artistic, poetic, dramatic, and musical modes of communication. The rector feared admitting to the text "a diversity of meaning where none really exists"; the cantor was inclined to discover in the biblical events an unlimited plurality of meanings, some of which are quite irreducible to abstract concept or to colorless prose. The rector gave primacy to grammatical analysis and rational deduction; the cantor, who took for granted the intelligibility of the text and the historicity of the events, used his imagination and musical language to disclose or to produce the free involvement of worshipers in the events narrated. Ernesti's approach stressed the full involvement of each text in the world; Bach captured in sound the paradoxical fusion of the temporal and eternal in the events narrated.

I believe the conflict between these two modes of interpreting the Bible is central to debates about the meaning of the Bible even today. If we focus attention upon the work of biblical scholars and even of some preachers, there can be little doubt that most of them are children of Ernesti rather than of Bach. Ernesti's emphasis upon rational philological and historical concerns is so dominant that not many exegetes consider any other alternative. But there can be heard voices of dissatisfaction, though they seldom come from card-bearing members of the biblical guild. As two sons of Bach, Joseph Sittler and Paul Ricoeur should be cited. First, Sittler:

> How, in the Bible, men grasped by the reality of God beheld and understood and dealt with themselves, their fellowmen, and the world is a fact that must be stated "beyond" the biblical mode if God and grace and contemporary men and their world are to be served.[9]

Bach's *Passion* is a superb example of Sittlerian exegesis that is faithful to the biblical reality by moving beyond the biblical mode of speech. Paul Ricoeur gives a more extended explication of the point:

> To understand a text is to follow its movement from sense to reference; from what it says to what it talks about. . . . The text speaks of a possible world and of a possible way of orienting oneself within it. The dimensions of this world are properly opened up by, disclosed by the text. . . . It is not the initial discourse situation which has to be understood, but that which . . . points toward a world which bursts the reader's situation as well as that of the author. . . . Beyond my situation as reader, beyond the author's situation, I offer myself to the possible modes of being-in-the-world which the text opens up.[10]

Here again I propose Bach as an exegete of Matthew who followed the movement of the biblical text as it opened up for listeners a possible world and a possible way of orienting themselves within it.

TWO AVENUES TOWARD CATHOLICITY

Having contrasted the two approaches to the Bible which, in somewhat latent and undeveloped form, emerged in the work of this cantor and this rector, we now move on to appraise their relative contributions to the ecumenical movement. We begin by observing that the work of each of these men resulted in making the Bible accessible to a much wider constituency, thus stimulating a movement toward universality.

Before Ernesti began his work, the study of the Bible had been severely restricted by dogmatic controls in which doctrinal considerations and allegorical distortions were allowed to displace the original intent of the text. The number of exegetes was more or less limited to those who would play the game according to rules set by dogmatic definitions of inspiration within traditional creedal boundaries. Ernesti's principles of interpretation immediately swelled the ranks of exegetes and freed them to place their interpretations within the context of ancient classical literature. The application to the Bible of the rules used for all other ancient documents gave to all humanistic scholars the full right to deal with the biblical books. The primacy given to philological and grammatical data likewise had the effect of excluding none and including all, since every literary document embodies the use of a lexicon and a language common to a community larger than those who share the author's stance. In principle, the Christian canon was thus opened for study by non-Christian scholars, as their literature was in turn open to Christians.

Similarly, the preference given to the use of objective reason rather than subjective emotion encouraged universality to the extent that all are capable of rational thought. *Solidarity with other students* who operate on the same basis of rational treatment of ancient books tends to supersede any earlier *solidarity with other believers*, whether with the authors of the New Testament, with their initial audiences, or with modern Christians. By reason of this "later" solidarity (which has expanded since Bach and Ernesti) modern scholars find that they can travel to other countries and visit members of other religions without leaving home—that is, without being subject to severe culture shock, so long as they stay on a university campus where Western patterns of historical study prevail. Far beyond his expectations and even beyond his approval, Ernesti's "elementary principles of interpretation" have, at least until the last century, been accorded virtually universal recognition. These principles of interpretation helped Christians win the battle against various obscurantisms of the eighteenth century and they have initiated a far-ranging and open-ended investigation of all religious literature.

No less influential, however, has been the work of Ernesti's rival, albeit Bach's universality possesses very different traits, relying as it does upon a musical rather than a verbal philology. Bach has spoken with tremendous power to people of many religions and cultures through his own mode of communicating biblical events and their meanings. Writing usually for a single audience, often a Christian congregation, Bach succeeded in establishing a solidarity in emotional response between the modern audience, the Leipzig congregation, and the biblical author—for example, Matthew—and his audience.

We have already observed Bach's concern to declaim the word of Scripture and to protect the autonomy of the verbal text. Now we see how that concern did not inhibit, but rather enhanced, the movement toward universality. His use of musical language was placed at the service of the biblical authors in the effort to help those authors address contemporary audiences. Just as modern biblical scholars find in every free university in the world a context in which their research can be presented to a heterogeneous and polyglot audience, so conductors of choirs and orchestras discover in every concert hall in the world a welcome for the explicitly Christian compositions of J. S. Bach.

Granted their parallel ability to speak to a universal audience, the contrasts between the methods by which Bach and Ernesti achieved a wider hearing become all the more obvious: one used an artistic mode, the other used a rationalistic perspective; one used a musical, the other a nonmusical, mode of expression; one was concerned to do justice to the multiple meanings of the text, the other sought out the single meaning; one stressed the uniqueness of the Bible, the other exploited its kinship to other books; one wanted above all to comprehend the mind of the ancient author, the other sought to share the responses to the event on the part of the ancient audience.

To sum up: Ernesti gave priority to recovering the ancient language, Bach sought to communicate the whole mode of being-in-the-world toward which that language pointed. Both assumed, of course, the unity of that world as God's creation, as witnessed by the Bible; they differed with regard to perceptions of how humans exist within that world. Yet, although both were convinced monotheists, Bach, I think, more than his rival, was alive to the many levels and forms of existence within the created order.

However that may be, with the benefit of hindsight we may discern the contributions of both men to the ecumenical phenomenon of our own day. Consider two areas central to recent discussion. First, consider the attitudes toward divine revelation in Scripture and tradition. Apart from the application of those historical methods bearing the signature of Ernesti, Protestants would not have been liberated from their captivity to ossified dogmas, nor Catholics from their obscurantist absolutisms. Because of the extent to which we have respected philological and linguistic canons, we have been able together to move toward greater catholicity by discerning the role of traditions within the Bible, the role of scripture within later traditions, and our own role as conservers and interpreters of both.

The second area in which these men have contributed to ecumenism is the impulse toward Christian unity provided by shared liturgical activity. Common worship has demonstrated to Christians of varying backgrounds the fact that they already "exist" in the same world, that their Lord has already made them one and has given them the task of manifesting that oneness. Music has proved to be a major ministry of reconciliation, and no music has been more efficacious in this ministry than that of Bach. His music mediates a mode of being-in-the-world that is inherently and contagiously catholic.

Both rector and cantor, then, have made major contributions to the emergence of ecumenism. In that process, however, both have had to pay a certain price in that their work has been subjected to the sweeping, and in some senses devastating, triumphs of secularization. These triumphs have affected the rich legacy in different ways, through changes we cannot trace in great detail here. In brief, the hermeneutical convictions of Ernesti have been radically altered, I believe, by the development of secularized universities in which the prevailing ethos and worldview are implicitly, if not explicitly, atheistic, in contrast to the Christian orientation of German scholarship in the eighteenth century. Likewise, I believe that the meaning of Bach's music has been radically altered by the fact that it is now produced in concert halls by heterogeneous artists for heterogeneous audiences. Let us explore further the effects of these changes.

TWO TYPES OF SECULARIZATION

The seemingly innocent and obvious statement that the Bible should be treated like other books meant something quite different in Ernesti's

Christendom from what it does in the secularized world today. Then, as we have seen, it was a form of rebellion against the monopoly held by formal dogmas that had inhibited study. To gain recognition, exegetes needed to present orthodox credentials and to produce results in accord with tradition. In that context Ernesti's little book was a new weapon in "the battle with stark orthodoxy," a battle that had to be won before other advances could be made.[11] This weapon effectively liberated scholars, widened the areas open to research, and produced vast alterations in the reconception of biblical history.

Today, however, that rebellion has become a new "establishment," with its own restrictive axioms. A "union card" is now virtually limited to scholars who have been professionally trained to apply objective methods and to restrict their conclusions to data which can be verified by those methods. All scholars are allowed equal access to the text, but believing scholars must take extra care not to "pollute" their findings by their faith. An historical methodology that finds in the Gospels nothing that distinguishes them significantly from Seneca, Epicurus, and Herodotus is not a methodology equipped to deal with the active presence of God in human affairs. It casts presumptive doubt upon the authenticity or accuracy of every verse in the Gospel of Matthew and especially on every verse in which the theological component, God's action, is central. It encourages readers to covet solidarity with contemporary historians at the cost of solidarity with Matthew or Matthew's intended audience. It appears often to limit the ground of faith either to a diminishing residue of authentic facts which remain in the historian's sieve or to a growing body of legends and myths which can be readily disjoined from historical reality. Matthew's own point of view, although allowed as a valid object of study, can no longer be accepted by the student as providing an essential basis for comprehension. Study can no longer be oriented or shaped by the features that distinguished the Bible from other books. Such matters as the presence of a book in the canon or the one-time claim to inspiration exert no noticeable influence on its interpreters. Thus the parochialism of orthodox dogma has been replaced by the parochialism of historical relativism, the inevitable result of a methodology that presupposes an atheistic view of historical process.

Surely Ernesti did not contemplate such consequences from his original protest. He took seriously the role played by the Holy Spirit in the Bible. He recognized that, in speaking of God, biblical authors used a figurative language to which later interpreters must be sensitive.[12] A secularized worldview embodied in the secularized methods of secularized schools has betrayed his intention and meaning. The price paid for achieving this kind of universality has been very high indeed, although many scholars have been happy to pay it. The vulnerability of the method depends, of course, not on the price but on its claim as an adequate means to the fullness of understanding.

Bach's interpretation of Matthew has also lost much as a result of the expansion of his audience. Originally he composed the *Passion* for a Good Friday service of worship in St. Thomas Church to accompany the sermon for the day. Thus at least a modicum of kinship between his audience and Matthew's was assured. Leo Schrade stresses the degree to which a lifetime goal of Bach's was the creation of a new liturgical service in which music would provide the organizing principle, the very structure of the congregation's praise and prayer.

It is therefore one of the strange ironies of history that when the *St. Matthew Passion* was revived after a century of oblivion it was performed in a Berlin concert hall, free of any association with sermon or church. Ever since then its use in churches has diminished in contrast to its use in concert halls, in part because of the demands of production and the standards of musical excellence. No longer do audiences join in singing the chorales as familiar confessions of their own distinctively Christian convictions. No longer does the sung text of the Gospel take the place of "the reading of God's Holy Word." No longer does an evangelical sermon intervene between the two parts, nor does the evening close with a congregational hymn and the benediction. Probably many who hear Bach's music have never participated in a Christian worship service. The secularization of the *Passion*, therefore, in spite of furnishing a larger audience for Bach since 1729, marks the reversal rather than the consummation of Bach's conscious intentions.

When devout Christians become aware of the irony of this situation and when they listen again to the *Passion* as fruit of Bach's heroic effort to develop a fitting liturgical celebration of Good Friday, they may be pardoned for finding in this secularization an institutionalized form of blasphemy no less shocking than other perversions of the cross. We should not dismiss too hastily the slogan that appeared as early as 1904 in the *Bachjahrbuch* (p. 25): "The church works of Bach for the Church."

Even so, something else must be said. Although the price of a universal hearing has been a secularization, which runs counter to Bach's intention, and although the separation of this art from the church has done

damage to both, we must in the end rejoice over the process of secularization from which Bach's music has gained more than it has lost. Why
so? For one thing, the boundary between the sacred and the secular has
become increasingly difficult to locate. The two realms have changed
their character since the days of Ernesti and Bach, changed in ways that
defy definition either by Lutheran dogmatists or by atheistic sociologists.
In producing this erosion of the boundaries, music has been one of the
most effective agents. Bach himself seems to have viewed all his work as
integral to his vocation under God. He used different texts and different
surroundings for his secular compositions, but he did not hesitate to
adapt secular music to sacred occasions or sacred music to secular
occasions.

Second, the secularization may be seen as an illustration of the intercessory character and vocation of the church. From this standpoint, the
concert in symphony hall may be seen as binding together believers and
unbelievers under the sign of Christ's atoning death, quite irrespective of
the conscious thoughts of conductor, choristers, instrumentalists, or audience. The power of the music to accomplish this miracle derives not
alone from the composer but from the evangelist and the Messiah, neither of whom wished to erect high walls around a sacred precinct.

Third, we may see in the secularization and universalization of the
Passion music a process implicit in the Matthean Passion story itself.
Better than performance in churches, the performance in concert halls
may dramatize the secularity of what happened in Gethsemane and on
Golgotha. Although it was written for the church, Bach's music correctly
interprets the unlimited range of Christ's atonement "for the sins of the
whole world." Like Matthew before him, Bach testifies to his faith in "the
providence of God as the ultimate environment of human existence."[13]

What are the implications of our study for the modern exegete? The
question becomes all the more pertinent if Bach actually was a better
exegete than Ernesti, as I think he was, and if in the *St. Matthew Passion*
he has taken us closer to the world of Matthew than have recent New
Testament commentators. If with Ernesti we acknowledge our obligation
to treat the Gospels as we treat other literature, with Bach we should
acknowledge our obligation to recognize the *distinctive* features of the
Gospels to which his music has done greater justice than have even the
best practitioners of our craft. We have too long denied the right of the
Gospels as literary documents to determine the kinds of interpretation
most apt and most adequate. We should also covet more eagerly the

potential contributions to biblical interpretation of other artistic forms of communication, including poetry, drama, fiction, visual arts, and liturgical celebration. There is absolutely no justification for our virtual exclusion of these from the processes of interpretation in the name of historical objectivity. We must seek liberation from the monopoly that discursive and analytic prose has established over biblical interpretation.

— 2 —
The Transcendence of God and Human Historicity

In the first chapter, I dealt with the conflict between two modes of interpreting scripture, one represented by the rector, Ernesti, a critic of ancient Greek and Latin texts, and the other by the cantor, Bach, a composer who set ancient texts to music. In this chapter I will explore the frontier between speculative thought, with its emphasis on divine transcendence, and historical thought, with its emphasis on human historicity. (The meanings of these key terms will emerge as we proceed.)

The exact location of this frontier is not easy to define because imperialistic theologians and equally imperialistic historians often contest each other's jurisdiction over this region as vehemently as did Bach and Ernesti. The struggle, however, does not really follow the boundary between these two academic disciplines. Biblical theologians are divided among themselves over how to deal as historians with apostolic claims to divine revelation. Dogmatic theologians are also divided, I believe, over how to deal as theologians with historical reality.

Speaking as a biblical theologian, I will confine myself to those developments in New Testament studies in which the problems of hermeneutics are debated. This debate points to the recognition that it is increasingly difficult for the historian, within the domain of conventional historiography, to deal with texts that claim to embody God's address to mortals. On the one hand, the Bible presents us with stories of God's eternal power working in, with, through, under, and beyond temporal events. On the other hand, historical methodology suggests that these stories are best dealt with as if that power were not present. This methodology is weighted in the direction of a historicism that A. E. Loen has described in these terms: "Historical reality is complete in itself and God as a transcendent reality must be bracketed out."[1]

SCIENTIFIC METHODOLOGY—A POSSIBLE ANALOGY

Leaving the construction of my argument for the time being, I should like first of all to examine the nature of methodology in the physical sciences and notice how alterations occur in that methodology. If we look away from the maelstrom of our own obsessions to see how changes take place within a quite different academic area, it may suggest a fresh approach to our own dilemmas. T. S. Kuhn provides one set of answers in *The Structure of Scientific Revolutions*.[2] Kuhn finds among scientists a gross misunderstanding of the development of their own disciplines. Their textbooks have taught them to view the past as the story of gradual, steady extensions in knowledge, the significance of each increment being determined by its contribution to modern thought. The historian serves them simply as a chronicler of the discoveries progressively made by individual scientists. But not so for Kuhn. He sees the methodology of each science determined less by "nature" than by educational institutions and research needs. This methodology assumes that "the scientific community knows what the world is like." Each initiate must accept that assumption. Professional education provides a set of "conceptual boxes," and research becomes the "strenuous and devoted attempt to force nature" into those boxes. The initiate is obliged to accept the set of boxes, the choice being always necessary and always arbitrary. Because it is necessary, the process of research tends to become bound by tradition. Because it is arbitrary, other boxes will in time prove to be superior, so that in time the progress of research will destroy the present filing system. The history of science is therefore an account not so much of steady increments in encyclopedic knowledge as of successive revolutions in views of the world.

Kuhn's book is an analysis of the nature of these revolutions. A chief tool in his analysis is the concept of the paradigm or model. The paradigm embraces the pattern of presuppositions, points of view, concepts, and rules that govern research in a given area. In fact, until a paradigm is adopted, the emergence of a science is quite impossible. A science emerges from its own prehistory when it begins to operate on the basis of a single accepted model.

A science is institutionalized when this paradigm is taken for granted, so that scholars need no longer argue those basic questions it has answered. It becomes the hidden foundation of "the establishment." Practitioners who do not accommodate their work to it are gradually eliminated. Those who adopt it can now devote all their attention to the problems it sets and the promises it makes. Because the area of research is now clearly defined, they can accomplish a greater depth of penetration, although this means that their language becomes ever more esoteric and their audience smaller. So absorbed are they in applying the paradigm to a particular problem that they become blind to fugitive phenomena which do not fit the paradigm. Their business is to demonstrate the efficacy of the paradigm, not to deal with its weaknesses, and even less to develop a new model which might better account for the fugitive data. Each paradigm exercises authority because it has become for a group of scholars the recipient of commitments, which are both methodological and metaphysical. These two types of commitments are so interdependent that any change in metaphysics ensures a change in methodology.

Such a change is inevitable simply because no paradigm takes into account all forces and factors. Research under one paradigm sooner or later induces change to another paradigm. In fact the better the paradigm, the more sensitive it is to its own failures and the more it conduces to its own obsolescence. Yet such failures do not in themselves produce change, nor do they overcome the resistance of scientists to change. "The establishment" does not surrender a paradigm immediately upon observing its deficiencies. A new paradigm must be available which circumvents those deficiencies. Scholars must test the capacities of this new theory to deal with the phenomena of nature. The new has not really been adopted until the whole industry has been "retooled," until textbooks, teachings, and laboratories have been redesigned. This transition from one paradigm to another, affecting simultaneously both metaphysics and methodology, is so radical as to justify the term revolution. (Thus far, Kuhn.)

RUDOLF BULTMANN AND HUMAN HISTORICITY

In presenting this analysis of revolutions in scientific methodology, I do not wish to argue that current methods for studying human history are entirely similar. Yet I believe that numerous similarities exist that are more than curious coincidence. In both historical and scientific fields, the paradigms are constructs of the human mind, modes of human response to the world. Scholars working within the same educational institutions have produced two kinds of paradigms within the same culture during the same epoch. Ours has been an epoch in which secular thought has produced naturalistic philosophies of history and historical philosophies of nature. It is not surprising that similar metaphysical assumptions should be woven into the modes of research in both disciplines. In both one may also observe the tenacity of old paradigms and popular resistance to new.

The historical paradigm is probably older, more inclusive, more flexible, and therefore less reducible to a limited formula than its scientific analogues. This paradigm, usually called the critical historical method, embraces the pattern of assumptions, perspectives, objectives, and procedures that are illustrated by most essays that appeared during the twentieth century in the *Catholic Biblical Quarterly* or the *Journal of Biblical Literature*, two of the most widely respected scholarly journals for biblical studies in the United States. At the moment we are especially interested in how this paradigm deals with the dimension of transcendence. The simplest answer is that the method encourages either antagonism or neutrality toward the presence of such a dimension. Altizer, for example, says, "We inherit the historical revolution of the nineteenth century, a revolution which stripped all historical events of a transcendent ground."[3] In the less enthusiastic words of A. E. Loen, the historical process has been "de-divinized," since the message of the Bible comes to be seen as "determined exclusively by historical factors."[4] The sequence of historical events is sundered from its metaphysical ground, so that "forgetfulness of the sphere of being robs history of its essence, just as it robs man of his."[5]

A method that is either neutral or antagonistic toward the presence of God creates a double dilemma for modern exegetes. In the first place, the biblical traditions that they must interpret are themselves pervaded by the awareness of God's presence in creation, his powerful activity in human affairs, and the revelation of his will to a chosen people. This poses the question whether the exegete can comprehend and deal justly with biblical writers with a method of research alien to their deepest convictions. In the second place, the exegete is in most cases a servant of the modern church. That vocation normally requires interpreting the message of the scriptures to a community that is listening therein for the word of God. Can exegetes transfer that task to the preacher and the theologian and limit their own work to the business of objective historical description? Should they do this, their decision will reflect their mastery *by* the paradigm of historical science as well as mastery *over* it.

The creative work in biblical exegesis has, I believe, been accomplished not so much by scholars who are content to expand the jurisdiction of the dominant method as by those who have wrestled with overcoming its deficiencies. A prime example is Rudolf Bultmann. He is widely known, of course, as a superb practitioner of historical science who applied with deftness and thoroughness the "objective" techniques that were developed during the last two centuries. It is this very mastery of method that to many scholars is the measure of his greatness.

What is more to the point, however, is the incisive critique which Bultmann leveled at the deficiencies in the usual application of the historical method. These deficiencies may be variously characterized as relativism, historicism, positivism, reductionism, and abstractionism. "The historiography of the nineteenth century . . . on the whole arrived at some form of *relativism*. It acknowledged change as historical law and denied the absolute value of judgments and knowledge, and it confirmed the dependence of all thinking and valuing on their time and culture."[6]

Mortals "[stand] within history." There is no way by which they can stand at its beginning or at its end or secure a vision of the entire historical process.[7] From such a stance it makes no sense to speak of a transcendent God. Biblical affirmations about such transcendence should be recognized as illegitimate absolutizing of the relative. But it also makes little sense to suppose that mortals can ever transcend their own times, places, families, or environments. The history of humanity is subsumed under the story of nature.[8] In this view much that is most genuine and significant, majestic and mysterious, is lost to view. The real self that persists behind and within all experiences, that recollects the whole of previous events, that asks and seeks and suffers and rejoices, that knows that it is known by Another—this self is drastically reduced to what can be weighed on the scales of the historians.

It is important to note that it is the metaphysics basic to contemporary historiography that Bultmann faulted. He remained an able practitioner of the prevailing paradigm, often using it to good advantage in order to destroy the claims of competing reconstructions of New Testament thought. One may even wonder whether his attack on the deterministic anthropology implicit in historicism ever noticeably changed the more technical side of his work. In any case in dealing with Bultmann, we must reckon fully with both his use and his critique of the prevailing paradigm. We must ask how he sought to supplement that paradigm so as to surmount its deficiencies.

Against the prevailing relativism, Bultmann defended the transcendence of God or at least certain aspects of that transcendence as expressed in the Bible. He saw the Eternal acting in history as the ever-coming, ever-encountering Other, whose sovereign Word demands obedience. God's will is absolute; obedience to him must therefore be radical. The message of God's action in raising Jesus from the dead remains the one point where the biblical saga cannot be demythologized. Whenever word of this resurrection is preached, it calls for a response so radical as to set a transcendental limit to the relativism of historical change.[9] This God who directs the historical process toward this goal speaks with indubitable authority; this speaking provokes an eschatological crisis that alone can restore freedom to the human person.

Although Bultmann thus defended the full actuality of God's action, he carried out this defense mainly by way of adopting an existentialist anthropology. Through the mesh of relativistic historicism both the transcendence of God *and* the corresponding historicity of the human person have dropped out. To Bultmann the second dropout is the more serious. Therefore, the exegete can restore the dimension of transcendence in the eschatological message only by restoring the radical nature of eschatological faith. A person is the rightful "subject of history"[10] who receives authenticity as a *subject* through the gift of freedom and the act of love. There is an inescapable paradox about this transcendence. On the one hand, we do not stand outside history; yet, on the other hand, in faith we do in fact receive a standpoint above history. It is by the decision of faith that this paradox is enacted. "Every instant has the possibility of being an eschatological instant and in Christian faith this possibility is realised."[11] It is through faith that we thus participate in the transcendent freedom of God. Since theology is faith's self-understanding, the theological analysis of transcendence must focus upon what happens to us in this *instant.* Since the kerygma (the gospel message) is what calls this instant into being, the work of hermeneutics, or biblical interpretation, is defined by the needs of preaching. Historicism has destroyed the credibility of first-century mythology, but historicity can yet be produced whenever the kerygma creates faith.

Bultmann makes much of the contrast between *Historie* and *Geschichte*. It is this concept of *two* histories that enables Bultmann to maintain both his loyalty to the historical critical method and his allegiance to a second, existentialist paradigm. *Historie* is a mode of historical being that is "objectively" studied in a secular way by means of the critical methods of academic science: "a self-enclosed, dynamic continuum of events which can be fixed as points of time." *Geschichte* is a second mode that recognizes our historicity and regards the moment of encounter with the Transcendent as revelatory of who we are and of what our historical reality consists.[12] Bultmann's historical work was based on commitment to the former, the historical paradigm; his theological work was based on the latter, the existentialist paradigm. Hermeneutics should translate the kerygma in such a way as to recognize the antithesis between first-century and twentieth-century modes of conceptualizing the activity of God in history and yet also to produce an authentic historicity wholly akin to the faith of Paul and John. It can do this without major change in the prevailing methodology. The only adjustment is the replacement of an implicit historicism by an effective existentialism, or historicity.

For many scholars, perhaps even today, Bultmann's treatment of hermeneutics provides the starting point for further discussion. There are, of course, theologians who deny the value of Bultmann's maneuver and who believe that a better starting point can be found. Although I belong to their number, I am now concerned with those who, starting with Bultmann's position, have tried to move beyond it in an effort to do fuller justice to the biblical witnesses.

THE LINGUISTICALITY OF EXISTENCE

Many post-Bultmannian interpreters have adopted as slogans the terms *language-event* and *linguisticality of existence*. The emphasis on language as the focal problem stemmed in part from Bultmann's Lutheran concentration on the moment of faith as the moment of a person's realization of authentic historicity. When the Word of God addresses us and we respond, we enter into eschatological existence—a realm in which our captivity to historicism is overcome. The words are human, and therefore relative; but the Word is God's and therefore transcendent. If language belonged wholly to us, revelation would be impossible; if it belonged wholly to God, our response would be impossible. What, then, is the character of that language-event that breaks through the walls of relativistic historicism and creates a new person in a new world?

Transcendence, we are led to suppose, becomes a function of this restored language. But this function must operate within a history that is perceived entirely in Bultmannian terms. The *text* that is accessible to the exegete is *not* God's word. It is only the medium through which God addresses us. Our transcendence of the historical order depends upon our hearing that address. The historian deals only with the text; it is the preacher and the theologian who preside over the process by which the Word of God becomes audible. Through their work the text is again enabled to become God's address, yet this work neither competes with nor qualifies "the crucial function of the critical-historical method."[13]

Thus we see that adherents of Bultmann's method accepted not only the current historical methodology but also the metaphysical axioms on which it was based. Fuchs, a student of Bultmann, for example, explicitly approved Bultmann's definition of history as "a unity in the sense of a closed correlation of effects."[14] According to Fuchs, history stands wholly under the law of causality, a power that operates as unconditionally in history as in nature. Any interruption by supernatural powers is quite inconceivable. Faith, in fact, must accept this view of history as an expression of God's will, as including all things under the law of death, and as a mode of divine judgment. Faith must therefore concede to the critical historian an exclusive jurisdiction over the text of Scripture so far as that text is viewed as a past bit of history.

It is, therefore, in their understanding of the future that Fuchs, a German scholar, and Funk, an American, both seek, like Bultmann, to free themselves from the determinism of the past. In certain respects, of course, they recognize the degree to which the historical critical method fails even to cope with the past. Because history is a system bound by the laws of causality, all phenomena whose effects are not discernible drop out of the historian's world. At best, therefore, written history is an "incomplete obituary notice."[15] But such deficiencies have for this school the positive value of turning attention toward the place where authentic freedom can alone be realized, that point in time where we face the future. By facing the future we can assume a concern for the whole of history, a sense of responsibility for history, and an experience of the end of history. But we can do this only in faith. And this faith takes place only in response to a message that is addressed to us.

Transcendence is therefore limited to this present moment of faith when we confront that future which addresses us in the form of the gospel. The transcendent is even more narrowly defined than this: it is that to which faith responds. Since faith is mediated by listening, God-talk must be limited to talk about this language-event. To an historian who respects this methodology, *no* credence can be given to transcendence as a factor in either nature or history. But the "language-event" is a necessary presupposition of faith.

Without language, Funk argues, there could be no contact with God, no true being for ourselves, and therefore no trans-empirical basis for theological reflection. Language empowers a person to exist as one who answers. Funk's appeal to transcendence springs from an effort on his part to understand faith's dependence on language. For example, the doctrine of the transcendence of Christ, based on confidence in his resurrection, is a way of affirming his presence in the kerygmatic language to which faith responds. Apart from such language, God would be made speechless. To Fuchs, Ebeling, and Funk, the traditional God-talk does, in fact, leave God speechless. To exorcise God's dumbness, if we may put it that way, the theologian must learn to speak of God godlessly—without presupposing God. The program of Fuchs and Funk appears then to equate theology with hermeneutics, since their common task has to do with the use of the biblical text. The historian, applying this method, has verified the text's imprisonment within the closed system of causality that embraces everything in the past. The historian hands over to the preacher and the theologian the opportunity and the obligation to preside over the process by which the text can again become the Word of God, encountering a person and producing faith.

THE TRANSCENDENCE OF GOD IN THE NEW TESTAMENT

I believe that to combine an historicist view of history with an existentialist view of faith fails to remedy the deficiencies in the historical paradigm. It accepts the reductionism that the historical method applies to the historical process. It advocates a theological reductionism that limits the transcendent to one component of speech and that limits faith to the experience of an individual responding to scriptural preaching. It does not, to be sure, translate theology wholly into anthropology, but by restricting attention to the "more than human within the human" (a phrase of Gregory Baum), the transcendent becomes so attenuated as to be trivialized.

What evidence is to be offered to justify this charge of reductionism? The varied witness of the New Testament to the corporate experience of transcendence. First of all, the awareness of God's activity is reflected in many syntactical and grammatical phenomena, such as the predominance of verbs of action, whether in the passive or active voice, in which God is the source and subject. Also, one may reflect upon the typical reliance on a wide variety of prepositional phrases: from, by, through, to, for the sake of, in. Without reference to the awareness of the transcendent it is difficult to account for the rich assortment of rhetorical forms: parable, dialogue, poetry, epiphany, allegory, vision, hyperbole, typological narratives, and archetypal symbols.[16]

Second, let me mention how the early Christians found in prayer a natural way to express their awareness of the interplay in all situations of the infinite and the finite. The divine command to pray and the promise to answer are found in all strata of the literature. The injunction to thank God for everything bespeaks a worldview in which every moment is permeable by God's power. The forms and the practice of prayer reflect an experience of the transcendent more continuous than momentary encounters with the future; they illustrate the linguisticality of existence, to be sure, but they resist limiting that existence to a series of discrete language-events.

Third, consider the variety of corporate liturgical forms in the New Testament and their robust, uninhibited vitality. The baptismal and eucharistic motifs embrace corporate memories of the old age and excitements of the new. Every *hallelujah* and *amen* is addressed to the Creator and Redeemer of all things, whose life transcends human distinctions between nature and grace, the past and the future. God is the only one who is worthy to receive all glory and power, wisdom and blessing. To limit God's speech to a word to which faith responds would sadly sterilize and prostitute the New Testament celebrations of his presence. A history of the early church that ignored its convictions concerning the powerful guidance of the Holy Spirit would not be recognized by that church as either authentic or germane.

Fourth, early Christian conceptions of transcendence were functions of a moral struggle that made human beings aware of the abysmal depths of their existence. Every situation became for them a time of temptation and testing, when an Evil One who was stronger than they were struggled for their loyalty. They could not understand the origin, course, or outcome of such a struggle except by referring to spiritual powers in heavenly places. They knew the hopelessness of living without God in the world—the skepticism of Ecclesiastes, and the despair of Job. Knowing well the weakness and transience of their own wills, they looked for strength to endure through the final conflict. It was because of this struggle that they could not conceive of a world in which either Satan or God had died, although they of course met fools who claimed that such a world existed. Instead, they knew themselves as heirs of a Kingdom that would never end. As God is the Alpha and the Omega, the kingdom of God reaches from the beginning before all beginnings to the ending after all endings. Yet this transcendence encountered early Christians within the context of the ordinary and the humdrum. It offered immediate freedom from the past, freedom from sin and death. It superseded the claims of the most holy and venerable institutions: temple, law, and priesthood. The whole ministry of Jesus became a parable of the mysterious presence of the Kingdom and of the gift of citizenship therein.

In the fifth place, in the New Testament every contact with any form of ministry was a contact with the transcendent, since each gift of ministry mediated God's power, whether to preach or to heal, to teach or to serve tables. Each member, in fact, was recipient of the powers of the resurrection; each congregation could think of itself as a temple of the Holy Spirit or the Body of Christ. Furthermore this self-understanding was not limited to a succession of language-events.

Finally, the genuine experience of the transcendent by New Testament authors is manifested by the constant reminders of the poignant inadequacy of human thoughts and speech, "Who has known the mind of the Lord? Or who has been his counselor?" (Rom. 11:34). They knew the dangers of idolatry in worshiping their own knowledge of things human or divine. They knew they were dealing with "what no eye has seen, nor ear heard," (1 Cor. 2:9) with a wisdom which seemed folly, with a mystery which could never be adequately translated into any language other than in some form of Passion story, some type of prophetic vision.

There is a huge disparity, therefore, between the character of the historical process as seen by New Testament writers and as seen in modern historiography. In this regard the deficiency in the dominant paradigm is no trivial matter. In part, the deficiency stems from its own set of metaphysical presuppositions. The paradigm embodies a repudiation of metaphysics all the while it offers an example of unexamined and untenable metaphysics. One sign of this is the arrogance with which it dismisses all other metaphysical positions as unacceptable. Among the positions so dismissed is that of the New Testament traditions. It is assumed that their concepts of transcendence are impossibly archaic and obsolete. In this case the judges may be more naive than those being judged. The New Testament writers were not unacquainted with deterministic theories of history. They were quite aware of the attractiveness of relativism, of positivism, of materialisms in various modes. They knew the anomalies involved in speaking of heavenly treasures in earthly vessels, of resurrection from the dead, of God's reconciliation of all things. Their choice of mythological language was due to this very knowledge. Surely this sophistication is one reason their God-talk has proved to be viable in every succeeding century, including our own.

I want, however, to argue that the deficiency in that method extends beyond its metaphysical (or antimetaphysical) presuppositions. It is deficient in accomplishing its historical objective, the recovery and description of past events in their original sequence and significance. When the historian succeeds, the story of the past remains in Fuchs's words, "an incomplete obituary notice." This incompleteness condemns the method. The net used fails to catch the data that to early Christians constituted the significance of the events in which they shared, while the data that the historian does recapture would have been to them of only secondary importance. The hermeneutical movements that we have analyzed have not removed these failures. Appeal to the eschatological character of faith is not enough to free present choices from the chains of causality. It is not enough by analysis of the linguisticality of existence to assert the power of God's word to bring life out of death. These movements have merit. They succeed in preserving a modicum of recognition of the transcendent as "the more than the human within the human." Yet none of them adequately challenges the current historical paradigm. And for the same reason none of them offers to historical science those distinctive contributions that should accrue from the revelation in Christ of what history is like.

In saying this, I do not mean that an academic science can translate the facts of God's transcendence into an alternate paradigm for historical study. Success in such an enterprise would indeed deny the reality of that transcendence. But historical reason is surely not restricted to a choice between two paradigms: a closed system of causality which enforces the denial of God on the one hand, or a historiography which would seek to demonstrate his activity on the other. There have, in fact, been many paradigms for dealing with history which have done less violence to the dimension of transcendence. And there will be other methods in the future more appropriate to the mysteries of revelation. There are few things of which we can be more certain than that there will be continuing revolutions in historical and hermeneutical methodology.

The task of contemporary exegetes is to allow Scripture itself to criticize both the assumptions and the methods that are used in its study. They must listen also, of course, to secular historians and to theologians. Success in their task will be possible only through a conviction that the temporal distance between this and earlier centuries is itself bridged by the eternal purpose of God and by the participation of the church in that purpose. But it will also be possible only if there is more effective collaboration between historians and theologians. Even the ideal cooperation among scholars, however, will never lead to reducing God's transcendence to the size of our various conceptual boxes.

> All the reasons given for crediting the proposition "God exists" cannot prepare one for the shock of His actuality. The Gospel administers this shocking mystery. Woe to theology [or historiography or hermeneutics] if it provide metaphysical insulation against it![17]

── 3 ──
Christian Eschatology
and
Historical Methodology

During recent years the impression has deepened that the science of historiography has reached a major turning point. In all areas of research and in all countries we find a sober questioning of the adequacy of prevailing methodologies. I do not refer to the attack upon individual scholars for their eccentric ways of applying the method, or to conservative protests that historians have invaded areas reserved for dogma. I have in mind scholars in many countries who have succeeded in mastering the method for dealing with the object at hand: history. The newer challenges appear most stubborn in regions where scientific historiography has achieved its most notable triumphs. They are therefore important wherever workers are proceeding with historical research.

Like other methods of historiography, the scientific method has proceeded by isolating a particular sequence of events recorded in literary documents, by observing the elements of continuity in these events, and by organizing these recurrent elements into a coherent pattern. In part this pattern is always suggested by the events and by the extant records. In part it is always suggested by the categories and presuppositions inherent in the observer's method. These categories and presuppositions implicitly convey a perception of time and an overarching perspective on history that dominate the cultural milieu of the historian. Every application of the method brings into play both the historical scene and the historian's mind. Every such application is a test of the method and, in turn, a test of the conceptions of time and history embodied in the method. Indigenous to modern historiography is a perception of time as impersonal succession, as unilinear movement, as an endless but measurable process. Indigenous also is a perspective that sees history as a single, unitary, and universal sequence of events, humanity-centered and humanity-propelled, although bounded by conditions of cosmic regularity and interruption. To understand the intrinsic meaning of any event, its location in time must be recovered so that its exact continuity with prior and later events may be established. To understand the significance for history of an event or a sequence of events, the historian must weigh its total effect on humankind.

Scientific historiography, together with all other sciences, seeks by a law of its own nature to establish increasing hegemony over all events that fall within its jurisdiction. Given its conception of time and history, this jurisdiction has been wide indeed. Clearly the Bible falls within this territory. All literature is historical; therefore the biblical documents must be studied by the same methods as other ancient records. All events narrated in the Bible, so far as writers claim that they happened, come within the purview of scientific examination. Generation after generation, scholars have claimed the right to explore new continents of historical life and, by their success, have vindicated that right. Advance scouts have opened up a given field. Technicians have followed. Gradually the field has been ordered in accordance with the demands of the science. The jurisdiction of the method has steadily increased until few indeed are the arctic lands not yet incorporated under the same flag. All this is at least a partial achievement of the necessary goal of any scientific method.

It would be folly, blindness, and presumption to deny the tremendous contributions made by scientific history to biblical studies. Among the successes must be included the recognition of the importance of eschatology in the New Testament, the steady advances toward understanding Jesus' message of the kingdom of God, the exploration of the connections between his message and earlier Jewish concepts, and the exploitation of analogies and contrasts in ancient Near Eastern cosmologies and mythologies. Modern historiography has succeeded in probing the alien historiography of biblical writers. It has succeeded in recovering, in part at least, the strange time-consciousness pervading the Bible. It has thus proved a measure of its objectivity by making clear the distance between the biblical and the modern outlook. All this has been native to its work of establishing hegemony over its legitimate territory.

Scientific historiography, like all disciplines of human reason, seeks to discover its own limits, that border where it must say, "Thus far, but no farther." It does this in part by ordering and governing the territories already explored. But it also extends its range by projecting hypotheses gained from earlier studies into regions not yet explored. It makes tentative claims of jurisdiction which only continued research can vindicate. At times these claims must be surrendered; at other times they are established, and the method moves toward a new frontier. Any method will initially be denied entrance into precincts that later become amenable to its techniques. For instance, the application of historical science to the Bible was resisted by many who defended a particular doctrine or an earlier picture of the events. One after another, many of these barriers were overcome, and this succession of triumphs seemed to justify the claim that no realm was independent and that no event would refuse to yield its meaning to a more exact application of the method. If historians failed to colonize a new territory, their failure would be remedied by a more scientific application of the accepted disciplines. Quite naturally, also, there has risen the fear that to admit the incompetence of the method to cope with any historical data would open the door to a new anarchy, in which a welter of prescientific methods would prevail. It is extremely difficult for any methodology in which post-Enlightenment conceptions of time and history are dominant to admit the existence of limits in the operation of historical reason.

Yet there are limits. And it is the business of any methodology not only to discover where those limits are, but also to review its own goals and disciplines in the light of those limits. The treatment of New Testament eschatology has demonstrated the existence of limits, although it has not yet led to a satisfactory delineation of them, nor has it yet produced sufficient reexamination of the method itself. The issues are becoming sufficiently clear, however, for us to grapple with them.

As I have already noted, the recovery of the shape and power of eschatological thinking in late Judaism and early Christianity constitutes one of the triumphs of modern historiography. We are now enabled to trace with increasing precision the roots of eschatology in the covenants with Israel, its place in the prophetic tradition, its apocalyptic forms during the Maccabean and Roman periods, its importance as context for the message of John the Baptist and Jesus, its complex influences upon early Christian writings, and its modifications and permutations during patristic times. There is a striking consensus among scholars in recognizing at least the presence and importance of eschatology, in tracing the development of its basic ideas, and in calculating some of its more tangible effects.

This consensus, however, tends to evaporate as soon as questions of significance and validity are raised. Immediately a profusion of "theories" and "schools of thought" appears. Historical study, informed by the best methods available, is unable to speak with a clear univocal verdict here. How, then, have historians faced this dilemma? Initially at least, this predicament has led to a more vigorous analysis of the field of study than of the methods of study. We are inclined to draw a line between the area preempted for historical reconstruction and the area left open to theological interpretation, assuming that the first area should remain firmly under the jurisdiction of historical methodology and gladly granting to theologians both the anarchy of theories of validity and significance and the task of ordering this anarchy. We have tended to accept the dictum of Lessing that accidental historical truths can never serve as proofs for eternal truths. We have distinguished sharply between history and faith, between historical and devotional treatments of biblical texts, between scientific research and homiletic proclamation. This tendency to locate the limits in the field of study rather than in the method of study is, of course, deeply rooted in our own modern outlook.

More recently this type of dichotomy has been carried over into the field of New Testament eschatology. Here the tendency is to distinguish the transhistorical from the historical process. We make use of the distinction between what lies within history and what lies beyond it, or the distinction between the historical and the mythological. Historians may or may not be deeply impressed with the historical value of a myth, or with the presence of suprahistorical realities, yet they find it difficult to escape the dichotomy itself.

These dichotomies originate, at least in their present form, in difficulties that have attended the extension of modern historiography. In part their *source* is that schism in the modern mind that has been created and encouraged by the categories and results of historical research. Their motivation is the desire to solve the dilemmas that are most real to historians. The dichotomies are apologetic efforts to overcome the skeptical results of research by assigning major significance to the territory left open by that research. Scholars for whom scientific methodology rightly claims ultimate sovereignty repudiate such efforts. Such efforts also fail to satisfy those who cannot draw so sharp a line between historical reason and faith. And even for scholars who adopt these dichotomies there remains in their own hearts and minds a deep hiatus between their work *qua* historian and their faith *qua* Christian.

What has been the net result of employing these dichotomies for explicating the New Testament understanding of God's kingdom? A number of excellent reconstructions have been produced, many of which are filled with valid insights and true observations. But if we take the best of these and read it in direct conjunction with the New Testament, we are not content, not even if that reconstruction is our own. Why do these reconstructions seem at one moment so faithful and the next moment so distant from the original? The background, the motivation, the form are different. As a result, these reconstructions fail to follow the line Paul draws between the old age and the new, or the line John draws between darkness and light, or the line in the Apocalypse between the kingdoms of this world and the kingdom of Christ.

This is the area where responsible historical study of New Testament eschatology is producing the greatest strain on methodology. It has made us aware that an eschatology radically at odds with the pristine Christian faith is implicit in our modern historiography. This is not an issue that affects merely the location of the outermost boundary of the historical process. It affects both the perception of each event in history and the interpretation of that event. This is perhaps most obvious in the realm of conceptions of time. We have noted how a scientific hermeneutical method operates with a clear set of attitudes toward time. Any change in these attitudes will condition the application of the method everywhere. What happens, then, when we discover in the Bible attitudes toward time which not only claim to be true, but which also commend themselves to us with increasing power? The entire hermeneutical system is placed in question. This perhaps is the basic reason biblical studies are still in the midst of a vast, exciting, unpredictable transition. Let me suggest three tokens of this transformation.

(1) The first token is the growing awareness that historical time is transformed by the actual appearance within time of an event that is ultimate. In an ecumenical symposium published in 1951, John Marsh presented many arresting observations regarding this collision of time and eternity within history. He defined history thus: "There is a human time and a divine time . . . it is when these two coincide that real history is made."[1] Or thus: "History consists not only of God's action, though that is the primary and constitutive thing, but it consists also in man's reaction. . . . The standards of judgment are to be found, not in our human nature, empirical

and fallen, but in the perfect humanity of the 'proper man.' "[2] Certainly, as Marsh insisted, historical criticism has proceeded from a vastly different conception of history, a conception in which the element of succession is primary and the standards of judgment are found in empirical human nature. By using "objective" methods we can recover the centrality of the eschaton in biblical thought. We can examine the amazing claim of the apostles that this eschaton has already been inaugurated. But does historical methodology make sense of that claim? We can observe that in the first century certain people viewed all history from this vantage point between the times. But can this methodology adopt that standpoint? It seems clear that it cannot do so without dethroning the image of time that dominates hermeneutics. The conception of endless, unilinear, one-way time must be modified if we are to accept the apostolic testimony.

If the end has actually been inaugurated, then historical time is capable of embracing simultaneously both the old age and the new. No methodology whose presuppositions on time are limited to the old age will be adequate to cope with the historicity of the new age or with the temporal collision between the two times.

(2) The New Testament not only confesses the manifestation of eschatological reality within history in the form of an event, it also proclaims this event in terms of a person. As Marsh put it, Scripture itself offers the major hermeneutical key that must be retained and employed. This key is "Jesus Christ himself, our incarnate, crucified, risen, ascended, reigning Lord."[3] Christ takes the central interpretative place not only in the Bible but also in all history. The event of Christ is the only fully real and really full event, or as Dorothy Sayers said so famously, "the only thing that has ever really happened."[4] Surely such a dictum is impossible for radical historicism to accept. It is not much easier for a confessing Christian historian to adopt it as a basis for study of the past. Implicit in this eschatological confession is the demand to adopt a thoroughly Christocentric exegesis. This at least is the conclusion to which Father Georges Florovsky was drawn (in the same ecumenical symposium):

> The tension between present and future has in the Church of Christ another sense and character than it had under the old dispensation. For Christ is no more in the future only, but also in the past, and therefore in the present also. This eschatological perspective is of basic importance for understanding the right understanding of the Scriptures. All hermeneutical "principles" and "rules" should be re-thought and re-examined in this eschatological perspective.[5]

This rapid reorientation in New Testament studies has brought a strange reversal of emphases. Once our methodology insisted upon studying the literature, persons, and events of the Bible by the same methods as those used for all nonbiblical history. Without denying the propriety of this, some pioneers in that same methodology now insist that we should view all historical persons and events in the light of this eschatological event: Jesus revealed as God's Messiah. If the field of historical study is found to begin and to end in this Person, the methodology of study will not long be content with an impersonal chronology or with theories of impersonal causation. The process of calculating "times and seasons" will be as incongruous in dealing with the past as in predicting the future. The substance of history itself becomes eschatological, existential, and personal.

(3) Biblical theology has been moving toward a consensus, recognizing the fact that to early Christians the ultimate hope was inseparable from the event of crucifixion.[6] The end that arrived in the person of the Messiah was an end that came nearest to mortals at the cross. Obviously such a conviction does not make sense unless suffering is inherent in the fabric of history and unless such suffering is the locus of both creation and redemption.

To the first Christians the cross constituted a once-for-all event but it also had the power of revealing the hand of God in all earlier and later events. Prophets who had predicted the sufferings of Christ had followed the guidance of "the Spirit of Christ within them" (1 Pet. 1:11). New Testament historians viewed the past in the light of an *eschaton* in which glory was inseparable from suffering. The Passion story of the Messiah was a true epitome and consummation of that history, which is constituted by the coincidence of God's time and our time.

> The prophets have left no doubt that the way of faith leads to suffering. The believing community does not charge forward from victory to victory; but through apparent defeat, suffering and death it bears the banner of its Master. . . . The meaning and success of [the believer's] obedient service consist not in what he does and achieves, but in the way in which his service bears witness to *God's* mighty action.[7]

Now few can doubt that this is an accurate historical observation of the outlook of both Hebrew prophets and Christian apostles. But not many of us have explored the implications of this outlook for historical methodology. If this outlook is a true appraisal of the inner meaning and the ultimate telos of history-as-lived, then any reconstruction which proceeds on contrary assumptions moves steadily away from the truth rather than toward it. And who can deny that the objectivistic perception of time moves in an opposite direction? Our view of death is itself the point where the two antithetical conceptions of time collide. The defeat, suffering, and death of the Messiah constitute, according to one conception of time, the end of the Messiah, the termination of his career in time, and the defeat of his earthly purposes. The primacy of the element of succession in the notion of time is in fact one of the factors which make his defeat a final defeat and his suffering a final suffering. The apparent defeat of the dying Messiah can become a real triumph only through the revelation of a new time in which all things become new. If historians recognize that this has actually happened, how can they remain content with an historical methodology that implicitly embodies a sense of time they recognize to be false? Will they not be forced to recognize that the historiography reflected in the Pentateuch or in Acts is superior to that of Herodotus or Tacitus? Will not a huge chasm be opened between their own historiography and that of their secular colleagues? What has changed is not simply the picture of early Christian history but also conceptions of time, of persons and events, and of success and failure. And this change is produced by faith in "the God . . . who gives life to the dead and calls into existence the things that do not exist" (Rom. 4:17).

— 4 —
Biblical Ontology and Ecclesiology

I have examined in chapters 1–3 the inadequacy of the prevailing historical critical methodology to deal with the insistence by biblical authors on divine revelation and transcendence, this despite the discoveries of the past century regarding the importance of eschatology to biblical history. However, nowhere has the silence of biblical scholars regarding the divine been more pronounced than with the topic of biblical ontology.

Should modern biblical interpreters deal with such a topic? Are they obliged to clarify the ontological assertions and assumptions of the biblical writers? From our colleagues in other disciplines we hear differing answers to this question. Some philosophers demand from us greater concern with ontology. Others warn us against such concern. Still other philosophers, absorbed in the discoveries of linguistic analysis, repudiate even for themselves the legitimacy of ontological statements. Whether it is encouragement or discouragement that we receive from our academic colleagues, it must be admitted that few biblical scholars are willing to venture into this realm.

Many cogent reasons account for this. We are historians, not philosophers. The whole momentum of historical research has drawn us away from metaphysical engagement. In our training and in our teaching, we wrestle with the sequence of events, not with the shape of metaphysical doctrines. This orientation has been strengthened by prevailing tendencies to locate the genius of Hebraic thinking in its preference for dynamic historical action over static ontological speculation and to assume that ancient cosmological thought is necessarily archaic and outmoded, requiring translation into some modern outlook.

I am on the side of the philosophers who believe that as biblical historians we should do more than we have done by way of clarifying the ontological outlook of biblical authors. I believe that this is an essential part of our descriptive task. Each biblical author has given some answer to the question of being. That answer reflects a perception of primal and ultimate reality. It either asserts or assumes the existence of links between the immediate and the ultimate, between the finite and the infinite, between the temporal and the eternal. It is the historian's business to recapture the pattern of those assertions and assumptions, so far as that is possible. In the case of the Apocalypse especially, I believe that this goal is possible.

By contrast, there is little surprise in the second term in the chapter title, ecclesiology. Here our own conception of the task coincides more closely with the expectations of colleagues in other disciplines. The church is obviously an historical entity, the existence of which was important to ancient writers. The historian must therefore explore with care the structure and dynamics of biblical notions of the church.

It appears, then, that exegetes are universally expected to deal with ecclesiology, though not with ontology. It is my contention, however, that they cannot deal with the one without dealing with the other. Ontology and ecclesiology are quite inseparable, at least for the New Testament writers. In point of fact, ontology and ecclesiology are quite inseparable too for modern definitions of what it means to be the church. The pronouncements of the Montreal Conference on Faith and Order (1963) is exemplary: "In the Scriptures we read of the glory of the Church as the new creation and the body of the risen Lord, and of the Christians' participation by their thanksgiving and praise in the victory of Jesus Christ. But what does this glory and participation mean?"[1] Delegates at Montreal asserted their faith in the church as God's new creation, and as the Body of the crucified and risen Lord, but they found it impossible to define satisfactorily the relationship between this new creation and those human institutions which are called churches. How do existing churches participate in the divine life? How is God's life present in the daily behavior of the churches? The very formulation of these questions demonstrates the strategic importance of this ontological question: How should we speak of an ultimate reality that conjoins the divine and the human?

Consider, as a second example, the *Constitution on the Church* of

Vatican Council II. In the first chapter on the mystery of the Church we read:

> The society structured with hierarchical organs and the Mystical Body of Christ are not to be considered as two realities . . . rather they form one complex reality which coalesces from a divine and a human element. . . . This Church, constituted and organized in the world as a society, subsists in the Catholic Church.[2]

Such statements do not solve the ecclesiological problem, but pose it in such a way as to call for ontological analysis. It eliminates some solutions as unacceptable. These two realities can neither be wholly separated (the visible and the invisible church, the earthly and the heavenly church), nor can they be identical and coextensive. But the formulation leaves undefined the mode of their *coalescence* into one complex reality, as well as the mode by which this one reality *subsists* in the Catholic Church.

We now turn to the task of analyzing and describing the thought of the Apocalypse in this regard. I do not attempt in this chapter to deal with the total conception of reality (ontology) or with the total conception of the church (ecclesiology), but with the conjunction of these two. In fact, I limit my subject even further, focusing upon selected passages of the Apocalypse and asking what those passages suggest concerning (1) John's situation vis-à-vis his readers'; (2) his mode of apprehending space-time realities; (3) his conception of the two cities; and (4) his way of locating the boundary between these two cities. In each of these four areas we will try to observe the central ecclesiological and ontological implications.

JOHN'S SITUATION VIS-À-VIS HIS READERS'

The most significant links between John and his readers are suggested by Revelation 1:9. John is writing to the seven churches in Asia. He identifies himself as "your brother." He locates himself on the island called Patmos. He indicates the basic reason for his being there: "the word of God and the testimony of Jesus." As both brother and prisoner he stresses the common bonds between himself and his readers. Their fellowship is described as being in Jesus and as consisting of three elements: persecution, kingdom, and endurance.

This verse requires taking with full seriousness the empirical situation thus depicted. John and his readers are united in sharing an actual tribulation including a real or potential imprisonment because of common obedience to their Lord. In this tribulation they have a common need for endurance and a common temptation to follow an easier course. Such a temptation and such a need conditioned John's thinking and writing. There is an undeniable *historicity* to this situation in life. Common participation in suffering is as fully historical as the existence of the churches themselves. Yet this common participation in suffering was traced by John to at least five invisible factors: (1) "Jesus," in whom these Christians shared; (2) "the kingdom" with its power and glory, which belonged to them in Jesus and to which they belonged in Jesus; (3) "the word of God" for the sake of which they were all placed in jeopardy; (4) "the testimony of Jesus," whether given by them to Jesus or given by Jesus through them; and (5) those redemptive events through which they had become brothers and sisters, kings, priests, and witnesses (see also Rev. 1: 6).

Each of these data is indubitably historical to John. Yet each datum is also indubitably ontological and eschatological. The sequence, "persecution-kingdom-endurance," characterizes the period of the messianic woes, and is therefore thoroughly eschatological. But the same sequence is just as thoroughly historical, at least in John's thinking. He is speaking of present, existent realities in such a way as to discourage a disjunction between the present demands for endurance and the future reward of life in the Kingdom. On Patmos and in the seven cities of Asia the eschatological reality and the historical reality had become fused in this fellowship with one another in Jesus. John could not perceive this reality aright either by driving a wedge between the two or by identifying the two. The meaning of "the kingdom in Jesus" was conveyed by "the persecution in Jesus," and vice versa. John assumed that this same interdependence was true for his readers in the seven churches.

JOHN'S MODE OF APPREHENDING SPACE-TIME REALITY

In the vision of the two olive trees in Revelation 11, a similar fusion is reflected. Here the mode of communication is different, since the prophet is describing a vision of the temple, its inner and outer court, and the conflict that takes place there. But the experiential components of the situation are much the same. Here the same Lord is present and the same community is bound together by worship at the same altar in the same temple. The task of witnessing provokes the same persecution and releases the powers of the same Kingdom. The two witnesses are faithful to their task and thus exhibit the same endurance and receive in Jesus the same vindication. The prophet describes not only a coalescence of heavenly and earthly forces; he sees also in a single situation the coalescence of many times and places.

Let us note especially the implications of Revelation 11:8, "their dead bodies will lie in the street of the great city that is prophetically called Sodom and Egypt, where also their Lord was crucified." The significant elements in this verse attach to the triple designation of the great city. The one sentence mentions three diverse places. The first of these is Sodom—a city, an epoch, a story, a typological symbol. As a story, Sodom connoted the rejection of God's messengers, the blindness of stubborn rebellion, and the awfulness of God's judgment. As a typological symbol, the city is defined by the behavior of its citizens. Isaiah had earlier accused the rulers of Jerusalem of becoming the rulers of Sodom (Isa. 1:10; 3:9). Early Christian teachers had associated with Sodom the cities of Israel that rejected Jesus' messengers (Matt. 10:15; Luke 10:12). Capernaum's response to Jesus had been called more culpable than Sodom's sin (Matt. 11:24). Thus God's judgment of Sodom had come to represent the final inclusive judgment on all cities of rebellion.

The second place mentioned by John in Revelation 11:8 is Egypt. It is virtually certain that by John's day Egypt had become a typological name for all anti-theocratic world kingdoms. We are all familiar with how the stories of the Exodus, preserved in scripture and celebrated in the cultus, had made Egypt an epithet for all the enemies of Israel.

The third place John mentions here is the city "where also their Lord was crucified." Some interpreters have argued for the deletion of this clause, but they find no textual support. Surely the most obvious meaning is right: *Jerusalem*, or better *that* Jerusalem that had killed the prophets and crucified the Messiah and had thus demonstrated its kinship with Sodom and Egypt.

A fourth city must be added to the three explicitly mentioned. In the vocabulary of John "the great city" carried a special reference to Babylon. In seven other appearances in the Apocalypse the phrase has this undoubted reference. In John's day Babylon was an accepted apocalyptic symbol for enmity against God and against his beloved city. In the Apocalypse Babylon as "the great city" is the antithesis to the city of God, which is normally called the holy city, or the beloved city (Rev. 20:9).

Because the prophet is speaking of Babylon in this verse, we may also include a fifth city, Rome. Unless most interpreters of the Apocalypse are wrong, John quite definitely had Rome in mind. Thus, in each of the five—Sodom, Egypt, Babylon, Jerusalem, and Rome—the definitive element is corporate response to God's witnesses and prophets.

Many commentaries devote primary attention to locating literary antecedents and parallel references to these five cities. Not often do they ask what conception of reality enabled John to see all these places as one place, all these epochs as one. How could he bring so many different events within a single frame of reference without destroying their historical specificity? He could do this in part by using a literary device, that is, by telling one story in such a way as to embrace many stories. But this is more than a literary device. It is a way of perceiving reality. He saw each story as fully historical, and yet as fully eschatological. There operated within his mind a "symbolism of the center" (*Mircea Eliade*), a perspective that accented simultaneously both the particularity of five cities and their common origin and destiny. For John, space functioned in such a way as to unite Sodom and Rome, not to separate them. Time did not separate the Pharaohs from the Roman emperors but brought them together. He perceived each separate place and time in terms of its content, that corporate historical action that "filled it." He discerned behind this action a transhistorical model that linked each story to the others.

This is a comprehensive rather than a disjunctive mode of seeing and thinking. It apprehends events in terms of their inner structure as responses to God's action. God's action in each epoch induced a recognizable pattern of reactions, and the prophet sought to discern that pattern for the sake of his readers. Egypt remained a distinctive name but it conveyed a symbolic richness of meaning neither limited by the original context nor scornful of it. Behind this mode of viewing was a distinctive ontological stance, to which we should give more attention than we usually do.

Two additional comments are in order. In the first place, because it is impossible to limit the identity of the great city to one geographical entity, I believe it is also impossible to limit the identity of the two olive trees to two specific prophets. We are familiar with efforts to establish their identity: Moses, Elijah, Enoch, Peter, Paul, and others. For each conjecture, some evidence can be cited in the text, but no conjecture has thus far convinced all exegetes. This impasse may be due not to the lack of exegetical ingenuity but to John's intention. If he had intended to construct an allegory, then the reader should be able to decode his system of algebraic equivalents, X=Moses and Y=Elijah, and so forth. But if his intention was to describe the transcendental model of all genuine prophecy, as most clearly revealed in the death and resurrection of Jesus, his description of the two lampstands would echo the stories of many prophets. Our difficulties in establishing the identity of two, and only two, lampstands simply demonstrate the disparity between our modes of viewing reality and John's.

In the second place, we should not forget the congruity between John's situation, as reflected in Revelation 1:9, and his description of the two olive trees in Revelation 11. On Patmos, John saw himself as bound to the conflict, the fate, the vocation of the two witnesses. His imprisonment because of "the word of God" enabled him to see that island on the map of the five cities and to understand his months spent there as part of the time of Sodom and the Exodus. This conjunction between John's vocation and that of the two prophets is strongly supported by the literary links between Revelation 10 and 11. John is ordered to prophesy to the very same audience (cf. Rev. 10:11 and 11:8). Thus the vision in Revelation 11 includes also the persecution faced by the churches in Asia. John and his readers shared the kingdom not only with one another, but with Lot, Moses, Elijah, Isaiah, Ezekiel, Jeremiah, and Jesus. The churches had experienced first-hand the work of true prophets (Antipas, Rev. 2:13), of false prophets (Jezebel, Rev. 2:20), and of the second beast (Rev. 20:10).

JOHN'S CONCEPTION OF THE TWO CITIES

Chapter 11 of the Apocalypse can be analyzed in terms of the five (or more) cities that are explicitly or implicitly mentioned, all of which can be described as the place where the witnesses are to be slain and where "their Lord was crucified." But the same chapter can be analyzed as well in terms of *two* cities, "the great city" and "the holy city" (verses 2 and 8). This division is more basic to the thought of John and to his literary and analogical method, since for him every event has its divine and demonic sides, expressive of the final conflict that constitutes the eschatological dimension of the historical decisions of God's people.

As "the great city" Jerusalem is the place of crucifixion. This is the place where the two witnesses complete or perfect their assignment (Rev. 11:7) and as such is reminiscent of the gospel sayings concerning the necessity for a prophet to perish in Jerusalem (Matt. 23:37; Luke 13:33-34) and for the Messiah to be perfected and to make his "exodus" there (Luke 9:31). His death makes this city the place where the beast rises from the abyss to make war upon the two emissaries. This text thus localizes in Jerusalem the great war with the devil, the messianic conflict in which the beast operates as the great adversary of God's people. The place is further described as the place for the exposure of the dead bodies, to be seen and laughed at by many peoples, tribes, tongues, and nations. This fourfold formula is one of John's favorite ways of expressing catholicity, both in space and in time. This universal audience is further described as the earth-dwellers, another typical formula of the apocalyptist. They are the citizenry of Babylon (Rev. 17:2) who worship and serve the beast (Rev. 13:8, 12, 14) as idolatrous enemies of the saints and prophets (Rev. 6:10), and as those whom the two prophets had tormented (Rev. 11:10). This same place, this same audience, provides the scene for the *anabasis* (ascension) of the prophets (Rev. 11:12) and their vindication by God. This is "the great city."

How does John describe Jerusalem as *the holy city?* He does not describe its location by reference to a different map. This Jerusalem shares the fate of God's messengers, being "trampled" by the nations for forty-two months (Rev. 11:2). This image of trampling is a vivid symbol of one power being visibly in control of another. Both the trampled city and the murdered prophets are signs of the beast's victory. However, John distinguishes the outer court from "the temple of God and the altar and those who worship there" (Rev. 11:1). The prophet is commanded to measure this *inner space*, not the outer court. Why this distinction? Perhaps to show that although the holy city is despoiled, it also remains immune to desecration, just as the two prophets are both immune and vulnerable. The inner sanctuary, that temple which belongs to God, that altar where true sacrifices are presented, and those people who truly worship in this temple, remains unscathed by the desecration of the outer court. The two lampstands that fulfill their vocation "before the Lord of the earth" stand in this temple, yet they stand at the same time in the streets of "the great city." Their story thus becomes an epitome of the collision between the two cities. The great city embraces all the places and times of rebellion and captivity; the holy city embraces all the places and times of prophetic vocation. Between the two cities is constant conflict, yet also a transhistorical resolution of that conflict. John is enabled to discern the reality of both cities by the light of the death and resurrection of Jesus

Christ. This event discloses to him the presence of "the great city" wherever mortals reject "the word of God and the testimony of Jesus," and the presence of "the holy city" wherever they are faithful to that word and testimony.

Having described the two cities, we should ask the ontological question, in what sense do these two represent ultimate reality? The answer depends on the relationship of each city to its God. The holy city is described as the temple of God, its altar, and those who worship there (Rev. 11:1). The other is described as the place where the earth-dwellers serve and worship the beast (Rev. 13:8). It is the enmity between the two lords that discloses the nature of both cities, and because this enmity is at once primordial and eschatological, the cities are seen to participate in whatever degree of ultimacy belongs to their lords.

The life of God is ontologically bound to the life of his holy city. This eternal kingdom is fully shared with God's anointed one and is embodied in the thrones and the worship of the twenty-four elders (Rev. 11:16). The temple, the altar, and the worshipers constitute one community (Rev. 11:1). This same ultimate reality is embodied in the authority given to the two olive trees, their immunity to injury, and their death and resurrection. Their story is a disclosure of the glory of the God of heaven. By its worship of God the beloved city inherits God's kingdom, glory, power, and eternal life. It transcends time by being at once a primal and an eschatological reality. Because its God and its Lord are rightly called Alpha and Omega, the city that bears their name is rightly seen as a city which is and was and is to come.

In a parallel way, "the great city" inherits its existence, power, and kingdom from the beast of the abyss. This reality, too, is transhistorical, in that it embraces the stories of Sodom, Egypt, Babylon, Jerusalem, and Rome. Its glory is inseparable from its false worship, its adulterous blasphemy. Its power is manifest in its victory over God's witnesses, its trampling over the outer court of God's temple. Such victory makes it the archetype for many historical triumphs. Thus the prophet views history in terms of two interlocking mysteries—the mystery of God's kingdom and of the devil's. Both claim to be the ultimate reality, yet only one can truly be such. Both of these realities represent a "coalescence" of divine and human wills and in both the superhuman reality subsists within the human. Yet only one of the two can be *Alpha* since the other is a reaction to its appearance (Rev. 11:7). The same city can alone be *Omega*, since its king alone has received an eternal sovereignty (Rev. 11:15). The two can be rightly distinguished only by the death and resurrection of this king as witnessed to by his prophets. The "testimony of Jesus" thus enables John to discern the boundaries between the two cities, as well as the true ultimacy of the one and the deceptive ultimacy of the other.

JOHN'S VIEW OF THE BOUNDARY BETWEEN THE CITIES

It can hardly be denied that John was immediately and primarily concerned with the dilemmas of the churches. He was commissioned as a prophet to interpret God's revelation in Christ and to mediate God's demands to the churches. We may therefore locate the boundary line between the two cities by studying these demands. Through the words of the prophet, the living Lord addressed those churches; this address took the form of explicit and implicit exhortations. The hortatory thrust was conveyed by a variety of literary forms. There are the easily recognized beatitudes, direct imperatives and hortatory subjunctives. There are also various catalogs or lists of those actions by which mortals are excluded from the holy city or included within it.

In the kinds of actions proscribed or enjoined there is also a wide range. The Spirit calls upon the seven churches to repent, remember, return, awake, watch, worship, bear witness, endure, keep Christ's works, follow the Lamb, bear on their forehead his name, don white garments, and be holy and chaste and faithful to the end. There is a kaleidoscopic variation in vocabulary, yet this variation is more verbal than actual. The same action can be indicated by different commands. To worship is to endure, to awake, to follow, and so forth. Each action is a form of bearing witness to the Lamb that was slain. All imperatives flow from the same source, the heavenly throne. All convey a sense of great urgency. None permits neutrality or compromise. The basic obligation is inescapable, though there is everywhere a temptation to escape.

This is particularly clear in the lists of citizens in the two cities. Here let us focus attention upon the catalog in Revelation 21:8, which includes: "the cowardly, the faithless, the polluted, the murderers, the fornicators, the sorcerers, the idolaters, and all liars." This list is a summary of typical actions against which John was exhorting the churches. Each of them is antithetically balanced by positive traits which characterize citizens of the holy city (e.g., against the cowardly may be set those who obey the command to be fearless, Rev. 2:10).

It is important to remember that John was addressing only the servants of Christ, and that he had in mind actual tendencies within the seven churches. Because these sins were constitutive of "the great city," John was concerned with them as the mode by which Satan was attacking, deceiving, and tempting citizens of "the holy city." It had been the appearance of the Messiah that had aroused the devil to combat. Now the existence of Christ's servants was activating the devil's most deceptive wiles. In this context the cowards (Rev. 21:8) are not those who have never known the glory of the holy city, but those who, having known it, are induced by their anxieties to defect. Liars are excluded from the new Jerusalem, but they become liars by betraying their confession (Rev. 14:4). Idolaters are excluded because, knowing the true God, they have been lured into worshiping his enemy. Fornication implies breaking a former wedding pledge. Pollution presupposes an avowed and intended chastity (cf. Rev. 21:8; 14:4). One reason the apocalyptic descriptions seem so grotesque and lurid is this: the bizarre antitheses underscore the deceptive coexistence of two orders that are originally and ultimately incompatible. The picture of the beast is a fantastic parody of the picture of the Lamb, as is the parody of the pure bride by the great whore.

John's concern throughout is with the behavior of persecuted insiders, not persecuting outsiders. He was assigned the bittersweet task (Rev. 10:10) of countering the invasion of demonic deceptions within the churches. The earthly life of those churches was coterminous with this warfare between the two cities. The eschatological glory of the heavenly city was coterminous with the death and resurrection of the churches, that is, with their apparent defeat by Satan but their actual victory over him. This is conveyed very clearly by the climactic promises in the seven letters (e.g., "To everyone who conquers, I will give permission to eat from the tree of life," Rev. 2:7).

I have been seeking to execute an historian's task of describing the pattern of thought characteristic of the Apocalypse. As a theologian I believe this pattern to be relevant, though not necessarily normative, for current discussions of hermeneutics, ethics, ecclesiology, and ontology. As a mode of communication, the Apocalypse is an example of the radical interdependence of these four aspects of biblical thought, an interdependence too often absent from current thinking. I believe that as biblical scholars we have a responsibility for making this interdependence as clear as we can. This sort of investigation of the ontological viewpoint of the Apocalypse should be extended to the other genres of literature in order to obtain a more complete idea of the ontological perspective that is in some degree paradigmatic for the entire New Testament.

The ontological viewpoint discovered here, because it includes a strongly ecclesial element, provides a good basis for analyzing church pronouncements regarding the essence of the church, its life and work, and for contrasting Catholic with Protestant approaches. This is true because such pronouncements, though they address an ecclesiological problem, pose it in such a way (as we have already indicated above) as to call for ontological analysis. This is an important, but often unrecognized or underutilized, function of biblical theology.[3]

For example, the Apocalypse provides a good basis for analyzing the Vatican II *Constitution on the Church*. The ontological perspective of the Apocalypse would support the effort of the framers of that document to orient thinking around the mystery of the church and to utilize the christological images of the New Testament in theological construction. It would also support the convictions that the earthly and heavenly aspects of the church's existence form not two realities but one, which coalesces from a divine and a human element. On the other hand, the ecclesiology of the Apocalypse suggests that greater importance should be accorded to the reality of Babylon. "The great city" may be far more present, far more threatening, far more definitive of the boundaries of "the holy city" than the framers of the Vatican II *Constitution* allowed. The stories of Babylon and Jerusalem may be far more subtly and dialectically intertwined in the history of the church than the *Constitution* suggests. Moreover, the actions of obedience appear to me to be far more constitutive of the church in the Apocalypse than in the *Constitution*. In John's message these actions are more genuinely episodes in warfare than they appear to be in the *Constitution*, where the enemies of the church are very hazily defined indeed. Comparison with the Apocalypse also raises the question of whether the transition from the mystery of the church to its hierarchical structures can be so readily and smoothly made as in the *Constitution* (between ¶ 17 and ¶ 18). John is not to be interpreted, of course, as attacking all churchly structures, but neither does he support unequivocal identification of hierarchical structures with the *militia dei*.

Where Catholic theology tends to stress the bond between the holy city and the empirical churches, the tendency of Protestant theology is to stress their separateness by drawing too sharply the distinction between invisibility and visibility or the more recent distinction between the historical level and the eschatological. The motive for this distinction is often quite in line with that of John, who, as we have seen, insists on the ontological importance of the criteria of death and resurrection. To John, every citizen of the new Jerusalem must share in the dying of the Lord Jesus. A common testimony is constitutive of the communion of saints. But for John the eschatological is not so clearly disjoined from the historical level as is true for many Protestant ecclesiologists. This reality is a city—a city that descends from heaven to earth. This holy city is more closely, more substantially, more permanently linked to the earthly churches than most existentialists admit. For John, the eschatological is also the primordial, the heavenly ground of being, apart from which the churches could not exist. The *subsistence* of this heavenly reality within the earthly churches is for John the necessary presupposition for his appeal to his readers, the basis of his understanding of history, and the truth without which the lies of Satan would be unintelligible. I believe that the Protestant tendency to stress the discontinuities between the holy city and the churches stems from deficiencies in ontological perspective that John can help to correct. The Catholic tendency stems also from an ontology different from John's. It is for this reason that the study of the interdependence in the Apocalypse of ontology, ecclesiology, ethics, and hermeneutics can be productive of fruitful results. John's ecclesiology does not fit easily within the traditional position of either Catholicism or Protestantism. It can therefore contribute greatly to contemporary discussions of the nature of the church.

I want especially to stress the contribution that a study of John's book can make to our descriptive historical work. Early Christian apocalyptic has been rightly called "the mother of Christian theology" (E. Kasemann). It should also be called the mother of Christian ontology because it viewed historical decisions and events in the light of an ultimate concern for their ultimate context in the purpose and action of God.

— 5 —
Divine Revelation and Human Knowledge

T

Today in the academic world professors and students alike assume that any address in defense of "revealed religion" is bound to be an attack on the liberties of the emancipated mind, however surreptitious and disarming the technique. They ask, is religion not a means by which professional priests exercise control over their people? And is not a claim to divine revelation essential in maintaining that control? There is undoubtedly a measure of fairness in these questions. Far too often revelation has been defended as a divinely authorized tariff wall that chokes the channels of intellectual commerce. I have been persuaded, however, that God's revelation in Jesus Christ is an ultimate guarantee of human freedom, including, most of all, the liberties of the mind.

To this matter we will return before the end of our discussion. In the meantime let me outline this discussion: first, the boundaries of academic knowledge; second, the Christian conception of God's revelation; third, the manner by which the church gains access to knowledge of God; and finally, the self-knowledge that God thus gives his people.

BOUNDARY QUESTIONS

Let us begin by visualizing that process we call the extension of academic knowledge. Here is a student in a library cell, scribbling away with cramped fingers and knit brows—a scholar at work. As commencement speakers insist, this student is the living center of the educational process. From this mind radiate lines of force bent on subduing stubborn data. These lines are focused not only on the immediate book, but also on a more distant goal—tomorrow's class assignment, a term paper, or an academic degree. As the student scrounges notes, this goal determines which quotes to crib and how these jottings are to be filed. Throughout the course of study, the movements of mind and pen are circumscribed by time. Each academic assignment carries a deadline. The library closes at ten o'clock. The watch warns him of the next appointment. But when a spark from the page ignites the fires of the mind, the rotation of the clock is forgotten. Time forgotten is time filled with meaning. When time is most full of meaning, the present is most alive. Yet this surcharged present is not isolated from the past or the future. Rather the past and the future come to life in a new way when the student, prompted by a particular goal, becomes absorbed in the process of discovery. There are limits, however, to this process, limits that can be described as the capacities of the student, the character of the goal, and the boundaries of the time.

From another perspective, the academic monk is not the center at all, but a denizen of a monastery. The school is a center in which, at least in a limited way, each participant, whether student or teacher, is a member of the others. The library, the classroom, the laboratory—these are corporate aids in the voyage of discovery. Discoveries in the realm of the mind are never purely private. The individual scientist may patent the result of a laboratory experiment, but the result is no less a fruit of collective effort. When the student is at his or her best, then, too, is the community.

Moreover, it is obvious that this community bears a unique sense of selfhood, seeks its own goals, and embodies a complex involvement in time. It lives in the now, but its life cannot be restricted to the mere present. Things past and things future meet in contemporary choices. The life of the group gives meaning to time, and yet it is also bound by time. On the basis of previous discoveries, this community provides maps of space and time on which the student locates individual discoveries. When the students march off their own self-made maps, they discover that they are still able to locate their bearings on the larger maps provided by academic disciplines. The power of the academic community to sketch maps covering both the atom and the galaxies has been firmly vindicated; its methods of inquiry have proved their competence over ever widening territories.

Even these maps, however, for all their accuracy and coverage, do not provide answers to all questions. There are both inward and outward landscapes that cannot be charted. Existential perspectives defy the best diagrams. The actual substance of the common life and the actual contours of its environment elude exact measurement and control. The existence of the community, no less than that of the person, is surrounded by profound and universal mysteries. It is easier, to be sure, to avoid recognition of mystery when dealing with corporate knowledge because the life of the monastery possesses greater solidity and continuity than does the life of the monk. It is more difficult to locate a vantage point from which to examine the axiomatic structure of group-consciousness. It is also more dangerous to examine the stock of assumptions by which the corporate ego has shaped its own world. Yet who will deny, on the ground of danger or difficulty alone, that questions must be raised which affect the inner core of community, the shape of it goals, and the significance of its time?

A mind lives and grows on its questions. But which questions offer the best nourishment? Some are rhetorical questions in which the answers are implicit in the questions themselves. Some are didactic questions, given by a teacher who knows the answers, for the sake of increasing or testing the student's memory and proficiency. Others are exploratory questions, which can be answered using appropriate reference books. Still others are maieutic questions, designed to force into consciousness the latent knowledge of truth. None of these is an ultimate question. An ultimate query eludes present capacities to answer because it emerges at the very boundary of human existence. Some boundaries are quite tentative because further accumulation of data and improvement of techniques will erase them. Some boundaries are temporary because the extension of present lines of progress will overrun them. But the outermost horizon persists, and no advance in accumulative knowledge can erase it. It is at such a horizon, where "there is only the flash of negative knowledge" (Auden), that we raise ultimate questions, even though we know too little about the boundaries to phrase the questions properly. It is a mark of the parochialism of the modern mind that these questions are so often called irrelevant. Actually only questions of this sort can be relevant in an ultimate sense. We have already intimated the burden of some of these questions.

First of all, what is the innermost status and structure of the self? Mental growth is, in part at least, a process by which knowledge of the self grows. But the more we learn about the self the more the self eludes our knowledge. It feeds on hidden sources that we cannot examine. It disappears behind every mirror into which we look and vanishes behind the eyes with which we look. The act of looking furnishes a sure hiding place for the pursued. Increasing knowledge may aid in detecting various masks and evasions, but it does not aid in apprehending the actual person, who always disappears behind a still more deceptive disguise. Yet this secretive self remains the active subject in all its knowing and doing.

Second, how is this hidden self related to its goals, its destiny? What is the connection between the potential future and the actual present? The typical posture of the person is one of leaning forward toward something that is not yet. As long as it is alive, the self is greedy and fearful of those unknown possibilities that we call tomorrow. It is both repelled and attracted by the crystal ball. It struggles to defend itself against the future, and to that end it jealously guards whatever hostage the past has provided. Or, resentful of the past, it looks forward toward its vindication. Tomorrow offers the twin possibilities of being and nonbeing, and the question of *which* it is to be affects the morale of the self today. Death, as Rilke repeats, is "the silent, knowing partner of the living." We all bear death within ourselves, as "the fruit which nourishes the whole." What our hope *is* we may not say; but *that* our hope *constitutes* our very *being* we cannot deny. And most of us are realistic enough to know that the true future, with its genuine possibilities, lies beyond the jurisdiction of our own knowledge and power. The relation of the self-that-is to the self-that-is-to-be remains a riddle.

Third, what does time have to do with the fullness of life? The person who hopes and fears becomes conscious of time. Time can serve as an enemy of our projects, an aid to our movements, or as a neutral tool of measurement. It provides both a parenthesis bracketing our dreams, and a rhythm punctuating our days.

Time continues in its irrevocable sequence, yet we know not what it is nor what purpose it serves. We may detect the beginnings and endings of limited periods of time, but the beginning of time and its end reach always beyond our vision. Unable to bound time, we postulate eternity as unconditioned by time, but how much this really means is dubious, for we are contrasting two unknown things that may be qualitatively different. Yet the self that is time-bound is also time-transcendent. It knows of a time that is relative to its purposes and its frustrations. It experiences "bright occasions" which are neither in time nor enslaved by it. It uses time, consumes it, fills it, redeems it. The clock that tells the passing of the hours tells also of those who use the clock to enhance and fulfill the meaning of life. But what is *time in relation to us?* And what are we *in relation to time?*

Fourth, what is the ultimate structure and function of community? Whatever we may say about the mystery of the self may also be said about the mystery of community. Awareness of the bounds of personal existence is accompanied by an awareness of abysses of meaning in the lives of others. We are able to increase a certain kind of objective knowledge about them by assembling observations of their behavior, by tracing sequences in their story, and by comparing their abilities with the norms of group achievement. Yet the more we know about them the more we know that in each person there is an inner citadel of selfhood that we shall never penetrate. There is a rich concreteness to their story that can never be reduced to words. There *are* chasms in social intercourse that we cannot bridge. What separates us, however, also makes us fellows, for we are united by the same boundaries of life and death, by the ultimate walls of a mutual strangeness, by the problematic character of the ground on which we all stand. The community is constituted by depths of individuality and mutuality that elude the research of any science. Fellowship we know, but what constitutes the ultimate ground of an eternal fellowship we do not know.

The borders we have described are not merely the limits of our perceptive faculties as finite creatures. They mark more than the line between the finite and the infinite, the relative and the absolute. What ultimately surrounds our life at its center and circumference, at its beginning and end, is not an "it," but a "Thou." Our contact with the boundaries of our existence is a personal encounter. Faith spells out the implications of this encounter with its skeptical question, "Who by seeking can find out God?" In this question all genuine questions are raised.

God is one whom we can neither find with our knowledge nor escape in our ignorance. Whether we take refuge in cynical relativism or in idolatrous absolutism, there is a hound who follows—follows after with "unperturbed pace" (G. M. Hopkins). The boundaries mark the place where he addresses us and where we turn in futile flight. That is to say, all ultimate questions are theological questions, and the answers, if they are to embody more than the shadow of our sin, must be given by God himself. When he gives the answers, however, we should not expect him to follow the pattern of our questions.

APOCALYPSIS

God answers in an action that we call revelation. It is of such revelation that Christian theologians speak. They begin not with abstract analysis, but with the concrete testimony that God has disclosed himself in a decisive way in Jesus Christ, once-upon-a-time and once-for-all-time. The key words for disclosure in the New Testament are *apocalypsis* (revelation) and *apocalypto* (reveal)—a noun and a verb, but in both the primary accent is verbal. The word refers to an event, to an act that discloses the hidden God who acts. The various uses of the word all rest upon the basic event narrated as good news: "In Jesus Christ God was reconciling the world to himself." What we are confronted with in revelation is not the "ontological exaltation" of some fragment of human knowledge but the historical humiliation of the true God.

In this humiliation the central events are Christ's death and resurrection. These events are central because they illuminate both prior and subsequent history. In them we are judged as guilty; in them we are summoned to enter into God's kingdom. The scriptures address us with the words, "God has made both Lord and Christ this Jesus whom you crucified. . . . Repent" (Acts 2:36, 38 [RSV]).

According to the New Testament, this revelation is not to be grasped first of all as the hypothetical solution to an intellectual riddle. Rather is it to be trusted as the action of a personal God sharing his love *with* persons *through* a person. It is not a sly way by which finite creatures build dream castles out of temporal frustrations; rather it is the means of proving the accusation that they have rejected the health and peace that God has offered. Revelation is not a gift to superior individuals, making them secure in a knowledge that has been arbitrarily denied to fellow-mortals; rather it is the majestic condemnation of all of us by a Messiah whom we join in crucifying.

Such a disclosure would be emptied of its redemptive power were it to become a device for buttressing the claims of one religion in its battle for dominance over others. What is revealed is not a religion but the Most High God whose justice and mercy encompass the histories of all. Nowhere does the New Testament encourage the use of the phrase *revealed religion*. It never uses the adjective nor does it speak of the content of revelation as *religion*. The gospel speaks of the disclosure *of God*, a disclosure mediated *by Jesus Christ* not as a Christian but as a human person, a disclosure that places on every person and every religion the

76

stamp of final judgment and final redemption. Through the work of Christ the God of hope consigns all creation to futility in order that he may include all creation in his adoption as children. In short, the revelation of which we are speaking is thoroughly eschatological.

Revelation is eschatological, in the first place, because it is a movement from the beyond into the here, from God's world into our world. Whenever he speaks finally about himself, the God who is Omega and Alpha "speaks finally about the world process" (J. A. T. Robinson). His purposive action moves from the coming age into the present and links contemporary events firmly to their consummation.

Revelation in the Messiah is eschatological, secondly, because of the finality of the events through which it is mediated—the death and resurrection of Jesus. His death was his own death, the death of a man who dies once and not a second time. It was also the death of Adam and the death of all, since "he tasted death for all." Such death is beyond doubt an eschatological category. So, too, is the Messiah's resurrection. His life-through-death is the life in which all shall be made alive. To him as first-born of the dead was given the power to beget the same life in those who "were dead through trespasses and sins."

The proclamation of the gospel is eschatological, thirdly, because it discloses the present moment as the fullness of time. The demand for repentance transforms the ordinary day into the dawn of the Lord's Day. Present isolation, present frustration, present despair, present idolatries of action—these are confronted with the Word of the cross, with the promise of life through death. The God who was disclosed to all on Golgotha and who will manifest himself to all in the Parousia is now pressing in on all and compelling them to a decision. Each present situation is laid bare as the scene of a critical choice. Wherever the Crucified is acknowledged as the reigning Lord, there the thoughts of many hearts are revealed, secrets which otherwise would never have been known. The Messiah's cross is God's sword, slicing through pious self-deceptions and frantic self-justifications. The fire that he kindles is the refiner's fire by which all works are tested. The warfare which he precipitates transforms human actions into fateful episodes in a final cosmic struggle between the Messiah and "the rulers of this darkness." Revelation turns the Now into a point where the transient world meets the Eternal Kingdom, where the ego must crucify its pride and be reborn into life with the Messiah, into the family of the poor in spirit.

Finally, God's self-disclosure is eschatological because it "pre-enacts" the coming of the Messiah, when he will complete his work of subject-ing every enemy. In Christ has taken place such an invasion of human life that nothing human and historical will in the end remain outside his kingdom. God has already given the Messiah dominion over death and life, over angels and principalities, over things present and things to come. In the end this dominion will be demonstrated to every creature. The gospel confronts us with the signs of this consummation and sum-mons us to participate in the final conflict. Revelation is always voca-tional—and because the revelation is final, this vocation provides an ultimate beginning and end for the pilgrim journey. All this is so sweep-ing, so inclusive, so grandiose, that it is easy to forget what must not be forgotten—that the event of revelation was the ministry of a humble Galilean carpenter who accomplished his messianic work on the ridiculed and obnoxious cross.

GNOSIS

We are now prepared to deal with the question: How does the church gain access to the knowledge of God? By what activities is its knowledge enhanced? It should be obvious that the manner of knowing God should accord with the event of revelation itself. Revelation is as closely linked to saving knowledge as is the death of Jesus Christ to his resurrection. Since the agent of revelation is personal, the church's relation to him will be personal—a relationship for which the bonds of human love are dim but suggestive analogies. The knower, like the lover, is able to know because the knower is already known and loved. The act of knowledge proceeds within the relationship of being known by God.

The revelation of God, as we have noted, carried with it the implicit and uncompromising demand: Repent. The act of repentance is an act of knowledge, an act of acknowledging and accepting God's judgment. God's epiphany thus becomes "the heart's epiphany" (Rilke). In the light of the cross the ego accepts itself as guilty, as estranged from God, yet now drawn by God within the circle of his mercy. In repentance the war-ring ego is brought to a total surrender, recognizing that its pride has been undermined by God's self-emptying. The ego-enhancing structures of community are demolished by the power of the cross, "towering o'er the wrecks of time."

The gospel is equally ruthless in its demand for mercy. Only by an act of forgiveness can the church know itself as forgiven. By acts of peace-making the church learns what it means to be children of a God of peace. Only in an act of self-forgetting and outgoing intercession can the beloved fully enter into the knowledge of what love actually is. Hidden within this knowledge is the door to self-knowledge. The segregated church is segregated not only from true knowledge of God, but also from a true understanding of itself. And knowledge of itself as loved is insepa-rable from knowledge of the world as loved. God's self disclosure always conveys an absolute imperative: obedience. The gospel proclaims each act of obedience as an act of knowing him in whom was perfect obedi-ence. It proclaims each taking up of the cross as a step toward fuller knowledge of the power that is made perfect in weakness. Such knowl-edge is too wonderful for the church, yet it is this very knowledge that makes the church the church. The church knows what revelation means when it obeys the summons to share the mission of God's Son, who through suffering redeems every time and brings every place within the orbit of glory.

The following, then, are ways by which the church enters into authen-tic knowledge of revelation: repentance, forgiveness, and obedient faith-fulness to its mission as Christ's body. Each act of knowledge is creative of new sinews of strength, new bonds of mutuality, and new motivation for continuing the reconciling ministry for the world.

It should be clear at once that the basic categories in this type of knowledge are incommensurable with the categories of our scientific dis-ciplines. Each increment of this knowledge is a work of grace that leaps across the ultimate boundaries of ordinary existence, from the beyond into the here, from the then into the now. Such knowledge is not some-thing gained once for all, something that accumulates until we are able to push beyond the bounds of time and space, but something that trans-forms the surface of things from the invisible center. It recognizes the sign of death and resurrection at the core of every situation, and this sign invests that situation with immediate importance stemming from Christ's eschatological action. His action does not negate the concerns of everyday life but imparts to them an ultimate and decisive significance. The knowledge of his kingdom does not lead to exaggerating the impor-tance of the transient present, but it enables the church to re-perceive each day in the light of God's abiding intention to rule within it.

What has been said about revelation should make clear the fact that the church's knowledge of God does not conflict with other forms of knowledge so long as these other forms do not claim unlimited autonomy. The church has not found an esoteric shortcut that replaces the tedious processes of research. It does not jealously guard a secret scientific formula. It does not claim exclusive jurisdiction over any province on the scholar's map. The relevance of revelation appears at the boundaries of accumulated human knowledge, but these boundaries, we repeat, lie within as well as without. The impact of revelation transforms the knower, transfigures the community of knowers, and orients the church's knowledge around a new center and toward a new goal. We come, then, to the question: What is the "content" of the knowledge that God's disclosure conveys to the church? And more specifically, what knowledge does the church receive concerning its own distinctive existence?

KOINONIA

The answer, I believe, may be indicated in terms of *koinonia*. The usual translation is fellowship, but this rendering is altogether too subjective, too sentimental, too weak. C. H. Dodd prefers the idea of shareholding: "*Koinonoi* are persons who hold property in common" as joint owners. Their solidarity is as objective and tangible as that. But *koinonia* goes much deeper than financial partnership, since Christians have been made partners with Christ and in him. They are joint heirs of a common life bestowed by him through the Spirit. This solidarity is so complete that what belongs to the whole community belongs to each member, and vice versa. Sharing in this life changes the status of each partner and decisively redefines what it means to exist.

The emergence of this solidarity is central to the church's knowledge of itself and also furnishes clues to the boundary questions that we have raised. In the first place, because of its partnership in Christ, the church knows itself to be one. He shared fully in human flesh and blood, in Adam's sinning and dying. His sharing with us established our solidarity with him. Or as the Epistle to the Hebrews phrases it: "The one who sanctifies and those who are sanctified all have one Father" (Heb. 2:11). He is not divided; neither is his Body. The togetherness of the church in his death is, however, a complex rather than a simple fact. There is a oneness in the guilt for his death—Adam is Judas. There is a oneness in the enmity for which he prayed forgiveness, in the lostness of the world for which he died. The church also becomes one with him when it truly proclaims his death as God's power and wisdom. It becomes one with him in dying with him—the daily dying in repentance and the daily dying of a reconciling ministry.

Second, the church's communion in the Body of Christ conveys its solidarity with the living and returning Christ. In witnessing to the revelation of God in the cross and the Resurrection, it witnesses to the coming epiphany of Jesus Christ with all who belong to him. The church has been delivered from darkness into the dawn of a new day. It lives by the ingressive powers of the coming day, strengthened by the firstfruits of the final harvest. The acts of repentance and love are acts of knowledge by which the church apprehends the love that will exercise the final power and the final justice. It knows that every revelation of his power brings surprising repudiations of those who rely on cheap grace and cheap substitutes for obedience. As the spearhead of the advancing Kingdom, the church knows that every fullness of time is marked by conflict and suffering before joy and glory are revealed.

In the third place, *koinonia* with Christ produces in the church a new solidarity with all other communities—the nations, races, tongues, and peoples that constitute the world. In every encounter with Christ the church meets a Lord "whose only concern is for others." His love is the point where the church sees God's omnipotence, omniscience, and omnipresence—the point where these divine attributes are redefined by the weakness, ignorance, and limitations of incarnation and death. His love is the measure both of God's distance and his nearness. There were no limits to the love of him who was hung between two thieves. He established a solidarity with humankind at its lowest denominator: sin, flesh, futility, death. He was raised as the firstfruits of God's harvest, a harvest that will finally include all creation. The only line between his community and all others is drawn by a love that is so exclusive only because it is also so inclusive.

Fourth, fellowship in Christ opens the door to a final freedom. The person who lives wholly for others is freed from self, for love brings the amazing gift of self-transcendence. The love by which the church is knit together unites it in an indestructible hope that frees it from the bondage to frustration. Its *koinonia* with Christ includes a gift of freedom, an eschatological freedom. In all other communities, the requirements of finite security create external restraints on personal freedom. Not so with the church. Here communal obligation and individual emancipation spring from the same person. The Lord who commands is the Lord who frees. The apostle who says, "it is no longer I who live, but it is Christ who lives in me" (Gal. 2:20) must also say, "For freedom Christ has set us free" (Gal. 5:1).

This knowledge overcomes human bondage in many subtle ways. The act of repentance liberates the church from group-egoism, from communal self-centeredness. The act of faith liberates it from anxieties of impending catastrophes and from dread of unknown possibilities. The act of expectancy tears it loose from preoccupation with the past, from the stingy clutch of dead traditions. The act of trust gives it the courage to accept itself, to forget itself, to spend itself. The act of love frees it from compulsions to retaliate against earthly enemies. All of the acts by which it acknowledges God's gift elicit an open heart, an open future, an open world. It shares the frustrations of mortality, but it knows that no work done in the Lord is done in vain. It lives under the constant pressures of conventional moralities, of ecclesiastical ambitions, of cultural ideologies, of economic systems, of totalitarian nationalisms, but each re-enactment of the Advent and pre-enactment of the Parousia restores its knowledge of a final freedom. Koinonia in that freedom makes the church the trustee of all those liberties to which the human spirit is rightful heir. Other human communities whittle down the freedoms of the individual when historical survival is threatened; the church celebrates a freedom given by God in the midst of catastrophe and death.

ADDENDUM

The following resources by the author are also relevant to those issues in biblical theology addressed in part 1:

"The Vatican II Constitution on Revelation," in John H. Miller, ed., *Vatican II: An Interfaith Appraisal* (Notre Dame: University of Notre Dame Press, 1966), 66-88.

"Barth's Commentary on the Romans, or Karl Barth vs. the Exegetes," in *Footnotes to a Theology: The Karl Barth Colloquium of 1972*, ed. H. Martin Rumscheidt (Waterloo [Ont.]: Academic Studies in Religion in Canada, 1974), 8-29.

"Gospel History: Celebration or Reconstruction," in *Jesus and Man's Hope*, eds. D. G. Miller and D. Y. Hadidian (Pittsburgh Theological Seminary, 1971), 13-27.

"Communication and Community," in *New Theology* No. 9, eds. M. E. Marty and D. G. Peerman (New York: Macmillan, 1972), 253-69.

"The Conception of History in the Prophets and Jesus," in *The Journal of Bible and Religion*, 11 (1943): 156-61.

PART II

The Churches' Memories
of the Messiah

Introduction to
PART II

It has often been observed that historians have the obligation to "carve history at the joints." We ask, then, where are the joints in the collection of twenty-eight diverse writings that form the New Testament? Most apparent is the contrast in literary form between the first four books and the others. This division is supported by the observation that the first four deal with the life and work of Jesus and the others with the life and work of apostles. Moreover, the first four end with the death of Jesus, where the others begin. So this joint in time appears to be the right place to carve.

We should ask, however, whether the early churches would have agreed. Consider the date of authorship. Many of the Epistles were written before the Gospels; others were written during the same period. The Gospels deal not only with Jesus but, beginning very early, also with Jesus' training of disciples for their future work. And the Gospels end not with his death but with Jesus' commissioning of his disciples. In fact, the death and resurrection are as essential to the epistles as they are to the Gospels. To be content with the usual sharp separation is to ignore this interdependence. The churches underscored this bond when they chose a title for the entire collection of Gospels and Epistles: The New Covenant of our Lord and Savior Jesus Christ. It is in recognition of this bond that we term part 2 "The Churches' Memories of the Messiah," and thus speak of the materials in the four Gospels.

In this section, each chapter deals with a different type of narrative, and each type presents its own dilemmas and discoveries to modern readers and especially to historians. All reflect post-resurrection faith in "the whole-Christ-event," to use a phrase of Leander Keck, but each reflects that faith from an angle of vision different from that of modern readers.

Chapter 6 deals with the stories that introduce the Gospels of Matthew and Luke, stories recounting the special initiatives and guidance from heaven at the birth of Emmanuel. Here we find a star moving in the heavens, messages delivered by angels, fulfillment of prophecies, visions of prophets, auguries of great dangers and narrow escapes. The origins of these stories are as impossible to trace as the origin of the Negro Spirituals. Little, if any, evidence is provided of the presence of eyewitnesses who would later report what they had seen. The events are recounted in such a way as to reflect heavenly initiatives. These stories are told and retold in communities that owe their salvation to similar initiatives.

Chapter 7 looks at a series of episodes in the midcourse of Jesus' career, episodes reflecting his relation to John the Baptist and to two groups, those offended by his activity and those who benefited by it. The material details the amazing but mysterious power of this humble-hearted man to create devoted followers and, by the same actions, equally devoted enemies. Though the episodes appear at first to happen diachronically (that is, at successive times), they are told synchronically (that is, at the same time) from the perspective of later faith in the crucified healer. Readers, including historians, find it hard to cope with the fusion of these two perspectives.

In chapter 8 attention focuses upon a series of narratives about Jesus' meals with both adversaries and friends, and their pregnant snatches of table talk. Such interest is not strange when we recall that the earliest groups of believers often met in homes, eating together and worshiping around simple meals of bread and wine. Here they were often made aware of the presence of the Lord, breaking the bread and blessing the wine. Memories of the crucifixion were inseparable from memories of the Last Supper, as memories of the victory accompanied stories of the disciples at Emmaus, belatedly becoming aware of the identity of their guest. It is not strange that the table talk should fuse together remembrance of the Passion and celebration of the Presence. Readers who separate them create confusion rather than understanding.

The final two chapters (9–10) in part 2 focus attention on the Gospel of John. In dealing with John, it is the entire Gospel that creates difficulties. In part this is due to the fact that the entire Gospel interprets every incident and every saying in the light of the understanding that this man Jesus is the Word that was "in the beginning with God," who "became flesh and lived among us" (John 1). Similar dilemmas and discoveries attend the efforts to understand the key assertion attributed to Jesus, "I am the resurrection and the life" (John 11). The conviction of the truth of that assertion permeates every verse of this Gospel, creating problems for every thoughtful modern reader but, at the same time, offering the promise of exhilarating and emancipating discoveries.

── 6 ──

The Preparation
(Matthew and Luke)

All four Gospels provide similar accounts of the work of John and Jesus when these men first emerged in "the public square." They also agree in stressing the reactions in that square among three groups: the glad reaction among "the poor in spirit" (usually anonymous); the hostile reaction among the powerful authorities (also anonymous); and the puzzled and unsure reaction of those whom Jesus called to share his mission (often named).

Matthew and Luke each devote two chapters to telling how God prepared the way for that mission. These preparatory stories did not arouse public attention at the time. Those who first responded to the messages of John and Jesus showed no signs of having known these stories. The stories seem to have been told by Matthew and Luke to help readers of their Gospels understand what would happen later in the life of Jesus and in the lives of his disciples. In all of these stories there is an initiative from heaven: Gabriel is sent on an errand to Mary; guidance is provided through dreams; angels sing to shepherds; a star moves in unprecedented fashion; and aged prophets see visions. These signs all indicated the divine initiative in the advent of God's Anointed One. The first human responses to such prevenient, divine action clearly anticipated subsequent human reactions: the humble gratitude of the elect; the violent reactions of the powerful; the increasingly hazardous prospect for Jesus' coworkers. In the study of these chapters, historians have much to teach, and from these chapters there is much to learn: my goal is to suggest both. I urge readers to have the texts at hand for constant reference (Matt. 1–2; Luke 1–2).

THE HISTORIAN'S ANALYSIS OF THE STORIES

Let us suppose that a reader begins the study with this objective in mind: to identify the original writers, to comprehend what they intended to convey to their initial audience, and to recapture how that audience understood this message. Once the aim has been stated in these terms, the reader encounters many obstacles. Modern readers will need the historian's help to overcome these obstacles:

(1) In dealing with the birth narratives it is particularly difficult to locate the original author. Today, everyone admits that to some degree these narratives are the distillation of a community's experience, an articulation of the multiple memories and hopes of that community. The problem of identifying the authors is similar to that of tracing the origins of a Negro Spiritual or a Viking saga.

(2) Even if we could name a particular editor, the matter of intention may elude us. Seldom does a writer of such stories have a single, conscious, definable purpose. Especially is this true in the work of a church leader, who fills a very complex role within the household of faith. (What we say here is true of both Matthew and Luke.) That leader stands between the people and God—speaking to God for the people and speaking to the people for God—as the steward of mysteries that cannot be stated bluntly in a single sentence. The leader is the channel of a tradition that speaks to the leader's own life at countless points before it can speak to that of the leader's audience. Having heard God speak through the tradition, through the total effect of the total story, the speaker in turn must tell the whole story so that others may hear the same voice, for the meanings of the story are inseparable from the story itself.

(3) The objective of recapturing the initial response of the intended audience is subject to similar obstacles. We do not know which community first heard the stories. In fact, they probably circulated in many places and in many forms before they were written down in one place and in one form. In oral tradition of this sort the responses of the listeners become imbedded in the tradition itself. And the studies of other folk literature have produced some helpful techniques, which the scholar may apply in an attempt to reconstruct the early meanings of the tradition. Let us examine three questions that should be asked in order to view these stories in their original context.

What was the original *life* setting for the stories?

The situation presupposed by the stories is not that of an apostle preaching the gospel for the first time to unconverted Jews or Gentiles; every facet of the tradition indicates that it was used by believers for believers. Nor is the primary context provided by the work of an apologete defending Christian convictions from the attacks of pagan adversaries. The stories presuppose faith in the basic christological formulas; they do not argue for certain dogmas but serve as testimonies of those who have been moved to glorify God for the gift of his Son. The narrators are seeking not so much to correct or to implement an existing stock of beliefs as to articulate the common joy of believers over God's saving acts. It is equally obvious that the birth narratives do not represent the official work of teachers whose function it was to train initiates in their new duties. The ethical dilemmas of individual disciples, as well as the usual forms and motifs of the catechism, are wholly lacking.

The exploration of the life setting also eliminates the thought that the stories were directed first of all to children, as winsome ways of appealing to their naive fancies; the tradition was produced by adults and for adults. Furthermore, adult use was not limited to an annual festival of Advent, as a periodical means by which parents might escape from the harsh realities of life to the romantic fantasies of infancy. No, this tradition reflects the mature and realistic understanding of the Christian life, based upon the cumulative, year-round experience of the Christian community as a whole. What, then, may we say more positively about the context within which the meanings of the tradition were set by the first bearers? The tradition itself assumes at least three major constituents in that context.

In the first place, the audience already knew the course of later events in the story of Jesus. The listeners were well acquainted with the preaching of John the Baptist and with the consequences of his ministry. The first listeners did not forget the significance of John's birth and work because of their special interest in Jesus. They also knew the character and sequence of the major episodes in Jesus' ministry. Narrators and listeners alike thought backward from the period after the cross and the Resurrection, and they frankly recognized that many of the implications of earlier events remained hidden even to Jesus' own family and closest disciples until after the climactic revelation of the Risen Lord (cf. Luke 1:32, 33, 45, 65-66, 80; 2:19, 46-51).

In the second place, the context for the birth tradition was provided by all the memories of the church, up to the time of each successive reading. The congregation vividly recollected its encounters with Herod and his successors. It saw in its own life the fulfillment of prophecies, the prevenient grace of God in his call of the humble. Some members testified that they too had been called from the mother's womb, that in them God had chosen "things that are not, to reduce to nothing things that are" (1 Cor. 1:28). These members of Christ's body knew how God's power appeared in the weakest vessels, how that power worked through signs and wonders, and how the Holy Spirit continued to humble the proud and exalt the meek.

In the third place, each individual disciple became the personal context in which to interpret the meanings of the tradition. At each new reading, each disciple heard the story as a Word addressed personally, even though that reading took place in a corporate assembly. Each one placed the story within the frame of a very personal history, orienting it around recollections of earlier encounters with God's mercy: an address by the word of the angels, initial doubt and scorn, rebirth through faith, and then certain faltering steps along the Via Dolorosa, meeting the resistance of the world, and learning the mysterious ways in which the Spirit offers power and wisdom. The life setting of these birth narratives thus includes the content of three stories fused together: the story of Jesus, the story of the new Israel, and the personal story of the disciple. To understand the original context, therefore, the exegete must stand at the point of convergence of these three stories. Here the life setting has become the faith setting, because to the original narrator and to the audience, each life-situation derived its meaning from its bearing on faith. The exegete must therefore rephrase the question to examine faith.

What was the original *faith* setting for the stories?

To the believing congregation each situation was a faith situation because its significance stemmed from the contemporaneous relationship between that congregation and God, a relationship that was controlled by the memory of Christ's work. The Father of Jesus was even now carrying out through Christ his program for the salvation of the world. Although the plan of this mystery was first disclosed in the death and exaltation of Jesus, the same invincible purpose had been at work secretly in all the preceding episodes. Since the heart of the mystery was the self-humiliation of God's Son, the initial act of descent as narrated by

Matthew and Luke carried within itself the whole plan of redemption, and should be understood as such (Phil. 2:5-11). Since each episode of humiliation concealed the whole eternal purpose, the eyes of faith discerned in each episode the major accents of that purpose: God's merciful invitation and stern judgment, the offense created by his Word, the creation of a new Adam and a new Israel, the powers of the new age at work in those who seek that new age with all their heart, and the manifestation of glory to the humble. It is thus that the whole gospel furnished the central motifs in the tradition concerning Jesus' birth. Four of these motifs are of particular interest.

First of all, these birth stories articulated the conviction that in the coming of Jesus, God moved decisively toward his people in the loving intent to save them. Over all the various incidents stood the sign "God is with us" (Matt. 1:23). Through all the happenings, God's power was at work: "Nothing will be impossible with God" (Luke 1:37); "the power of the Most High will overshadow you" (Luke 1:35). It was God who drew each actor into the drama, either with or without the actor's consent. He called those with whom he was well pleased and gave them the blessing of heavenly peace. His visit among them fulfilled the oath that he had sworn to the ancestors (Luke 1:55, 70-73), yet it caught his people unaware for he appeared in a humbler guise than expected. Nothing was too lowly to be hallowed by the descent of God's Spirit to a dwelling place among them (Luke 1:48-53). The hand of the Spirit wove all the separate incidents together on a single loom. All the happenings participated in the same miracle; all were transfigured by the light of a single mystery. Nothing appeared to have changed in the balance of human fortunes, but God's visit nevertheless produced a total change in the significance of all history. The story of the Son's descent to earth became for faith an epitome of how all history is permeated and directed by one invincible purpose, all incorporated into a single grand design.

A second major motif of the stories when placed in the context of the faith setting was to express the varying responses of creation to this divine activity. In Zechariah believers glimpsed spontaneous doubt, an unwillingness to trust the good news, and a demand for more convincing proofs. In Elizabeth and Anna they recognized the power of patient, prayerful expectancy, which refused to be cast into despair by the long chain of unanswered prayers (Luke 1:6, 24-25, 43-44; 2:36-38). In the wary cruelty of Herod they saw the fear of God's kingdom and the blind efforts to protect one's own autonomy (Matt. 2:13-18). In the reference to the census, an event which for Jewish nationalists symbolized the abyss of shame, they observed how God used the humiliation of Israel as the opportunity for its rebirth (Luke 2:1-7). In Joseph they were led to appreciate the temptation to be offended by prevailing moral standards and to overcome that temptation by trusting in the heavenly command (Matt. 1:20-24). Mary was likewise quite aware of probable slanders, but demonstrated pure receptivity to the Holy Spirit and instant readiness to let the Word of God have its way (Luke 1:34-38). This symphonic score had a place for all sorts of contrapuntal variations (for the dissonances of unbelief), but penetrating all these could be heard the dominant chords. Each movement was the occasion to magnify and glorify God (Matt. 2:2, 11; Luke 1:47; 2:13, 20, 28), to stand in fear and trembling before him (Luke 1:12, 29, 65; 2:9), to give thanks for his mercy (Luke 1:64, 68; 2:38), to rejoice greatly (Matt. 2:10; Luke 1:14, 44, 47, 58), and to receive his peace (Luke 1:79; 2:14).

Moreover, we should not forget the tensions under which the congregation was living as it awaited the return of its Lord. Not having seen him, they loved him, and the price of this love was patience and suffering, temptation and endurance. To them, the story of how the faithful had responded to the first coming of Jesus became a paradigm of how they themselves should await his return. They must now be ready to receive him in the same mood with which faith had always received him. Ever and anon these stories reiterated the promise: "where meek souls will receive him still, the dear Christ enters in." By reiterating the promise, the stories elicited that meekness.

A third dominant motif in the faith setting was a clear recollection of Jesus' place in the whole history of salvation. In the Babe in his cradle was realized the solidarity of Israel: all the generations of faith met here in a final unity. The stories declared how in Christ God had fulfilled his promises to the fathers: to Adam (Luke 3:38), to Abraham (Matt. 1:1, 17; Luke 1:55, 73), to Jacob (Luke 1:33), and to David (Matt. 1:1, 17; Luke 1:32; 2:4, 11). They linked the ministry of Jesus to that of prophets and kings (Matt. 1:23; 2:5; Luke 1:17, 32; 2:4, 11, etc.). They related the new covenant to the sacrifices in the temple (Luke 1:8-9; 2:22, 41-42) and to the fulfillment of the Torah (Luke 1:6; 2:22, 27). They constituted one way of saying with Paul that the Son of God was born of woman, born under the law, born of the flesh. Yet at the same time the narrative expressed the conviction that Jesus was born both of the flesh and of the Spirit, that he was a son of Israel "according to the flesh" and of God "according to the spirit" (Rom. 1:3-4), for in Jesus the two became one. On the one hand the birth of the flesh countered the tendencies that later developed into Docetism; on the other hand, the birth of the Spirit countered the tendency that later developed into Mariolatry. Believers were moved to cry "Blessed is the womb that bore you" (Luke 11:27), but the stories make clear that Mary was qualified for motherhood simply by her eagerness to hear and obey the Word of God. Furthermore, the stories suggest that if one must look for the important earlier events that prepared the way for the incarnation, one should consider the work of John the Baptist rather than the history of Mary. In John's birth, the Spirit was preparing for the birth of Jesus. Elizabeth, through her faith, was the real predecessor of Mary (Luke 1:36-63). It was through John that God would "turn the hearts of parents to their children" (Luke 1:17).

A fourth aspect may now be mentioned, albeit too briefly. Those who told and heard the stories of Jesus' nativity were themselves ministers of reconciliation. They were sent to proclaim the gospel of God's peace, a proclamation by deed as well as by word. They were themselves signs to an evil generation of what God was doing. Just as God's coming had taken place through the birth of Jesus, so to a later generation the reenactment of Christ's coming took place only through the instrumentality of his witnesses. Wherever the disciple or the congregation stood, there the evangel was being manifested and the old age was undergoing the first collision with the new. The stories served to illuminate this missionary situation and its problems, for the Christians were witnesses to the birth of Jesus in a deeper sense than that of repeating the stories verbally. The witness shared the poverty and obscurity of the stable, the infamy and scorn to which Joseph and Mary were subjected. The witness also struggled with the contradictions between God's wisdom and the wisdom of the world. One wisdom spoke of power, wealth, and glory in terms antithetical to those of the other wisdom. On one side were the Herods and all the forces of evil; on the other was a babe. In this context the stories sounded a shout of defiance at the enemies of the cross, and a shout of victory over their power.

All these, then, are aspects of the faith situation that provided the context for the birth narratives. It is clear that these aspects came to the sharpest focus as the Christian congregation met for worship. In corporate prayer and praise all the dilemmas and paradoxes of the Christian situation were concentrated. The faith situation became most explicit in the worship situation, for there the complex communication between God and his servants was the central fact.

What was the original *worship* setting for the stories?

To the most casual analyst it is obvious that the birth narratives were woven from materials that had been frequently used in worship. They included familiar readings from the lectionary, petitions drawn from common prayers, and verses from hymns and chants. These materials refracted all the basic moods of Christian fellowship and were used to celebrate God's wondrous help. The stories served to make the Spirit's presence vivid, to bring the life of worshipers within that realm where God's sovereignty was again realized. It should be equally obvious that materials so produced and used had a richness of connotation derived from this recurrent situation. The stories developed a rhythmic dignity and imaginative symbolism of their own. They articulated the most sacred memories and the most ardent aspirations. They were instruments for the confession and forgiveness of sins, for the realization of the weakness of the old Adam and the strength of the new. They conveyed messages from the Master to his slaves, regarding their present duties and temptations. They conveyed messages from the slaves to their Master, regarding his mysterious ways of ordering their affairs and of guiding their growth in grace. The stories thus belong in the very "holy of holies" of the early church, there at the altar where communication took place between God and his people.

The stories have led the historian back to their original context, through the life-situation to the faith-situation to the worship-situation, where they belong and where their significance is still to be grasped. Now what are exegetes to do here? How will they fulfill the function of reconstructing the original meaning of the historical data? Let us suppose that they now realize several things. They realize the intricate interdependence between the narratives and the life of this community, so that any interpretation of the stories, to be genuinely adequate, must evoke a repetition of this situation. They recognize that such a repetition is something that they must share as worshipers before they can describe God's works as interpreters. At this point, they may find that the stories themselves begin to exert an unexpected and curious judgment upon their previous outlook as historians. We should look briefly at some of the forms this judgment may take and the changes it may produce.

THE STORIES' ANALYSIS OF THE HISTORIAN

One may perhaps trace all the changes in the historian's orientation to the transposition of contexts. On beginning a study, I, as an exegete, place the object of study within the context of my own thought-world. I set this event into the frame of historical process. I relate the data to my previous body of knowledge as a whole. I think of my task as one small segment in my professional assignment. All of this is necessary and justified because the birth of Jesus was an event like all others in its particularity as historically conditioned. But when in faith and worship I hear God speak afresh through these stories, an entire frame of meaning is disclosed that establishes itself as the rightful context for all work. I now see that God's purpose, as revealed in the incarnation, encompasses all history: Christ is even now extending his sovereignty through all events of space and time; the Christian community is the pattern according to which God is reconstituting all communities; and my own vocation as an historian belongs within this context. How then, does this affect my perspective as an historian?

Let it be said that the vocation as an historian continues, as does the selection of the best methods for study of ancient literary documents. In fact, I am now under greater obligation to be an accurate and competent historian in the task of preserving, correcting, and enhancing the memories of the church. The more seriously I consider my work as a service of the Lord, for the edification of the Lord's body, so much the more vigorously will I seek freedom from my own self-centered ideas and wishes. I know how easily the memories of the church may be corrupted and how, especially in its sentimental use of the birth stories, the Christian congregation cloaks its unwitting heresies under romantic platitudes and dogmatic truisms. In counteracting the current misunderstandings concerning the narratives, I will find ample use for the sharpest tools.

Certain objectives, however, which I formerly held may now seem to be condemned. To the extent that my motives have been those of enhancing my own professional reputation, gaining a public, or establishing superiority over other scholars—to that extent the stories themselves may call me to repentance. To the extent that I assumed an elevation above the materials, an ability to judge, to select, or to condemn, thus sharing modernism's implicit disdain for the ancient, sophistication's supercilious attitude toward the primitive, or rationalism's suspicions of the imaginative truths of sagas and poetry—to that extent the stories will call for a new mind.

There also may take place a revision of the central questions with which I began the study. No longer is it enough to ask: What happened? No longer is it enough to try to delete from the record the secondary elements, leaving only such facts as I may rate as authentic. Rather, considering the wealth of meaning disclosed by the stories, I may ask: How can I mediate to my own generation an effective understanding of what God has done for the world in Christ? How can I remove the hindrances that prevent my congregation from hearing in these stories the same message that God spoke to our parents in faith? How can I grasp afresh the meaning for history of what God has done in history? Such a transposition of questions may well humble the historian.

The changed outlook may also affect my choice of methods. Is the former method so oriented that it can only produce results which faith would consider quite trivial or irrelevant? Would that method at its best simply lead me to the position of Zechariah: "How shall I know this?" Does the method adequately deal with the quality of inspired imagination that produced the stories? Is it congenial to the truth about life expressed in prayers and hymns? Does it take account of that level of experience where the Holy Spirit is at work? Does it damage the message that the stories tell by forcing it into purely objective categories (what could be photographed and televised), or by reducing it to purely subjective categories (fanciful ideas and fleeting feelings)? Only a method that is adjusted to the message will be adequate for it. Perhaps any methodology produced by an alien worldview will therefore be ineffective. By contrast, perhaps the original narrators chose the best way, the best methodology for conveying the message of the incarnation—superior to both the formulas of the theologian and the factual prose of the historian. However that may be, if the birth narratives have succeeded in humbling the historian, that humility will affect the methods and the reliance upon those methods.

Such changes, however, as are produced by a fresh impact of the history should make better historians. It should create historians who are able to enter more fully into the life of the distant past and give a better report on the inner structure of that life, who are able to assess the work of ancient writers more accurately by viewing that work within the writers' own perspective. This should permit them to see their own work as a work of the whole church, in the effort to keep in order the church's memories of its past. More significantly, greater knowledge of the original relevance of the birth narratives should make historians more effective critics of current misconceptions of those narratives—misconceptions that are more dangerous to the church's health than its people are likely to admit. Now, however, when historians condemn unsuspected heresies among the devout, they will be speaking on behalf of the original authors. They will be arguing for a more disciplined listening to God's voice, a more flexible alertness for receiving the gift in surprising places, a greater openness to the joy and peace of the patient Anna and the trusting Mary.

These exegetes may find a new role for themselves, injecting a tone of freedom and vitality into methods that have become fixed and sterile. They may criticize prevailing objectives and assumptions, not from the desire to champion outworn shibboleths of fundamentalist bibliolatry, not from the fear of subjecting the Bible to rigorous examination, but from the experienced realization that they are dealing with truths that enter human history on a level too deep to be measured by rationalistic historicism, objectivistic empiricism, or the tortuous paths of antiquarianism. They need to be liberated from the limitations of their methodologies, not simply in order to hear angels tell glad tidings, but also in order to deal with an historical process that is guided by God's purposes.

Perhaps they will also be freed from the tendency toward archaism from which much orthodoxy suffers. Though the original authors told the stories in such a way that they could communicate God's message most effectively to their audience, and though each repetition of the message requires the context of Christian worship, yet leaders of that worship must do what they can to tell the message in the idiom of their own congregation. The prayers and the hymns, if they are to be genuine, must be the deepest and most spontaneous expressions of the congregation's heart. The conversation with God must draw the whole gamut of the congregation's experience into the story of incarnation. Interpreters will present the message to the greatest advantage by making it contemporaneous, by showing how modern history belongs within its context. For only when the stories are the medium for a new encounter between God and believers, for a new recognition of God's descent into the form of our existence—only then will they be rightly interpreted.

— 7 —
The Offense
(Matthew)

In this chapter, I examine matters of theological and historical perspective raised by specific aspects of Matthew's Gospel. These thoughts on perspective are stimulated by one of the greatest of the world's paintings, the gigantic fresco Michelangelo created on the wall behind the altar in the Sistine Chapel. I want first to comment on that mural. I will rely on observations made by art critic Roberto Salvini. He stresses that Michelangelo rejected any use of a frame for his fresco. A frame would have implied "a fixed distance with a fixed viewpoint."[1] It would have presupposed a limited space and time, whereas the painting was designed to cover a range of reality from the highest reach of heaven to the deepest zone of hell. The subject was too big for the room, for any room, for it pictured heaven with its dense population of angels and demons as the essential and eternal source and context for everything that happens on earth, from the creation of the first mortal to the end of the age.

In the fresco, the focus of vision falls on the vindicated and powerful Judge. Near him on one side is a vast company of the patriarchs and prophets of the old covenant and, on the other, an equally vast company of apostles, martyrs, and saints. At the bottom, on one side, are the blessed who are being raised from their graves and, on the other, the cursed, being assigned to Hades. Among the latter is "the extremely bitter self-portrait that the artist included in Saint Bartholomew's empty skin."[2] Essential to an understanding of the drama are the two lunettes at the top, one showing the cross and the other the pillar, two symbols borne by angels to suggest the qualifications that enabled the crucified Jesus to serve God as the final judge.

Let me make two additional comments. The entire fresco enables viewers to see synchronically (i.e., simultaneously) the long story of earth within the context of God's creative activity. It also enables them to locate a single center for that story in the person of Jesus, a human whose humiliation and exaltation embodied the power of God, thus qualifying him to serve as the judge of all. Because of the conjunction of these two, simultaneity and centrality, every episode in the long story points toward that center, which, in turn, yields an ultimate significance to each episode. The very scope and depth of this bond between detail and center justifies the location of the fresco behind an altar where it invites worshipers to see, once again, both the story in its unimaginable diversity and the center in its inexplicable synthesis of defeat and victory.

These comments introduce an explanation of the initiation and purpose of this essay, dealing as it does with selected incidents in the Gospel of Matthew. Let me state that purpose in various ways. Just as worshipers in the Sistine Chapel are being silently urged to hear again the witness of patriarchs, apostles, and martyrs when they see men and women in the fresco, so, too, readers of the Gospel stories are being subtly urged to relate each scene to the central scene in the Gospel—the Crucifixion. To put the same point more technically, as Michelangelo provides a synchronic vision of a long tradition that happened diachronically (i.e., successively), so Matthew edits a diachronic collection of stories in a way that calls for synchronic vision.

But to see the Gospel in these terms is far from easy because of the emergence of modern attitudes toward history, the development of the historical sciences, and the subjection of every verse in the Gospel to tests employed in those sciences. Those tests give priority at every point to the demands of diachronic reasoning. Every past event must be located at a specific point on a fixed chronology, after some events with their possible influences and before other events with their possibly warped interpretations. A chain of successive events must therefore be reconstructed before hypothetical influences and meanings can be ventured. Whenever Matthew relays events out of their original order, any interpretation becomes hazardous. Only a strictly diachronic reconstruction can lend credibility to the causes and effects within the story. And such causes and effects are limited to things observable in time and space.

References to interventions by angels or demons arouse either outright disbelief or nervous skepticism. Even more embarrassing are appeals to heavenly kingdoms, whether divine or satanic, or to warfare between those kingdoms. Faith in a God from whom, to whom, and through whom are all things, yet a God whose closest link to human history is by way of human hearts—such faith can only complicate historical narratives and their understanding. Yet that very faith is essential both to Michelangelo's *Last Judgment* and to Matthew's Gospel.

In spite of such difficulties, I want to challenge readers to *see* the Gospel in ways analogous to Michelangelo's vision. And there is no inherent difficulty in meeting that challenge. In writing his Gospel, Matthew was himself seeing all its contents in retrospect. Like all memories, retrospects are by nature synchronic. All such retrospects receive their unity from being viewed by a single set of eyes that interpret earlier events in terms of present significance, whether destructive or constructive. This holds true also for Matthew's first readers or listeners. They were believers who had accepted from Jesus, as their Lord and Savior, an exalted and dangerous vocation. That vocation established the image of God's crucified Servant as the pivot for all their thinking. That pivot provided them the key to unlock significance within all the stories and teachings that stemmed from Jesus' own mission. This significance, concealed when viewed diachronically, became obvious only when viewed synchronically.

What was true for that original conversation of writer and readers is also true for some Christians today. They often listen to these stories during times of worship, introspection, and inward imagination. At the same time, they are facing an altar on which a cross continues to provide for that imagination the detailed recollection of the Passion—a recollection that is synchronic in the fullest sense. These worshipers are at times prompted by the presence of the cross to see the connections between two moments: the moment of the Gospel lesson as read from the pulpit and the moment of that terrible crucifixion. Such a vision may well remind these worshipers that the church has placed in its canon of authoritative scripture the Gospel of Matthew rather than some historical distillation of events that might seem more credible.

Now let me illustrate Matthew's synchronic perspective by examining three episodes selected from chapters 11 and 12. Viewed diachronically, these sayings have proved very baffling to historical exegetes; but viewed synchronically, with the Passion story as the center, they give a clear and coherent witness to the good news.

THE BLESSING AND THE OFFENSE

Now when Jesus had finished instructing his twelve disciples, he went on from there to teach and proclaim his message in their cities. When John heard in prison what the Messiah was doing, he sent word by his disciples and said to him, "Are you the one who is to come, or are we to wait for another?" Jesus answered them, "Go and tell John what you hear and see: the blind receive their sight, the lame walk, the lepers are cleansed, the deaf hear, the dead are raised, and the poor have good news brought to them. And blessed is anyone who takes no offense at me." (Matt. 11:1-6)

Historians find many difficulties in interpreting this story. The story-teller shows virtually no interest in the original participants. None is named. There is no clear location in space or time. No concern is shown for John, his reason for raising the query, or his response to Jesus' answer. Jesus gives no direct answer to the question that John has asked but instead leaves to others the responsibility for answering. In fact, he places the emphasis not on his identity but on the judgment of others about him. Six groups are mentioned as having profited from Jesus' work and having responded to his message, but none of them is present and none speaks. Only a few things seem to be common to these six groups. They have accepted the good news through a repentance stimulated by their helplessness. Nothing is said about their political status. The only economic factor recognized is poverty, though the kind of poverty is unspecified. All six groups appear to be disadvantaged religiously, being considered according to certain sanctions as unclean and thus disqualified from a full share in the worship at the synagogue and temple. None is in a position of power, or in a position, when healed, to exercise power. In short, the characters in this story and their place in society are as undefined as the crowds in Michelangelo's *Last Judgment*.

Little wonder that the historically minded exegete finds it difficult to establish a context within which the story can be interpreted. Such a context is partially provided by "what you hear and see," but the very next statement of Jesus proves that this context alone does not fully answer the question. Jesus' final statement, a natural climax, points the reader toward the proper focal point. What is the offense? Who are offended? Who are not offended? What is their blessedness? The Gospel as a whole provides clear and convincing answers to these four questions.

What is the offense? Jesus himself is the offense. It is not the signs that offend, but the person. Not his power to release captives, but his failure to present the evidence that would fit the expectations of "the one who is to come." He appeared rather as "a glutton and a drunkard, a friend of tax collectors and sinners" (Matt. 11:19). He was too meek and humble in heart to qualify (Matt. 11:29). He did not "wrangle or cry aloud," did not step on a bruised reed or extinguish a flickering lamp (Matt. 12:19-20). He was an ordinary man, a member of an ordinary workman's family, who received no special respect in his hometown (Matt. 13:55-57). Last of all and slave of all, he was of all penitents the most humble in heart (Matt. 11:30). All these offenses were telescoped into one: "he must go to Jerusalem and undergo great suffering at the hands of the elders and chief priests and scribes." That offense was too much even for his closest follower (Matt. 16:21-23). Jesus not only lacked the expected credentials, he rejected them. His offense was to reverse all human measures of greatness, of freedom, of wisdom—and of history. When God struck down this shepherd, all the sheep in his flock scattered (Matt. 26:31). All definitions of the offense meet in and are reflected from the forsakenness at Golgotha: Jesus *is* the offense.

Who are those offended? The Gospel mentions diverse groups. One is "this generation," which, like children playing in the marketplace, rejects the calls from John as well as from Jesus (Matt. 11:16-19; 21:28-32). Another group includes the residents of Chorazin, Bethsaida, and Capernaum who refuse to repent, thus sharing in God's judgment on Tyre, Sidon, and Sodom (Matt. 11:20-24). Blindness to the presence of God's grace unites those proud people from different places and times in a single obtuse generation. The offended include "the wise and the intelligent" whose self-esteem prevents them from seeing things revealed to infants (Matt. 11:25). One must also include Pharisees, who, blinded by their own place on Moses' seat, could not accept the priority God placed on mercy (Matt. 12:1-14). The key to all these offenses was something internal in the offended themselves, a self-assurance that inhibited complete honesty before God. They could not repent because of blind eyes, deaf ears, and hearts that could not understand the possibilities that opened up on the far side of complete humility before God (Matt. 13:1-9). Nowhere is this definition of the offense more inclusive and more devastating than when the Passover blood was being "poured out for many for the forgiveness of sins" (Matt. 26:28).

Who are not offended? One detail in the painting identifies the six groups who are specified in the response to John's question (Matt. 11:5); in another detail are the weary and overburdened who respond to Jesus' promise of rest (Matt. 11:29). Also included are those who, bedeviled by demons, are freed from their blindness and inability to speak (Matt. 12:22). Others, because of their abundant and understanding hearts, receive healthy eyes and ears (Matt. 13:15-16). The parable of the seeds adds to our list those who hear the sown word, who understand it, and who yield God's intended harvest (Matt. 13:24). Finally, we must include those members of Jesus' school of prophets who, after being offended and scattered at his arrest, are humbled enough to accept his final assignment on the mountain in Galilee.

As Matthew paints the picture, this scene permits only two options: to be offended or not. Such a perspective permits only two results: to be blessed or cursed. The only ultimate source of blessing and curse is both invisible and inaudible: the eternally creating God. It is to God's approval that Jesus refers in his declaration: "Blessed is anyone who takes no offense at me" (Matt. 11:6). In what, then, does this gift of blessedness consist? One inclusive answer is this: inheritance in the kingdom of God and its opposite, rescue from the power of the evil one (Matt. 6:13). But there are many closely related expressions for such inheritance and rescue: the vision of God, the gift of an ultimate mercy, comfort for sorrow, life as children of God in the family of God's Servant-Son, the healing of infirmities, freedom from fear, the strength and wisdom of the Holy Spirit, treasures in heaven for those who store them there, courage to save life by losing it, and, finally, the promise "I am with you always" (Matt. 28:20). Each detail in the vast mural is painted in such a way as to point to its luminous center and to be illuminated from that center. Matthew invited all readers to share his synchronic vision of that reciprocal reality.

BEFORE AND AFTER THE VIOLENCE

As they went away, Jesus began to speak to the crowds about John: "What did you go out into the wilderness to look at? . . . A prophet? Yes, I tell you, and more than a prophet. This is the one about whom it is written,

'See, I am sending my messenger ahead of you,
who will prepare your way before you.'

> Truly I tell you, among those born of women no one has arisen greater than John the Baptist; yet the least in the kingdom of heaven is greater than he. From the days of John the Baptist until now the kingdom of heaven has suffered violence, and the violent take it by force. For all the prophets and the law prophesied until John came; and if you are willing to accept it, he is Elijah who is to come. Let anyone with ears listen!" (Matt. 11:7-15)

This entire paragraph consists of an address given by Jesus to the crowds (possibly the groups mentioned in Matt. 11:5). The climactic disclosure is signaled by the assurance of an authority from heaven: "Truly I tell you." That this manifesto contains a mysterious message is suggested by the warning against deafness: "Let anyone with ears listen!" Between the *truly* and the *listen* comes a puzzling reference to *violence*, separating the time before from the time after. Yet, although this mystery is uttered with dramatic intensity, there is no indication of any immediate response, whether from the crowds, the disciples of John, or the disciples of Jesus. Apparently, this narrator was more interested in the responses of his own readers or listeners. Did they have the ears to penetrate the conundrum? There is no mistaking the presence, the intentional presence, of a riddle. After praising John the Baptist as the greatest of those born of women and, in fact, as the expected Elijah, Jesus identifies the least in the kingdom of heaven as greater than John. How can these who are the *least* be *greater* than the *greatest*?

The riddle serves to focus attention on three successive periods: the time "until John came"; the time during which the kingdom of the heavens is under violent attack; and the time of the least in that kingdom. Let us examine them in that order.

(1) *"Until John came."* Obviously, this period embraces all those born of women, that is, since Eve. It was a period when the law and the prophets constituted a time of prophecy. That period had reached its term in the prophecy of John, who was none other than Elijah, sent ahead of Jesus as God's messenger (Matt. 11:10). That errand established John as "more than a prophet." All this, of course, was intelligible only to those willing to accept it.

(2) *"From the days of John the Baptist until now."* This is the second period, with its beginning clearly identified. The text places Jesus as standing within this period, along with his audience (and with Matthew and his audience as well). This second period, this *now*, describes the kingdom of the heavens as under attack from violent forces. That attack

seems to have been initiated by John's announcement of the Kingdom, by his baptism of those with penitent hearts, and by his identification of the "brood of vipers" (the progeny of Eve's serpent?). An early clue to the violence had been the struggle of Jesus in the wilderness with Satan, a struggle that had been provoked, in turn, by his true penitence at John's warning (Matt. 3:13–4:11). An early instance of violence had been John's imprisonment (soon to be followed by John's murder [Matt. 14:3-12]).

The rest of the Gospel so fully documents the human violence against Jesus as the spokesman for God's kingdom that its mounting intensity need not be reviewed here. In simple truth with abundant proof, this prophet came to earth in order to bring a sword (Matt. 10:34). In fact, this early period in his ministry leads to a single conclusion: His adversaries conspired how to destroy him (Matt. 12:14).

So much for the violence that was aroused on earth when the good news was announced. Behind and within that war, Matthew discerned the outbreak of violence in the heavens between the two invisible kingdoms—one of God, the other of Satan. This conflict had been going on since "the foundation of the world" (Matt. 25:34). The *now* marked the time when both John and Jesus could disclose the advent on earth of God's victorious kingdom. In that disclosure was the assurance that God had cast Satan out of heaven so that his kingdom could no longer stand (Matt. 12:25-29). Through this invisible victory of God, Satan's house had been entered. Its owner had been tied up and his possessions plundered. Of that plundering in heaven, Jesus' exorcism of demons provided the visible earthly evidence.

(3) *"The least in the kingdom of heaven is greater than he."* This is the third stage in the sequence. We should not read this declaration as if it canceled Jesus' tribute to John. During the government by the law and the prophets, no one could be greater than Elijah. John's greatness was in his being a witness to the unprecedented opportunity now open to all those born of women. Their banishment from Eden had ended in the mercies of God's kingdom, inasmuch as the powers of the serpent were overcome. The good tree on the good earth again produces good fruit (Matt. 12:33). Something greater than Jonah or Solomon is here (Matt. 12:41-42). Eyes can now see what the prophets had long hoped to see (Matt. 13:16-17). In fact, the descent of God's kingdom from heaven to earth has made the object of the prophet's longing within reach of a simple petition by the community of disciples, for example, their rescue from

"the evil one" (Matt. 6:9-13). The gift of that kingdom constituted God's blessing on those who were not offended at Jesus. It was that gift that defined the greatness of the least.

It is the severity of the violence that is the measure of the greatness of these "least." They are greater than the greatest in the pre-Elijah age, than all those born of women. They have been freed from the kingdom of the evil one by the power of the Holy Spirit (Matt. 12:28).

SOMETHING IS HERE GREATER THAN . . .

Matthew next paints two scenes that reflect the same radical shift from one realm to another. In the first realm, the law and the prophets have reached their term. In the other, things concealed from the wise and intelligent are made visible to infants (Matt. 11:25-30). Conflict emerges at the point of transition. Here is the entire first scene:

> At that time Jesus went through the grainfields on the sabbath; his disciples were hungry, and they began to pluck heads of grain and to eat. When the Pharisees saw it, they said to him, "Look, your disciples are doing what is not lawful to do on the sabbath." He said to them, "Have you not read what David did when he and his companions were hungry? He entered the house of God and ate the bread of the Presence, which it was not lawful for him or his companions to eat, but only for the priests. Or have you not read in the law that on the sabbath the priests in the temple break the sabbath and yet are guiltless? I tell you, something greater than the temple is here. But if you had known what this means, 'I desire mercy and not sacrifice,' you would not have condemned the guiltless. For the Son of Man is lord of the sabbath." (Matt. 12:1-8)

The narrator assumes that his listeners will understand Jesus' reply better than the original actors did. It is not so much a story as a scene from a larger tapestry. What the actors see depends on their residence. The Pharisees, as residents of one realm, see only the infractions of the law that they are responsible for correcting. The scene documents the guilt of the disciples and requires condemnation by the judges. But in Jesus' response, the government of the other realm appears. He declares the disciples innocent and their accusers guilty, a guilt that stems from not knowing what had taken place. *Something greater than* David is here. The Pharisees do not recognize these authentic successors of the priests in the temple, who are exempt from Sabbath regulations. *Something greater than the priesthood is here.* More decisive still ("I tell you . . ."), *something greater than* the temple is here (compare Rev. 21:22). To mark that shift from one realm to another, Jesus repeats what God had said through Hosea: "I desire mercy and not sacrifice" (compare Hos. 6:6). *Something greater than* the need for sacrificial offerings is here. The desire for mercy has been realized in this Sabbath of which the Son of Man is ruler. *Something greater than* the Pharisees' Sabbath is here.

All this, of course, lies beyond the horizon of the Pharisees. Not only had Jesus broken the law; he had defended such violations as a mark of the fulfillment of God's design for Israel. His opponents began to plot his destruction, thus making very clear the kind of violence that is the gateway between the two "ages."

There follows a climax of all three incidents that is given entirely in the words of Matthew himself (Matt. 12:15-21). First of all, he stresses the fact that the plot to destroy Jesus did not dissuade him from continuing his work of mercy. "Many crowds followed him, and he cured all of them." Such defiance of the scribes' challenge virtually guaranteed the success of the conspiracy. Moreover, Jesus continued the practice of encouraging—in fact, commanding—those who were healed not to advertise their cures. He did not want to be hailed as "the one who is to come" (Matt. 11:3)—at least, not yet.

Matthew then affirms that all this happened in fulfillment of Isaiah's prophecy (Matt. 12:18), in his eyes a final proof that Jesus had not come to destroy the law and the prophets (Matt. 5:17). This fulfillment proved that Jesus was a better interpreter of the Scriptures than were his enemies. Moreover, Matthew underscores the fact that someone other than Isaiah is present, in that it is God now speaking through Isaiah: "Here is my servant." That is to say, "These acts of mercy are acts not of my servant alone but of me, since he is only following my orders." As indications of God's will, those acts indicate God's design for all creation. Such is Matthew's confession, the witness of Isaiah, and the manifesto of God—a fitting conclusion to the three incidents.

Again, readers should visualize the Gospel of Matthew as a vast fresco with the crucifixion at its center and with every scene pointing toward it and defined by it. To use a phrase from a well-known hymn, the Gospel "is the heaven-drawn picture of Christ, the living Word."[3] The assertion that this picture is heaven-drawn is not simply the idea of the writer of this hymn; it is what God says through Isaiah and through Matthew. But first of all it is the word-picture of the works of mercy done by the servant. Earlier on, I commented on one major contrast between Michelangelo and Matthew: the former paints a picture that focused on Jesus as Judge; the Gospel picture centers on Jesus as the Crucified. I am now corrected by this very text. Matthew here portrays the crucified servant as being himself both Judge and Victor (Matt. 12:20).

─ 8 ─
The Covenant
(Luke)

In the study of eucharistic origins, an epoch of polemical theology has left its mark on New Testament scholarship. Historians have been impelled to ask of the text questions that have been crucial to liturgical debates, and to bring back answers that distort the text in order to buttress partisan arguments. A premium has been placed on recovering the exact words and meanings in the earliest account of the Lord's Supper, on the assumption that the original record should be accepted as normative for contemporary Christian worship. The results have not, in fact, settled dogmatic issues, but have rather illustrated the paradox: The more knowledge, the more doubt. Nor have the Gospels profited from this kind of treatment. Their answers do not match our questions, since they were not written with reference to our debates.

If we would profit from Luke's thinking about the sacrament, we should approach his two-volume work looking for glimpses of the apostles at the table, and asking what significance Luke attached to those occasions. It is, for example, important that the genuine climax in the story of Pentecost, when the church was baptized with the Holy Spirit, is to be found in the picture of all the disciples breaking bread in their homes. Devotion to the common meal was related to acceptance of the apostles' teaching and fellowship (Acts 2:42). Table companionship was associated with prayers, with rejoicing, with the inclusion of all in the common budget, with generous care for the needs of all. Daily worship was followed or accompanied by daily meals together.

At Troas, Paul and his traveling company broke bread with the congregation, an occasion where a speech, prolonged until midnight, really put a man to sleep, with the well-known consequences. It is hard to know if the meal at daybreak was a continuation of the supper, and if so, whether it celebrated the man's return to life or the apostle's departure, or both. But it is clear that to Luke the offer of hospitality at table and the covenantal act of breaking bread together conveyed great symbolic significance.

We learn enough from Acts and Paul's epistles to know that many of the early congregations met for worship in homes of members and that a common meal was part of the worship. The Pentecost story provides assurance that the breaking of bread together was viewed as a direct sequel and response to the apostles' teaching and fellowship. In that teaching, of course, the unfailing nucleus was witness to Jesus' death "by the hands of lawless men," his resurrection to the right hand of God, and the descent of the Spirit on the church.

We can learn something more from the distinctively Lukan focusing of the accounts of the appearances of the risen Lord on the Emmaus journey and the meal with which it terminated. Various scholars, in their study of the Lukan authorship, have become convinced of the strategic importance of this story. It is a summary not only of the gospel of the Messiah's suffering and glory but also of the testimony of the law and prophets to those saving events. It is an essential prologue and promise of the life and expansion of the church as recounted in the Book of Acts.

The trip to Emmaus, with the climactic meal, was the occasion for the apostles to express their shattered hope for the redemption of Israel. It was the occasion for displaying their disappointment, their confusion, their slowness of heart to believe. All this, however, was transformed "when he was at the table with them" (Luke 24:30). When he took and blessed and broke and gave the bread (the four ritual actions so weighted with meaning), "their eyes were opened, and they recognized him; and he vanished from their sight" (Luke 24:31). Now, and only now, were they enabled to understand his earlier exegesis of the Scriptures. Now, and only now, could their despair and confusion be replaced by joining the eleven in their witness to the Lord's resurrection. What had happened was disclosed to them at the table where the actions of the stranger had opened their eyes to recognize him, and where this recognition was so decisive that they no longer needed his visible presence to convince them.

This episode is extremely valuable in setting forth Luke's sacramental theology, not only in its central doctrinal substance but even more in the mode of thinking about the Supper. Luke depicts each table scene as an event where, because of the presence of Jesus, things happen that release power in the participants for the vocation to which they are called. Now we must note the sequence of earlier meals in the Gospel of Luke to detect the character of this vocation and this power.

The host for the first meal is Levi, the tax collector (Luke 5:29-39). Jesus goes in with his disciples for a supper with Levi, and immediately controversy breaks out over two basic questions: Why do you eat with sinners? Why so much levity, so much frivolity, so much joy, when there should be fasting? The conversation at table answers those two questions. Why eat with sinners? Because only those who are sick need a physician. Why so much frivolity and joy? Because the bridegroom is present with the wedding guests. In each of Luke's stories of talk at table, controversy breaks out, a redemptive controversy, for out of it comes an opportunity for fuller understanding of the gospel itself by a recognition of the difference that the presence of Jesus made.

The second example of table talk is an occasion where a Pharisee was host (Luke 7:36-50). As Jesus and the Pharisees (and to most of the early Christians *Pharisee* was a word for sinner just as it is for most of us) were sitting at table eating, a woman of the city, a notorious sinner, came, and standing at his feet weeping, began to wash his feet with her tears. Again controversy broke out. Can Jesus accept this defiling contact with this notorious sinner? Again Jesus makes the conflict an occasion for teaching. "Who will love more? The person who is forgiven more." What is the measure of forgiveness? The measure of the sin; that is the measure of grace, and of gratitude. Here again Jesus chose to be reckoned with transgressors, some of whom were blind to their sin, and others overwhelmingly penitent.

On a third occasion as well a Pharisee invited Jesus to dinner (Luke 11:37-52). Well aware of the strict laws about foods and meals, Jesus did not wash, taking this as an opportunity to challenge the deep religious convictions of his host. In response to the host's amazement, Jesus seized the opportunity to announce a basic truth: "Did not the one who made the outside make the inside also." This priority establishes "the inside" as the source and test of cleanness before the Creator. By this test "justice and the love of God" are mandatory, while pride, greed, and violence (even the murder of prophets) are excluded, along with laws for cleansing "the outside." Such an answer insulted the lawyer friends of the host.

But it would later serve as guidance for the house churches, when they failed to remember Jesus' teaching about "the inside" (e.g., Rom. 14).

Then in Luke 14:1-24 a story is told of a meal at which Jesus uses many parables and parabolic gestures. Jesus is again dining at the house of a ruler who is a Pharisee. It is the Sabbath, and there is a man there who has the dropsy. Enemies watch Jesus to see whether he will heal the man, and he does. Then comes a parable concerning guests. When you are invited, which seat should you take? The least honored and the most shameful. Then a parable concerning hosts. Whom should you invite to your meal? Not your friends or brothers but the poor, the maimed, the lame, the blind. Why? Because they cannot repay you. This policy is then illustrated by an allegory of God's banquet at his great homecoming celebration. God's servants, bearing invitations to the feast, have discovered that the righteous decline the invitations for various reasons. God therefore commands his servants to bring in guests from the highways and hedges—the poor, the maimed, the lame, and the blind. God chooses the company of sinners who cannot repay his generosity.

Several important motifs are common to these episodes. In them all there is a controversy over the fellowship between Jesus and sinners. The charge against Jesus is indeed well documented: "A glutton and a drunkard, friend of tax collectors and sinners" (Luke 7:34). The action of Jesus gives to the penitents a release from guilt, from sickness, and from bondage. It destroys the barriers between the honorable and the disreputable, between the poor and the rich. But the action also brings intense controversy, which is buttressed by mistaken reliance on the law, the prophets, and the traditions of the elders. This controversy, however, is taken by Jesus as an opportunity for clarifying such matters as his own vocation, God's forgiveness of sinners, the proper constituency of the church, and the reversal of earthly fortunes in the kingdom of God. The table becomes a place where human need meets divine grace, where the presence of Jesus transforms the sad remembrance of things past into the glorious promise of things to come. One might with confidence assert that every major component of the good news of salvation is disclosed in the action of Jesus at table. Surely his action at table elicits that joy which in the parable of the prodigal son marks the feast with which the father welcomes the resurrection of his son. The same action is seen on a larger scale in the story of feeding the five thousand, which Luke interprets as an example of Jesus' hospitality and as an example of how the kingdom of God provides healing for the sick and food for the hungry

(Luke 9:10-17). Luke is quite aware that such meals are no insurance against final rejection. The returning Lord may well refuse those who say, "We ate and drank with you, and you taught in our streets" (Luke 13:26). Yet, on the other hand, Luke can think of no higher blessedness than the promise that the master "will fasten his belt and have them sit down to eat, and he will come and serve them" (Luke 12:37). Yet when a dinner guest said, "Blessed is anyone who will eat bread in the kingdom of God!" (Luke 14:15), this beatitude was accompanied by the terrible warning that "none of those who were invited will taste my dinner" (Luke 14:24).

All these references to the table furnish data to be considered in recapturing Luke's sacramental theology. The most useful data, however, may be found at the table that is prepared in Jerusalem for the Passover feast (Luke 22:14-38). It is no wonder that Luke presents the story of the Last Supper as the occasion for the most important teachings concerning sin, repentance, and forgiveness. This is the only meal of the six where Jesus serves as the host, although in a borrowed room. This is the only place where he, serving as host, takes the initiative in offering a covenant in the wine and bread. In this story the center of gravity lies not in the words of institution but, as at earlier tables, in the four key dialogues between Jesus and the disciples. Each of these dialogues has its own sequel in the later story. Luke has placed these four dialogues at this point in the story to give them maximum emphasis.

Christian communicants at the Last Supper are seldom aware of an explosive announcement that in Luke immediately follows the words of institution. Every church gives voice to the words of institution, "this is my body . . . my blood." No church, so far as I know, includes Luke's sequel in its sacramental liturgy, for they recognize the severe shock that would be caused by the sequence in the Lukan text: "my body . . . my blood. . . . But see, the one who betrays me is with me, and his hand is on the table!"

It is this shock that provokes the first dialogue, for none of the other disciples knows the traitor's identity. (The readers, of course, know [Luke 22:3-6].) Uncertain, they begin to discuss: "Who is it?" But Jesus saw the betrayal as a fulfillment of prophecy: "The Son of Man is going as it has been determined, but woe to that one by whom he is betrayed." Earlier, of course, Luke had made it clear that Judas's action had been Satan's work. So the final meal of Jesus with the twelve marks the apparent triumph of Satan. Jesus ate with Satan's pawns.

Now let us look at the second controversy (Luke 22:24-27). This, like the previous episode, involves all the disciples. In the other Gospels this dispute appears in other contexts, but Luke with real intent and genius locates the story at this particular point. "A dispute also arose among them as to which one of them was to be regarded as the greatest." Another betrayal! The answer is familiar: "Who is greater, the one who is at the table or the one who serves? Is it not the one at the table? But I am among you as one who serves." Luke, and every Christian reader, would see this as a picture of transgressors, of those disciples who at this very moment had not begun to understand the rule concerning service and greatness. Jesus knows that they lack understanding, but he eats with them; he serves them, knowing that they had not yet begun to understand what service meant.

Where is the sequel to this episode? When Jesus said, "I am among you as one who serves," he pointed to his death. The saying also refers to this very occasion, when Jesus shares with them the bread and the cup. It also points to his promise that they will eat again with him at his table in his kingdom. In all these situations, whether past or future, he is among them as the one who serves.

In the third dialogue, Jesus is concerned about all twelve disciples, yet this concern is focused on his discussion with Simon Peter. "Simon, Simon, listen! Satan has demanded to sift all of you [the plural, i.e., the twelve] like wheat, but I have prayed for you [singular] that your own faith may not fail; and you, when once you have turned back, strengthen your brothers" (Luke 22:31-32). The futures are intertwined: the twelve, Peter; Peter, the twelve, "strengthen the brethren." The fate of *all* is at stake in this dialogue.

This brief interchange reveals a fascinating behind-the-scenes struggle. Satan also has been petitioning for something. Satan has prayed to God for the right and the opportunity to sift them. And Satan has been granted his request. God has told Satan, as he told Satan at the time of Job's temptation, "All right. You have the power to sift them. Go ahead." Now Jesus interposes his own prayer that Peter's faith, after the sifting, would be restored. Then Peter would have power to strengthen the whole group of twelve. In the sequel it becomes clear, of course, that Jesus' prayer is stronger than Satan's prayer. Satan's prayer is answered. Satan does have power to sift them. He does sift them in Gethsemane and later on in the trial, but Jesus' prayer proves stronger. Again, notice that the central theme has not been abandoned, "He was counted among the lawless" (Luke 22:37). But the purpose of this counting is irresistible and will not be denied. The burden of this prayer is to be fulfilled.

Now we come to the fourth and most difficult of the dialogues. There is great dispute among commentators about this passage, and I present a minority judgment. Because this comes at the end of the sequence, I think this was intended by Luke as a climax to the others.

> He said to them [that is, to the twelve], "When I sent you out without a purse, bag, or sandals, did you lack anything?" They said, "No, not a thing." He said to them, "But now, the one who has a purse must take it, and likewise a bag. And the one who has no sword must sell his cloak and buy one. For I tell you, this scripture must be fulfilled in me, 'And he was counted among the lawless'; and indeed what is written about me is being fulfilled." They said, "Lord, look, here are two swords." He replied, "It is enough." (Luke 22:35-38)

The pattern of this dialogue is the same as that of the others. All twelve are involved in an encounter with Jesus. We have from them a clear confession that they had lacked nothing so long as they had accepted total insecurity, so long as they depended totally upon the grace of God through the Holy Spirit. But now, in this crisis, when they have heard from Jesus that imprisonment and death lie ahead, they have already bought two swords. The difficulty here, of course, lies in the command, "The one who has no sword must sell his cloak and buy one." My interpretation here is that this is still another betrayal. It is worth noting that this is not a command that the disciples obey. They have already disobeyed the previous command concerning swords and bags and purses and cloaks. The purpose of this command is not to secure obedience, but to reveal the fact that they have already disobeyed his rule. "Here are two swords." Jesus already knew that they had defied his principle. Their possession of the swords indicates their transgression. "He was counted among the lawless" has its fulfillment in this very scene. Two swords are enough to prove it. The swords become the two witnesses that must be heard, according to Deuteronomy, before a man is judged guilty. "It is enough."

Now let us look at the sequel, for swords are used almost at once. The scene occurs after Judas had come up to identify Jesus with a kiss,

> when those who were around him saw what was coming [notice how their fears disclose his fearlessness], they asked, "Lord, should we strike with the sword?" And one of them struck the slave of the high priest and cut off his right ear. But Jesus said, "No more of this!" [Satan has asked to have you.

He has sifted you. You have become his tools. Thus far, but no farther.] And he touched his ear and healed him. Then Jesus said to the chief priests, the officers of the temple police, and the elders who had come for him, "Have you come out with swords and clubs as if I were a bandit? When I was with you day after day in the temple, you did not lay hands on me." (Luke 22:49-53)

Jesus rebukes the police, the priests, and the elders because of their reliance upon the sword. He rebukes the disciples as well. "No more of this!" And he heals the ear. What more effective rebuke could be given than this act of canceling out the wound caused by the sword? "This is your hour, and the power of darkness." This is the hour that belongs to you. This is the hour in which Satan as the ruler of darkness can wield power. That power is demonstrated by the swords of disciples and captors alike. "He was counted among the lawless."

Thus far this fourth table scene, and the aftermath, seems a rather bleak picture. What about the frivolity, the feasting, the rejoicing of the earlier suppers? The picture, however, is not wholly dismal, for it is in the very context of these dialogues that Jesus promises to these transgressors that they will sit with him at his table in his kingdom. He appoints them to thrones judging the twelve tribes of Israel (Luke 22:28-30).

The continuity of ministry is here: "You are those who have continued with me" (RSV). But this is continuity in his trials, in his temptations—for they are temptations by the same tempter. Yet he has prepared for them a table in the midst of their enemies. He has eaten with them. In eating with them, he has pledged their health, their salvation: "Take this [cup] and divide it among yourselves."

To Luke the symbolic center is taken by Jesus as the *diakonos*, fulfilling his diakonia. "He was counted among the lawless." Only so could his destiny be fulfilled. Not simply because transgression is an inevitable element in human life, but because transgression must be overcome before there can be joy and celebration. And how can it be overcome except by forgiveness? How can Jesus save transgressors except by eating with them?

In summary, there are four ways in which biblical scholars may profit from cooperation with their counterparts in liturgical theology. First, we can pursue more fruitfully together how Luke and other New Testament writers thought about the eucharist. Luke interprets the words about the cup and the bread by providing a context of stories in which what is written about transgressors and their forgiveness is fulfilled. Second, we can study more effectively the way in which the table fellowship with Jesus, both then and now, becomes God's way of revealing the secrets of human hearts. In those hearts the battle continues between loyalty and treason, between truth and self-deception; and apart from the re-enactment of the Supper, such a battle cannot be won. Third, we can be led toward a more illuminating understanding of how the battle between God and Satan reaches its decisive expression at the table, not in debates over the prescribed manner of celebration or the literal preservation of the words of institution, but in the power of Jesus both to accept the indescribable treacheries and at the same time to issue his promise of a table in his kingdom. Fourth, we can learn much about how to interpret the whole life of the church in the light of this Passover meal; and more than that, we may be enabled to discern the pattern of the eucharist in the life of the world. Luke is not engaged (and neither was Jesus) in providing a basis for understanding the symbolic significance of the liturgy as an iso-lated ceremony in the Christian calendar. He was using the Christian experience of table fellowship with Jesus as a basis for understanding God's kingdom, God's warfare with Satan, the transformation of human society, and the mission of the church in history.

The mystery of the presence of Jesus at the table is an essential expres-sion of the mystery of the church itself, the origin of its life, its invisible means of support, the character of its fellowship, the joy and generosity which occasion its meetings. Here the heavenly and the earthly, the eschatological and the historical become one reality. This is why we should think about the sacraments not simply as an illustration of theo-logical doctrine, but even more as the point of approach to all doctrines, so that their sacramental character is fully recognized and they are seen as modes of describing the miracle of bread and wine. The liturgical theo-logian needs the exegete; the exegete needs the liturgical theologian; the church needs both if it is to properly understand not only the sacrament but also the whole existence of the church as an encounter with God, an encounter in which Jesus Christ is reckoned with transgressors for their salvation.

These texts in Luke constitute a judgment on interpreters who ignore that encounter and an even more severe judgment on descendants of the original disciples. Such judgment is inescapable when we notice that the flight from Gethsemane is designed by Luke as the conclusion of the table dialogues.

9

The
Creative Word
(John)

In Luke the words of Jesus, whether in speaking to enemies or to disciples, carry unusual authority. In the Gospel of John the source of that authority is made clear at the very beginning, for Jesus is introduced as the Word (*logos*) of the Father. In this Gospel it is impossible to understand any segment of the story without dealing with this concept because the logos thought pattern pervades the later chapters as clearly as it dominates the prologue. And in these later chapters it is a major star in the constellation of ideas—the ideas of God, the world, the church, and salvation.

We should first recognize the intricate subtlety and baffling complexity of John's symbolic language. It is no simple matter to adapt one's own linguistic habits to his elusive vocabulary or to restructure one's mental processes into some degree of conformity to his. Virtually every word in his lexicon carries a range of foreign reverberations; our ears must therefore be very sensitive. John's unit of thought was not separate words but entire sentences, indeed often entire clusters of symbols. Each verbal image evoked many antonyms and synonyms. The affiliation of one idiom with its neighbors provides better clues to the structure of John's thought than do the fixed definitions of the separate words. This means that we must explore each cluster of concepts as a whole, taking soundings of the deeper levels rather than mere samplings of the surface. Thus we will take six soundings from passages in which the logos concept is affiliated with other concepts in illuminating patterns.

FIRST SOUNDING: JOHN 5:19-38

This text demonstrates that the *logos* concept is virtually synonymous with several affiliated expressions. Although the noun *logos* appears here only twice, the verb *to speak* appears five times, three of which are introduced by Jesus' prophetic exclamations, *amen, amen*. Three times the term *voice* is used, and each time with emphasis on the power of this *voice* to give life to the dead. Four times this voice announces a final judgment. On nine other occasions in this same text witnessing refers both to God's speech and to that of Jesus. In some instances speaking and doing redemptive works merge as images; the word becomes a deed, and the deed becomes a word. Throughout the passage, verbs are as strategic as nouns, actions as significant as speech.

Now we should examine the two explicit uses of *logos* in this text, in two verses that, although separate, provide a carefully constructed antithesis.

Very truly, I tell you, anyone who hears my [logos] and believes him who sent me has eternal life, and does not come under judgment, but has passed from death to life. (5:24)

The Father who sent me has himself testified on my behalf. You have never heard his voice or seen his form, and you do not have his [logos] abiding in you, because you do not believe him whom he has sent. (5:37-38)

From the construction of these statements, and from their intended contrasts, we can draw several inferences:

- There is a one-to-one correlation between hearing the logos, believing in God who sent Jesus, and having the abiding presence of the logos.
- Speaking or hearing Jesus' logos is equivalent to speaking or hearing God's logos.
- The difference between hearing and believing, and not hearing and not believing is the difference between being freed from God's condemnation and being bound over to final judgment.
- There is a one-to-one correlation between condemnation and death, between freedom and life.
- The transition from death to life takes place simultaneously with hearing the logos, along with its coordinate actions of believing, witnessing, and so on.

- This transition creates a strong bond between God as sender, Christ as the one sent, and the hearers as believers.
- The same transition creates a communal habitat for the logos; the community that hears becomes the antithesis of the community that does not hear.

In tracing the correlations of the logos we have entered a distinctive universe. The logos has served to establish an ultimate *inclusio*. In being spoken by Jesus, God's logos is as primal as God's first word on the day of creation; linkage to that day is never far from John's thinking, as 1:1-4 demonstrates with its clear echo of Genesis 1:1-3. Similarly, God's logos is as final as the day of judgment, with its implicit reference to the curse of death and separation from the tree of life in Genesis 3. Whenever the logos is spoken by Jesus, it forces hearers to situate themselves between those ultimate boundaries, which can no longer be viewed as distant possibilities but must be respected as immediate actualities. The choice between life and death remains the same as the choice made by Eve and Adam; the consequences of that choice are measured by the image of the final judgment. God's voice is fused with God's works "from the foundation of the world." All this gives to the simple word *logos* many dimensions: protological and eschatological, theological and christological, ecclesiological and soteriological.

SECOND SOUNDING: JOHN 6:48-71

John 6 represents one of the major shifts in the narrative, a pivot in which the conflict between Jesus and the leaders of Israel reaches a climax and in which many disciples, on learning what discipleship demands, are so offended by the difficulties that they turn away. The debate with the leaders centers in understanding how Jesus could be "the bread of life."

> I am the bread of life. Your ancestors ate the manna in the wilderness, and they died. This is the bread that comes down from heaven, so that one may eat of it and not die. I am the living bread that came down from heaven. Whoever eats of this bread will live forever; and the bread that I will give for the life of the world is my flesh. (John 6:48-51)

That declaration appears to result in complete incomprehension among

Jesus' adversaries: "How can this man give us his flesh to eat?" (John 6:52). His disciples understood a bit more; they understood enough to be offended, so shocked, in fact, as to reject their leader.

It is easy to miss the reason for their rejection. "This [logos] is difficult; who can accept it" (John 6:60). It may help us to grasp the force of this response if we interpret both this logos and the word for accepting it in consonance with the thrust of 5:24 that we analyzed in the first sounding. What did this logos refer to that made it so difficult, so impossible, for these disciples to accept? Only two things can fully explain their apostasy. First, the identification of the "bread of life" with Jesus' "flesh and blood" made it clear, at least to John's readers, that this bread was nothing less than Jesus' death for the life of the world. Second, the acceptance of this logos was a commitment to join him in that voluntary dying. The conjunction of those two things (in the messianic Passion to be shared by the disciples) made this logos offensive; yet that same double truth made Jesus' words the source of "spirit and life" (John 6:63). Jesus' word was simultaneously death-demanding and life-giving. So difficult was this logos that, as Jesus rightly said, "No one can come to me unless it is granted by the Father" (John 6:65). Judas's betrayal was a good index of this difficulty, one that the devil was quick to exploit (John 6:71).

Here then, is another mysterious cluster of interlocking images. John's thought passes smoothly from the single word *logos* to the plural, and as smoothly from hearing to seeing, from bread to flesh and blood, from drinking blood to abiding in Christ. The clusters of symbols point to an enduring, complex system of associations that constitute the habitat of John's thought. Each metaphor retains its own distinctive affiliations, yet the meaning of each figure is directly contingent on those affiliations. The total stream of consciousness is much greater than the sum of its parts. This is surely due in part to the fact that the entire stream is dominated by Christian memories of the Passion story. As a consequence, when a congregation, in celebrating the eucharist, reads this text, each of these metaphors calls into play a rich symbolic resonance. And whenever the congregation joins in the Lord's Prayer, the petition for daily bread may be enriched by the Johannine version: "Sir, give us this bread always" (John 6:34). The bread is the logos of life that is spoken through voluntary dying.

THIRD SOUNDING: JOHN 8:31-47

In John 8 the debate between Jesus and the Jews continues with even greater intensity. It is in the midst of this debate that Jesus declares, "I am the light of the world" (John 8:12), a manifesto that reminded readers of the first command in creation, "Let there be light" (Gen. 1:3). Now, as then, the creation of the light dispersed the darkness. In this case the light impelled a division of the Jews into two communities, believers and unbelievers. Only one of these two could be the true family of Abraham, the community in which the logos dwelt:[1] "Then Jesus said to the Jews who had believed in him, 'If you continue in my [logos], you are truly my disciples; and you will know the truth, and the truth will make you free' " (John 8:31-32). These are Abraham's descendants. And what of their adversaries? "Why do you not understand what I say? It is because you cannot accept my [logos]. You are from your father the devil, and you choose to do your father's desires. He was a murderer from the beginning" (John 8:43-44).

In both of these citations "you" is plural; Jesus separated two communities by using the logos. Where the logos dwells, a family bond is formed; members of this community are at once children of Abraham and children of God. The logos liberates this community from slavery, makes it immune to death, and commissions it to continue Jesus' mission. The symbol of an indwelling logos carries this entire panoply of implications; they will become clear, of course, only after the Son of Man has been lifted up from the earth (John 8:28).

Conversely, there is nothing bland about the dereliction of the community in which the logos finds no home, a community of slaves believing they are free and of fornicators persuaded of their own purity. No children of Abraham, these, but rather children of the devil, that archetypal progenitor of lies and murder. The reference to this "murderer from the beginning" (John 8:44) summons up memories of the first human murder, when one son of Eve killed the other in a religious dispute (Gen. 4:1-8; also 1 John 3:4-17). The polemic is fierce indeed. But it is not merely the animosity between two religious communities, each claiming to be superior to the other. This is a polemic between their two progenitors. God's curse had rested on one community because of its complicity in the serpent's deceit and its participation in fratricidal violence. That shedding of blood could be remedied only by the giving of blood; that darkness could be overcome only by light. Only a savior from the beginning could defeat a murderer from the beginning, by giving his flesh for the life of the world.[2]

So the appearance of the logos disclosed a chain of being that reached from Eden to the present, revealing the inner definition of every community, its freedom or slavery, its truth or illusion, its participation in life-taking or life-giving. One community lifted Jesus up from the earth, crucified him; the other testified that the logos of Jesus had been the logos of light and life from the first day of creation.

FOURTH SOUNDING: JOHN 12:44-50

This passage in John 12 is the final appeal that Jesus made to the authorities, an appeal that clarified the results of receiving or rejecting the logos. The chain of being that we noted earlier becomes here a closely linked chain of sending and, in fact, a chain of eternal life.

> I have come as light into the world, so that everyone who believes in me should not remain in the darkness. I do not judge anyone who hears my words and does not keep them, for I came not to judge the world, but to save the world. The one who . . . does not receive my word has a judge; on the last day the logos that I have spoken will serve as judge. . . . The Father who sent me has himself given me a commandment about what to say. . . . His commandment is eternal life. (12:46-50)

Here Jesus identified the logos with God's commandment. To obey this word is to obey the commandment. But the commandment is rather unusual. Does the word refer to the commands in the decalogue or to the commandment to love, with all its implications? No, here the command is eternal life, a life that comes in the form of light. A strange correlation is this: logos = command = life = light. But it is not so strange when we notice the same correlation in the prologue (John 1:1-3) and in the Genesis saga of creation (Gen. 1:1-3). In Genesis, too, the command was obeyed, and as a result light was separated from darkness. That is the command that John identified with eternal life. Logos thus forges a bond among believers in Christ that also binds them to the primal action of God in creation, before human sin had corrupted God's design—that is, before God had said to Adam, "You are dust, and to dust you shall return," cutting off access to the tree of life (Gen. 3:19-23). The curse was a command; its remedy was a command.

This command also specifies the other half of the cosmic *inclusio*, the eschatological function of the logos to match its protological function. In the last day the same logos will judge everyone who rejects the commandment of light and life. It could hardly be otherwise, if what Jesus said was faithful to what God commanded him to say. It could hardly be otherwise, if the logos had the function of revealing the descendants of Adam, Eve, and Cain. The use of this *inclusio* reflects a universal range of thinking, orienting each response to the logos within the farthest horizons, the first day of creation, and the last day of judgment—both days lying far beyond the reach of human tinkering. Yet those far horizons lose their distance at the moment when the logos is spoken afresh by those whom God sends. The logos brings the command nearer than either yesterday or tomorrow.

FIFTH SOUNDING: JOHN 17:6-26

Both old and new affiliations come to the surface in the prayer of Jesus in the seventeenth chapter. Here the logos is seen as the bond between God, Jesus, and Jesus' messengers. To God Jesus says, "I have given them *your* [logos]" (John 17:14). The reception of this logos creates a continuing vocation on the part of these messengers: "They have kept *your* [logos]" (John 17:6; emphasis added). The logos forms both the source and strength of their vocation, thus uniting Christology and missiology. "As you have sent me into the world, so I have sent them into the world" (John 17:18). The gift to them of the logos entails hatred by the world to which they are sent (John 17:14), but this hatred cements the bond of self-giving between sender and sent: "They are yours. . . . Mine are yours . . . yours are mine" (John 17:9-10). In fulfilling their assignment they will be sanctified in the truth. How does John think of this sanctification, this "being made holy"? The norm of holiness is, of course, provided by Jesus' self-sacrifice. His path to the glorification of God is theirs as well. As God is glorified in Jesus, so, too, will Jesus be glorified in them (John 17:1, 10). These corollaries may be added to our list: logos = sanctification = glorification = crucifixion.

The concluding petitions in the prayer bring into view an extension of the chain of life, a fourth link to be added to the earlier links: God, Jesus, and Jesus' apostles. Now appears the generation of those who believe through the work of Jesus' messengers. All who believe through the logos of the apostles learn that God loves believers "as you have loved me" (17:23), a love, it must be noted, that existed before the creation of the world and that is designed for the salvation of the world (John 17:24).

SIXTH SOUNDING: JOHN 1:1-18

That action, the salvation of the world, of course, is the point at which John began his story.

> In the beginning was the logos
> the logos was with God
> the logos was God. . . .
> All things came into being through the logos. . . .
> What came into being was life. (John 1:1-4, paraphrased)

These words can be read as a prelude to the entire Gospel, but they can as easily be read as a summary. In our various soundings we have noted echoes of these opening words, indicating that these verses were written by someone who knew what was to follow. Readers are confronted first of all with a logos theology: "The [logos] was God." Readers are also confronted with a logos zoology: in this symbolic universe where all things are made through the logos, life (*zoe*) is defined for the children of God by their birth from above. This is a very different zoology, to be sure, but its importance to John cannot be denied.

> The life was the light of all people. The light shines in the darkness,
> and the darkness did not overcome it. (John 1:4-5)

As we have seen, the entire Gospel recounts this struggle between the light and the darkness. Victory was won by the light when the logos, rejected by way of crucifixion, disclosed the truth that this logos-God was the parent of Jesus and of Jesus' logos-born siblings (John 20:17).

The prologue was carefully structured to accentuate the antithetical relationship to the logos on the part of two communities (a logos sociology, if you wish). One community was defined as those who accepted the light, received the logos, believed in the name of the logos, and became children of God through its power. The other community was defined as allies of the darkness who unsuccessfully tried to overcome the light, as the *kosmos* that did not know the light, as the people who did not accept the light, and as those who had a contrary birth and parentage. The entire Gospel then spelled out in detail the conflict between these two communities and thus disclosed who belonged to which family.

The ultimate punishment of the first human parents had been exclusion from the garden and the tree of life, and a return to the earth, dust to dust (Gen. 3:19, 22). In this regard the prologue of John celebrates a total reversal, in that those who are born of God enter the realm of life and light. They are now heirs of the truth; they are, by implication, no longer the dupes of the crafty serpent's lies (John 1:14). By implication, they receive "grace," not the curse. Their reliance is not on the law, but on the knowledge of God, the vision of God, and the fullness of divine glory. In this conception of life and light, Genesis may have shaped the basic vocabulary, but the story of Jesus determined the understanding of what happened when the logos came to the logos' own and was rejected. The logos' crucifixion and glorification won the victory for all who were born of God (John 1:13): "The Word became flesh and lived among us, and we have seen his glory" (John 1:14).

Here, for the first time in this carefully constructed and highly significant prologue to his Gospel, John uses the first personal pronouns *we* and *us*. This use of the plural pronouns provides an important guidance to readers for interpreting what follows. The Gospel is more than the product of a single author's mind; it is the result and the substance of conversations among the many who are logos-born, containing their meditations about their own genesis as children of God. It is neither a biography, nor a history, nor a collection of doctrines, nor a segment of scripture—and it is clearly not a theological essay on Christology. It is a series of conversations among those who have received God's grace and seen God's glory.

These conversation partners have been made aware of the frontiers that separate three contiguous worlds of thought and that illustrate three different sets of relations between children and parent. One of these is the empirical, visible world where children can simply identify their parents as John and Mary Doe. In a second world, equally empirical yet invisible, the children think and act in accordance with the desires of their parent, the serpent or devil. In a third world, always new and yet always the primal creation of God, the thoughts and actions of God's children are empowered and directed by the love disclosed in the first-born Son. Logos is *group-binding* in the sense that it constitutes the cohesive element in this third realm where all children are one in the same sense that God and Jesus are one (John 17:21). This binds the present community with both its ancestors and its progeny, all those who have received Jesus' "fullness" (John 1:16). Within this realm no generation can be superior to any other generation, because the very term *generation* is defined genetically and not chronologically.

The logos is *time-binding* in that all children receive a sense of time that links them to the beginning and end of God's work of creation and redemption. Those who live in this realm find that what happened in the beginning and what will happen at the end are more decisive than what happened yesterday or what will happen tomorrow in the realm of John and Mary Doe. This sense of time relativizes the significance of sacred calendars with the annual repetition of holy days and holy seasons. Logos measures and punctuates time in a very different way.

By living "among us," the logos has created a different sense of space; it is genuinely *space-binding*. Jesus prayed that all who accepted the logos would be with him "where I am" (John 17:24). After his death, one of the most agonizing confessions was that of Mary: "I do not know where . . ." (John 20:13). But the disciples came to know the truth of his promise: "I will come again and will take you to myself, so that where I am, there you may be also" (John 14:3). This transcendence of geographical space relativized the holiness of holy places as well as the importance of living in a selected city or nation.

So when John wrote "we have seen . . ." (John 1:14), he and his readers entered a realm of space and time, of birth and death, of conflict and victory that was the antithesis of the serpent's realm of deceit and death. Here the verbal symbol of logos fused their memories, duties, and hopes. It strengthened their will to accept persecution, while discouraging any martyr-complex by giving absolute priority to the power and demands of love. By the birth it shared with God's first-born, this community received a sense of its distinctive identity and vocation. "In the beginning was the Word."

— 10 —
The Resurrection
and the Life
(John)

Those who search the Gospel of John to find the central theme of the entire document can scarcely do better than to focus attention on the declaration Jesus made to Martha at the heart of the Lazarus story. This statement is one of the most mystifying and tantalizing ever attributed to Jesus. In it he fused one declaration and two promises into one interlocking whole:

The declaration: "I am the resurrection and the life."
The first promise: "Those who believe in me, even though they die, will live."
The second promise: "Everyone who lives and believes in me will never die." (John 11:25-26)

It is obvious that this sentence was carefully crafted; John showed its importance by adding the peremptory challenge to Martha, "Do you believe this?" By implication, John addressed the same challenge to his readers. John's readers identify with Martha's experience: She seems to have been made uncomfortable by the necessity to answer. She thought she believed, but was her belief what he intended? Did she comprehend fully that mysterious "I am" of Jesus? Did she accept without hesitation the two promises? As we shall see, this declaration, like many others in this Gospel, seems to have been intentionally designed to arouse and to feed uncertainty, and thereby to open the door to greater clarity. In what follows, we will try to recapture that design.

When most readers and commentators analyze these two verses, they look for clues primarily in the long succession of dramatic scenes in John 11: Jesus receiving the word of Lazarus's illness, the call for help from the sisters, the delay in Jesus' response, the dialogue with the disciples about the reasons for the delay, and the subtle intimations that there was a hidden linkage between Lazarus's death and his own (John 11:1-16). Then come the poignant meeting between Jesus and Martha, her reproach over his delay, her ambiguous confession of faith in him, and her affirmation of hope for Lazarus's resurrection "at the last day" (John 11:17-27). What most readers assume to be the climactic scene followed: Jesus' prayers to the Father, his command to Lazarus, the emergence of the bound corpse from the tomb, and the command to the bystanders to unbind him and let him go (John 11:28-44). Here the interest of most readers ends (as do many lectionary snippets). But that was not the narrator's intention. The epilogue tells of immediate consequences: belief, confusion, hostility, a hasty meeting of the Council, in which it becomes clear that the freeing of Lazarus from the bonds of death guaranteed Jesus' death, in Caiaphas's prophetic words, "for the people" (John 11:45-54). In one sense, the declaration of Jesus in John 11:25-26 articulates the ultimate truths that were hidden within this entire story; readers should therefore read the story as one of the earliest midrashic interpretations of the declaration. In another sense, that same declaration articulates the plot of the entire Gospel, for it relates the life and death of Jesus' followers to his own life and death. In this essay, we will explore the multiple connections between Jesus' declaration and this wider linguistic context of the entire Gospel.

As the first step, we will examine the form and structure of the "I am" declaration and the promises dependent upon it. That structure justifies the following inferences:

- The predicates to the "I am" are "the resurrection and the life." They both presuppose the truth of the "I am" statement, and extend its range of reference.
- The words "I am," like other Johannine uses of this formula, assert the oneness of the Father and the Son. Only as the Son could such an assertion be made.
- The assertion is expressed in the present tense, an "eternal present" that covers the beginning, the now, and the forever.
- The two promises assert an eternal bond between this "I am" (Jesus himself) and those who "live and believe in him." If they live, it is

in Jesus' life that they live; if they are raised, it is by sharing in Jesus' resurrection.

- The bond between Jesus and his followers, expressed in the eternal present, is made possible by his eternal bond to the Father.
- The first promise is based upon the first "I am" predicate: Jesus is the resurrection. It is he who is qualified to make such a promise to believers who die.
- The second "I am" predicate is the ground for the second promise. As the life, Jesus is qualified to promise that those who live in him will never die.
- It is assumed that the double declaration, with its dual promise, defines the essential core of the term "believe." Jesus' question to Martha proves that this constitutes his own definition of faith.
- The narrator assumed the same for readers of his Gospel. If they believed, this declaration and its promises formed the substance of their belief. Later in the Gospel, the Evangelist indicated that such belief on the part of his readers was his objective in writing the Gospel (20:31).
- The formulation of the two promises appears to make belief in *both* of them difficult if not impossible, since one contradicts the other. One asserts that believers will die; the other that they will not die.
- Such a contradiction appears to be intentionally designed to raise important questions: For example, did Jesus promise death (and resurrection) to some believers while other believers would avoid death entirely? Did he thus intend to divide all believers into these two groups? Or were both promises addressed to all believers and thus designed to call attention to two quite different concepts of death? The text assumes that any such contradictions can be resolved, since both promises are based on a single truth: one person is both the resurrection and the life. In him and in his story, the contradiction is both embodied and resolved. Accordingly, the story calls readers to search for the resolution.

Such an understanding of the formal structure—and of the importance of the seemingly contradictory two-part promise as the substance of faith—has induced me to canvass the entire Gospel for clues to the inner logic of the declaration. I will divide this search into three segments: (1) Because the declaration "I am the life" appears to serve as the basis for the promise that believers will never die, I will call on other texts to elucidate that declaration and promise. (2) Because "I am the resurrection" undergirds the promise to believers who die, I will call on texts that help us comprehend such a dying and resurrection. (3) Finally, I will comment on the results of this research and the ultimate resolution of the contradiction.

LIFE

The declaration "I am the life" personalizes all thinking about this life. Before readers say life, they should think of this particular speaker and his whole story from an invisible beginning to an invisible end. This is not the only text in the Gospel that makes this claim (e.g., John 14:6). In addition, concrete images occur that discourage thinking about this life in wholly abstract terms: the bread of life, the light of life, the water of life. All such images remind us of the eternal dimensions of this life. Seldom does the word "life" appear in John devoid of this complex and rich resonance, this aura of overtones that emerges from all chapters of the Gospel (e.g., "Before Abraham was, I am" [John 8:58]).

This life is, of course, explicitly identified with the life of God who has "life in himself"; like his Father, the Son has "life in himself" (John 5:26). Father and Son share in the same work of giving life to those whom they choose, those whom they send (John 5:19-21). Each gift of life is a work of creation that responds to God's command (John 12:50). One such work is "the lifting up" of the Son, an event in which both Father and Son are glorified.

We fall short of catching the full resonance of this term *life*, however, unless we grasp its significance in terms of the Johannine prologue. There John traced this life to the Word, that was in the beginning with God, and that, in fact, was God. Without that Word, nothing whatever had come into existence. The life that was the light of his creatures was in this Word. To those who accepted it, God gave the power to become his children. Begotten not of violence and not of the will of human parents, they were begotten by God, coming from heaven, not earth; and from the Spirit, not flesh. This life is truly archetypal, from the beginning and continuing now and forever. It is within the ambiance of the prologue that the declaration of John 11:25 must be seen.

We also need to push behind the prologue to the early chapters of Genesis, where all light and life also originated in response to God's command. Everything that came into existence was a work of God: the separation of light from darkness, the victory over darkness, the goodness of all his works, the gift of dominion to humankind, God's blessing of everything thus made. It is that same blessing that echoes in the grace bestowed on the family of God in John's prologue. This is the context that alone provides the full range of meaning to Jesus' declaration, "I am the life." And this same range lies behind his promise: "Everyone who lives and believes in me will never die" (John 11:26).

We find in the Gospel no fewer than twenty-five variations in describing what it means to live in Christ and to believe in him. The following are some of those variations:

> —to come to Christ (John 5:40)
> —to be chosen by Christ (John 5:21)
> —to hear, accept, keep, and obey his word (John 5:24, 8:51)
> —to follow him wherever he goes (John 8:12)
> —to eat his flesh and drink his blood (John 6:54)
> —to work for the food that endures (John 6:27)
> —to drink the water he gives (John 4:14, 7:37)
> —to hate their life in this world (John 12:25).

Belief is thus defined. If one's belief does not include these elements, one's thinking has left the Johannine orbit. These various descriptions aid interpreters in comprehending the necessary conjunction between Christ's action and the disciple's response, between gift and work, between water offered and water drank. It is only at the conjunction of election and decision that this life is created and inherited.

There are also many significant alternatives to the promise that these believers will never die.

> Believers have already passed from death to life (John 5:24).
> They no longer stand under God's judgment (John 5:24). ·
> They are no longer condemned as the object of God's wrath or curse (John 3:18).
> They no longer walk in darkness but in the light of life (John 8:12).
> Out of their hearts flow rivers of living water (John 7:38).
> No longer are they slaves of sin or dead in their sins (John 8:34-36).
> They are freed from lies and deceptions that characterize children of the devil (John 8:42-47).
> As sheep in this shepherd's flock, they will go in and out and find pasture (John 10:9).

All these promises help to define that immunity to death that Jesus promised in John 11:26. Life in the *Word* is clearly not subject to death, and that is the life of which believers are heirs.

RESURRECTION

It was axiomatic with John that only God could raise the dead and give them life (John 5:21). It was to such an action of God that Jesus pointed on his first visit to the temple, when zeal for his Father's house so consumed him that he challenged the authorities with the words "Destroy this temple, and in three days I will raise it up" (John 2:19). That statement does not make sense unless (1) the *I* who speaks was God; (2) the temple was Jesus' body; (3) its destruction was the work of the religious authorities; and (4) its raising was God's act in glorifying Jesus as his beloved Son and in saving others through him. All this was a promise that Jesus would himself die and be raised, a promise that the disciples believed, though only after Jesus' death.

In its immediate sequel, Jesus announced to Nicodemus, a teacher of the Jews and a Pharisee: "Just as Moses lifted up the serpent in the wilderness, so must the Son of Man be lifted up, that whoever believes in him may have eternal life" (John 3:14, 15). Here, as in the later parallel (John 12:32), the lifting up referred both to the kind of death Jesus would die and to the resurrection that would accompany that death. He would be lifted up by both his enemies and his Father. Those who believed in him must accordingly believe both in the crucifixion as human rejection and in the glorification as divine vindication. It would be this action of the Father that would enable "the dead" to hear the voice of that Son (John 5:25). It was because the Son saw what his Father was doing in raising the dead that the Son was also empowered to raise the dead and give life to "whomever he wishes" (John 5:19-21). So, it was God's will that Jesus should at the last day raise up all who saw the Son and who believed in him (John 6:39-40, 54).

This lifting up of Jesus was, of course, a measure of the Father's love for this Son, and the basis was clear: "For this reason the Father loves me, because I lay down my life in order to take it up again" (John 10:17). Such a sacrifice was made out of this Shepherd's love for his sheep, a love that fulfilled the will of the divine Shepherd. Jesus was himself "a grain of wheat [that] falls into the earth and dies" (John 12:24). He thus carried out the prophecy of John the Baptist: "Here is the Lamb of God who takes away the sin of the world" (1:29), an obvious allusion to the sin of Eve, Adam, Cain, and their progeny.

For John, it was Jesus' own story that permanently defined the death from which Jesus was raised. In his words, it revealed "the kind of death" he would die (John 12:33). This identification had several implications. It was a death by crucifixion. To doubting Thomas and the other disciples, the identity of the exalted Lord would be secured by his pointing to his hands and side. It was a death that embodied the Father's love for the world in the Son's love for the world. It was a death that marked a climactic struggle with darkness and the devil that secured victory over those primeval foes.

THAT LIFE, THAT DEATH

Jesus declared unequivocally that servants are no greater than their master (John 13:16). One image that enforced this commonality was that of washing the feet of one another. When their master washed their feet, he conveyed the necessity of similar behavior on their part. When they demonstrated solidarity with his self-sacrifice, not only would they be blessed but those who received them would receive both Jesus and his Father (John 13:17-20). To honor this Father, they too must plant their seed in the earth so that through death it might yield a harvest. By hating their life in this world, they would keep it for eternity. The logic of the entire Gospel requires that we define *this* dying by the death of Jesus. The Son of Man forever defined eternal life by the dying life of the Crucified. To believe was to follow, and to follow was to be "where I am" (John 12:23-26). It is in the believers' case that the promise makes sense: "Those who eat my flesh and drink my blood have eternal life, and I will raise them up on the last day" (John 6:54). In that promise, we should notice the shift from present to future tenses. Those who follow Jesus in sacrificing themselves for others already "have eternal life"; only in this way can they be promised resurrection.

We are now in a position to resolve the apparent contradiction in the two promises given by Jesus to Martha. As the life, Jesus promised believers that they would never die; as the resurrection, he indicated the kind of dying that would lead to resurrection. The death from which believers were promised immunity was the death in sin on the part of Adam and his heirs, the wrath and condemnation of God as pictured in Genesis 3 (not the death of Gen. 5:5). Those who live "in Christ" would never suffer that death. The death that followers of Christ would die was another thing entirely. Their death was a death for the sins of the world, incarnating the love for that world of the Father and the Son. This dying was measured by the self-giving of Christ, not the self-seeking of Adam. Through such dying, they would be with Christ: "where I am." The apparent verbal contradiction was an intentional one, meant to puzzle readers until they penetrated the mystery of a deeper truth. So understood, the double declaration of Jesus with its two corollaries is the epitome of the entire Gospel.

MISUNDERSTANDING AND UNDERSTANDING

We have thus far used the entire Gospel rather than the Lazarus story itself to interpret the key saying, but our discussion sheds light on that story as well. It would seem that one of the concerns of the narrator was to exploit the misunderstandings of Jesus on the part of successive groups: the disciples, the sisters, their Jewish neighbors, and the Council. In his teaching, Jesus had meant things that those people did not grasp; the narrator wanted his readers to grasp Jesus' meaning more clearly.

Here, as elsewhere, the narrator wanted them to penetrate the mystery of who Jesus was and what his mission involved, a mystery that reached its climax in the decision of the Council to put Jesus to death. Step by step, various titles were used in speaking of this man: rabbi, teacher, Lord, Messiah, and Son of God. Although each of these titles was used with seriousness, each proved to be vague, ambiguous, and even misleading. Jesus was not satisfied with any of those titles, and neither, we assume, was the narrator of the Gospel. The narrator wanted his readers to gauge the validity of their own believing, not by reference to formal titles, but by this rich and resonant declaration.

The people around Jesus were also mistaken in their varying perceptions of death. John 11 presents a parade of such perceptions: Lazarus's sickness would not lead to death since he had fallen asleep; Jesus will die at Bethany if he goes there; if Jesus had been present our brother would not have died; Lazarus's resurrection means that Jesus and Lazarus must both be killed. It was against this list of wrong perceptions that the narrator set Jesus' declaration, introducing two *other* definitions of death. In one case, death is God's judgment on the sin of Adam and his heirs; in the other case, death is the self-sacrifice of the Son of God for the sins of the world. Understanding these uses of the term *death* will enable readers to understand the sense in which Jesus is the life and the resurrection.

Of all the characters in the story, the one who came closest to penetrating this mystery was Caiaphas, with his prophetic revelation that Jesus would die for the people. Yet Caiaphas had not had the slightest premonition that the deaths of both Lazarus and Jesus would lead to the glorification of God.

We now ask whether John anywhere illustrated this double promise of Jesus to Martha. A search discovers a possible illustration in John 21, in the very last, and therefore potentially significant, conversation of the Gospel. Here, too, we find a final example of a misunderstanding that leads to an understanding.

John 20 describes the fulfillment of Jesus' promises about himself. Though he died, yet he lived. He ascended to the Father whom he had been with in the beginning as the life (John 1:1-5). Having been lifted up on the cross he had disclosed "the *kind* of death" he would die and its vindication by his Father. In John 21 Jesus wanted to show the fulfillment of the earlier promises *to the disciples*. Seven disciples are mentioned, yet only two are chosen to serve as their spokesmen (the beloved disciple and Peter). Their conversation with Jesus was an intended climax, not only to Peter's story, but to the entire Gospel. We will see that it illustrates the double promise of John 11:25-26.

First comes the account of the renewed fishing in the Galilean lake. Interpreters are certainly right in taking this account as a symbol of their later success as Jesus' messengers. Frustrated throughout the long night, their efforts in the early morning yielded abundant results. That success, of course, was caused by Jesus, once the disciples obeyed his instructions. It was amazement at the huge catch of fish that prompted the beloved disciple to recognize the stranger as the ascended Lord. This identification prompted Peter, in turn, to leap into the sea and swim to shore.

If we listen to this account with the whole Gospel in mind, we hear the echoes of many promises of Jesus: "The hour is coming . . . when you will be scattered, each one to his home, and you will leave me alone" (John 16:32); "I will not leave you orphaned; I am coming to you" (John 14:18); "I will . . . reveal myself to them" (John 14:21); "My Father will love them, and we will come to them and make our home with them" (John 14:23); "The one who believes in me will also do the works that I do and, in fact, will do greater works than these, because I am going to the Father" (John 14:12). The fishing story fits smoothly into the world of John's thought as an anticipation of how the apostles would learn the truth of such assurances from their subsequent work.

Next comes the description of breakfast, with the ascended Lord presiding and providing bread and fish. Now all seven of his followers recognize the presence of the Lord (John 21:12). Again, interpreters have seen here a symbol of Jesus' presence at table with disciples. In John's mind, that breakfast was the anticipation of many such meals in which followers would receive from his hands nourishment for the day's tasks.

So evocative and dramatic were these stories of fishing and eating that readers often find the dialogue between Jesus and Peter to be anticlimactic. But such an impression is dispelled when we recognize that the narrator has arranged this final dialogue to illustrate the double promise of John 11:25-26, and that in such a fulfillment the two apostles represented all followers of the ascended Lord. Since the two represent all followers, the disappearance of the other disciples from the scene goes unnoticed.

It is clear that, to John, Simon Peter was an important figure, though we should not confuse his portrait with that which appears in the other Gospels. Earlier glimpses of this follower betray several characteristic weaknesses. For example, in the foot-washing scene, Peter at first refused to accept an action by Jesus that symbolically anticipated Jesus' final sacrifice: "You will never wash my feet" (John 13:8). He finally consented, when the price of refusal was repudiation by Jesus. Even so, at the time, Peter misunderstood the requirement that disciples must make a similar sacrifice. Soon after that, Jesus made a double prediction: "Where I am going, you cannot follow me now; but you will follow afterward" (John 13:36). This made explicit what had only been implicit in the exchange over foot-washing. In any case, the disciple immediately rejected this first prediction, saying, "I will lay down my life for you"; almost at once, however, the truth of Jesus' prediction was registered in Peter's fear-driven denials in the high priest's court. (The second brief prediction would find its intended confirmation only at the very end of Peter's story, in John 21.) Readers next glimpse Peter in the Garden during the arrest, when Peter drew his sword and severed the ear of the high priest's slave. Jesus explained this disobedient action as an effort to prevent Jesus from drinking the cup that the Father had placed in his hands, further evidence that Peter did not understand the scriptural necessity for that death. Without such an understanding, Peter's denial was entirely logical. Then, Peter is seen returning home after his visit to the empty tomb, again without understanding the scripture (John 20:9-10). Apart from John 21, that was Peter's last appearance on the Johannine stage, and that would have been a very strange conclusion to a carefully planned scenario. Without John 21, John's readers would have read nothing about Peter's role in the church except for the brief prophecy in John 13:36.

But in that final chapter John brought Peter back to center stage. After his return home to Galilee, Peter took the initiative in a return to fishing. After his fellow fisherman identified the stranger on the beach as Jesus, Peter responded impetuously by putting on his clothes, by jumping into the water, and later by dragging ashore the net full of fish. All this was prelude to the final conversation with Jesus, a true climax not only to Peter's story but also to the Gospel.

> "Very truly, I tell you, when you were younger, you used to fasten your own belt and to go wherever you wished. But when you grow old, you will stretch out your hands, and someone else will fasten a belt around you and take you where you do not wish to go." (He said this to indicate the kind of death by which he would glorify God.) (John 21:18-19)

Peter's earlier desire to *follow* Jesus would at last be realized. He would prove his love for Jesus by feeding his sheep, a ministry that would end in helplessness, captivity, and a martyr's dying (although Jesus did not here label it as death; John did). By that dying, Peter would glorify God in ways similar to Jesus' glorification of his Father. John made the point so clearly that no reader could miss it: "He said this to indicate the kind of death by which he [Peter] would glorify God." (This phrase had been used to refer to Jesus' death in John 12:33 and again in 18:32.) Hating his life in this world, Peter would keep it for eternal life (John 12:25). Peter had been the first to confess: "You have the words of eternal life" (John 6:68). Now he would become the representative of all those followers (shepherds, fishermen, etc.) whose confessions would lead to the same kind of dying. This was precisely the kind of death that was embraced in the first promise of John 11:25: "Those who believe in me, even though they die, will live."

In a similar fashion, the role of the beloved disciple throughout the Gospel is clarified when we consider his place in John 21. Here we find a fulfillment of the second promise in John 11:26: "Everyone who lives

. . . in me will never die." Because the evidence for this hypothesis is less obvious, we must look at this text very closely:

> When Peter saw him, he said to Jesus, "Lord, what about him?" Jesus said to him, "If it is my will that he remain until I come, what is that to you? Follow me." So the rumor spread in the community that this disciple would not die. Yet Jesus did not say to him that he would not die, but "If it is my will that he remain until I come, what is that to you?" (John 21:21-23)

The narrator used Peter's question to turn attention to the future role of the beloved disciple. Jesus' answer has baffled readers ever since, and the text shows that this bafflement began with the first readers. Everything is made to depend upon the meaning of Jesus' reply, which was repeated precisely because of the misunderstanding. The brothers (which in the NRSV becomes "the community") thought that Jesus had said that this disciple would not die; but Jesus had not said that. Again a misunderstanding, a misunderstanding over different perceptions of death, and a misunderstanding that John used to advance an insight into Jesus' will. The narrator skillfully used this misperception; he forced readers to ponder what Jesus had really intended by "if it is my will." If they understood that clause, they would understand the destiny of this representative and beloved disciple. Let us examine this clause carefully.

The speaker who said "if it is my will" (literally, if I will) is the one who had declared "I am . . . the life." This Son of God was able to give life to anyone whom he wills (John 5:21). The *I will* of John 21:22 is the same as the *I will* of John 5:21. As we have seen, anyone to whom he wills to give life "does not come under judgment [the sin-death of Adam] but *has* passed from death to life" (John 5:24). So that clause "If I will" carried echoes of many promises that Jesus had made, and by which he had challenged universal human perceptions of death. In taking away the sin of the world (1:29), the Lamb of God had removed God's curse on Adam and could declare in effect, "Whoever lives in me will never inherit Adam's curse." The misunderstanding of the brothers in chapter 21 was the same as that of the two sisters in chapter 11: "If you had been here, our brother would not have died."

John's use of the verb "to remain" (*menein*) also contributed to the misunderstanding. Did Jesus have in mind simply physical survival? The other occurrences of this verb help to remove the misunderstanding. *Menein* appears in John with many meanings that vary according to the context. Its weight is especially great when used to characterize the

intimate, power-laden union of God as Father, and Jesus as Son. Because
the Father abides in the Son, the Son can be said to abide forever (John
8:35; 12:34; 14:10). The Spirit that came from heaven was said to abide
on the Son (John 1:33). The most telling analogy here is that of a vine
with its branches. Their mutual abiding is an index of vitality and fruit-
fulness (John 15:1-5). Whenever that abiding ceases, a fiery judgment of
the branches follows. This kind of abiding is best realized in sacrificial
love: "As the Father has loved me, so I have loved you; abide in my love.
If you keep my commandments, you will abide in my love, just as I have
kept my Father's commandments and abide in his love" (15:9-10).
Abiding is loving; loving is abiding. We should not forget that the disciple in chapter 21 is "the disciple whom Jesus loved"; his abiding (or
"remaining") was defined by the Master's will, by his love, and by keeping his commandments. Elsewhere in the Gospel, such an abiding is
defined by keeping the divine *logos*, dwelling in the Messiah's house, and
eating his flesh, the food that endures (*menein*) to eternal life. The opposite of this life is to abide in God's wrath, to walk in darkness, to remain
dead in sin under the condemnation of God. It would be strange indeed
if in John 21:22 "remaining" denoted only the physical survival of the
disciple whom Jesus loves and who *abides* in him. It is such abiding that
helps also to grasp the meaning of the phrase "until I come."

We do not do justice to this phrase by applying it to some apocalyptic
cosmic event. The basic force in this context surely derives from the
same mutual bonds between the exalted Lord and those whom he loves,
those whom he has sent into the world to love that world in his name.
The "I" who comes is the Master who is "the life"; those to whom he
comes are "his own" because they have received him and loved him. The
best clue to the nature of this coming may be provided in John 14:3: "If
I go and prepare a place for you, I will come again and will take you to
myself, so that where I am, there you may be also." Both his going and
his coming are the expression of love. The purpose of his coming is
reunion, so that beloved disciples may be "where I am." Here space and
time are being defined by the presence of the Father, by the vision and
knowledge of God, by Jesus as "the way, and the truth, and the life." The
revelation of *this* coming was not made "to the world" but only to those
whom he loved and to whom he gave the Spirit of truth (14:22). This
way of understanding his *coming* identified his advent with their own
action of obedient self-sacrifice for others. The words "until I come"
are virtually the equivalent of "until you have fulfilled your mission."

So when we read that the community misunderstood the prophecy of Jesus in John 21:23, we should remember the long chain of such misunderstandings: Nicodemus's misunderstanding of "being born from above"; the failure of the Samaritan woman to recognize the time of the Messiah's advent; Martha's conception of the resurrection simply as a future event; and Peter's repeated miscalculations of his own faithfulness. "Until I come" did not mean until some date on the calendar of the world or until the date of a disciple's death as recorded in human obituaries. His statement "if it is my will that he remain until I come" did not mean that this beloved disciple would not die; rather it meant that "everyone who lives . . . in me will never die" (11:26). In the design of the Gospel as this narrator planned it, the story could end only when readers understood that they, too, could count on the fulfillment of Jesus' double promise to Martha.

Addendum

The following resources by the author are also relevant to those issues in biblical theology addressed in part 2:

"New Starting Point," in *Interpretation* 10 (1965): 3-15.

"Propheten Gottes: das Wesen ihrer Berufung," in *Oekumenische Theologie in den Herausforderungen der Gegenwart, Festschrift fur Lukas Vischer,* eds. K. B. Gerschwiler, et al. (Gottingen, 1991), 175-91.

"The Home of the 'Our Father,' " in *Worship* (May 2000).

"The Beloved Disciple in the Fourth Gospel," in *Novum Testamentum* 19 (1977): 105-23.

" 'We Don't Know Where . . .' (John 20:2)," in *Interpretation* 30 (1976): 125-39.

PART III

The Messiah's Presence with the Churches

Introduction to
PART III

Both historians and theologians recognize the importance of contexts in conditioning how humans think. There are thousands of possible contexts, some very trivial but some very powerful, some of which we are conscious and some of which we are quite unconscious. They range from the intimate and immediate influences of family and daily work, through more distant economic and political involvements, to ultimate life-or-death crises.

The texts of the New Testament are set within contexts that are at once immediate, powerful, and inclusive. The following chapters furnish five examples of these texts in context. In addition, the biblical authors consistently identify one context in particular, the heavens and the earth (with both elements of the image always present and interacting), as their *ultimate* context. They find this image attractive because, like the sky (the same Greek word is used for both), the heavens, with their unlimited height, are everywhere equally near the earth and all of the earth's inhabitants. The heavens provide a powerful and final setting for all earthly failures and achievements. The heavens are nearer than the closest living human being, yet "the company of heaven" includes all the generations of Adam's children, armies of angels, and an endless variety of principalities and powers. The heavens contain all the lords whom earthlings serve and all the gods whom they worship. These earthly servants are bound to these heavenly lords by shifting fears and hopes, hates and loves, betrayals and trusts. Quite literally, their heaven is where their hearts are. It is this fact that invites frequent and easy communication between the heavens and human hearts by way of prophetic visions and supliant petitions. The curtain separating these heavens from this earth was altogether more porous for the biblical authors than we suppose—we who are so fully absorbed with the day's newspaper.

When the God of Israel enthroned the crucified Messiah in heaven, that enthronement increased the nearness of this Lord to his servants and thereby the frequency of their two-way conversations. When his servants gathered for worship, he was present in their midst, identifying them as his family and enrolling them in his war with the Great Deceiver (chapter 11). When they worshiped him as Lord, the heavens became their homeland (chapter 12). This double residence (they were heaven-dwellers and earthly pilgrims) obligated them to love all on earth whom he had loved and for whom he had died (chapter 13). This new existence gave to the family of the Messiah on earth a peace that the world could not give (chapter 14) and a hope that nothing could destroy (chapter 15). Their life on earth thus received an ultimate anchorage that was intimate, powerful, and enduring, that is, so long as they shared their Lord's humility and courage.

— 11 —
The Family
(Hebrews)

The terms *poetry* and *theology* do not appear in the New Testament, but both are present, often in unsuspected places. When present, poetry and theology are usually so blended together that they cannot readily be separated. Amos N. Wilder called this union of the two *theopoesis* and *theopoetic*. He attributed this combined art to Jesus, to Paul, to the stories of Jesus' birth and resurrection, and to the Apocalypse.

In this essay I wish to nominate as a practitioner of *theopoesis* another theologian, the author of the Epistle to the Hebrews. I am well aware that such a nomination may turn into a specious *tour de force* in which massive contrasts between the centuries are ignored and tenuous similarities are artificially induced. My motive is neither to vindicate Professor Wilder by documenting his biblical orthodoxy nor to exalt the author of Hebrews by proving his modernity, but simply to test these hermeneutical rubrics to see whether they transcend in any significant degree the admitted chasm between then and now. The more fully we recognize vast cultural distances between ancient Rome and modern America, the more weight we should give to genuine correlations in the exegetical perspectives and perceptions of these two authors.

The basic perception of *theopoetic* is the insistence that creative poetic vision must be accorded a major role as prelude to theological construction. This is succinctly stated in one of the epigraphs to Wilder's *Theopoetics:*

Before the message there must be the vision,
before the sermon the hymn, before the prose the poem.

Because the poem and the vision were prior for the biblical author, they must be prior for modern interpreters as well. The hierophanic visions of New Testament authors gave to their words a dramatic intensity that was intrinsically revolutionary.[1] These visions were able to release from the depths of human sensibility new "coordinates of time and space," new "calendars and geographies"[2] that provided the "resources and criteria for consciousness changing." The consequence is clear: a modern exegete must do justice to the original axis that connected these revolutionary hierophanies to the structures of faith. Because biblical writers employed "primordial language and dynamic symbol,"[3] interpreters must beware of the stultifying effects of conceptual abstraction and prosaic stereotype.[4] In our day it is distrust of imagination that characterizes both biblical literalists and rationalistic critics.

Turning now to a particular New Testament author, and selecting from his entire work a single homily (Heb. 2:5–3:6), we will assess the degree to which, in his thought, creative vision served as prelude to theological construction. In this homily the author of Hebrews was himself acting as an interpreter of scripture for his readers. In Hebrews 2:12-15 he was commenting upon verses from Psalm 22 and Isaiah 8. These texts were poetic; so was the exegesis. The original use of the texts had been in liturgical and prophetic contexts; so too the exegesis in Hebrews. Notice first the quotation from Psalm 22:22.

> I will proclaim your name to my brothers and sisters,
> in the midst of the congregation I will praise you.

In Hebrews, the speaker is Jesus, as a living brother addressing his brothers and sisters in the church. The homilist would not have discerned the dramatic relevance of this text to his own situation apart from a prior hierophany, in this case a christophany. He had himself experienced a vision of Jesus standing in the midst of the ecclesia. He had himself heard the Son of Man speaking to God and to the congregation. He had himself recognized the strategic importance of that presence, that voice. It was the concord between that vision and the psalmist's confession that prompted him to use the quotation in a context that provided its own interpretation. Notice the triangular conversation. To his brothers and sisters Jesus discloses God's name; as their spokesman Jesus praises God. Thus Jesus as an unseen liturgist in the midst of a worshiping congregation evokes the presence of God; in fact, it is by way of sharing in the vision of the homilist that this congregation *becomes* the ecclesia, linked through the poetic-liturgical traditions of the synagogue to the psalmist. For Christians, this same psalm reverberated with memories of the suffering of Jesus on the cross, and with continuing conflicts between faithful servants of God and their enemies. It conveyed a call for those servants to fear and to praise the Lord by courageously enduring those conflicts. It reminded them of the blessings which the Lord's presence imparts to the meek and afflicted. We can almost retrace the steps by which the imagination of this Christian author transmuted the ancient hymn, poem, and vision into a prose sermon designed to induct his listeners into the presence of the risen Lord.

We now ask why this preacher included the two quotations from Isaiah 8:17, 18.

> I will put my trust in him . . .
> Here am I and the children whom God has given me.

It is of course impossible to be absolutely sure of an answer to our query. The homilist could have chosen various appropriate texts. Why then did he choose only these two lines? We observe that these lines provide a precise parallel, a double witness as it were, to the verse from the Psalm. They also preserve the triangular conversation—Jesus, God, and the children. More significantly, they retain the priority of the poetic vision of Jesus standing in the midst of the congregation. The moment Jesus is identified as the speaker of these lines, the words become an epitome of God's relation to the church. The Father is trustworthy; they are his children, his gift to Jesus.

We should note how this vision gives dramatic intensity to the prophetic exclamation *idou*. (The translation "Here am I" weakens the ejaculation.) Whereas we place an exclamation mark at the end of a sentence, this word announces in advance a command to stop, to listen, and to look: "See!" The text from Isaiah, reverberating through the vision of the homilist, thus becomes a summons for the congregation to share in that vision, alerting them to the presence of the triumphant Lord in their midst. It is the vision, not the doctrine, that communicates to them their identity as God's children and Jesus' brothers and sisters. I find in this christophany a central clue to the thought-complex as a whole. The word "children" in the Isaiah text is a verbal link to what follows (Heb. 2:14-15); so, too, the "brothers and sisters" of the psalm text links the vision to the preceding verses. This bit of exegesis in Hebrews illustrates another epigraph from Wilder's *Theopoetics:* "The structures of faith and confession have always rested on hierophanies and images."

The authentic religious imagination, in Wilder's accounting, makes bold and deft use of mythology. This is no optional matter for the exegete because our struggle with principalities and powers is continuous with the struggle of the early Christian. The human future depends on the outcome of that struggle. Furthermore, Wilder stresses the liturgical character of the cardinal myths: "The Christian myth is only properly at home in the liturgical mysteries of the church." Exegetes can of course recognize this linkage and still reduce myth and liturgy to sterile prose, as if these had little bearing on historical or ontological issues. This they will not do if, with Wilder, they realize that this liturgical myth is a potent weapon in communal conflicts. The early Christian movement "was a guerilla operation which undermined social authority by profound persuasions. . . . It was a case of liturgy against liturgy, of myth against myth."[5] This means that the interpretation of myth is not so much a matter of conceptual ideas or subjective experiences as it is a matter of sharing power. In this regard Wilder asserts the deficiencies of two groups: scholars who are so engrossed with the aesthetic potentialities of the parable that they ignore the "grander scenarios" of the myth,[6] and enthusiasts so absorbed in charismatic spirituality as to cut themselves off from communal traditions of worship and their disciplined sense of "the awe and the abyss."

Let me now turn to the exegesis of Psalm 8:4, 5 in Hebrews 2:5-11 as an example of bold and deft use of mythological and liturgical material. It should be obvious that in the synagogue this psalm had for centuries articulated a fusion of the mythological stories of human origins with the liturgical practices of God's people.

> What is man that thou art mindful of him,
> or the son of man, that thou carest for him?
> Thou didst make him for a little while lower than the angels,
> thou hast crowned him with glory and honor,
> putting everything in subjection under his feet. (RSV)

We may ask what motives impelled the homilist to select precisely these lines for extended comment. It seems likely that he wished to stress the solidarity between these mortals and this mortal, Jesus. We recall how central this unity was in the vision of Hebrews 2:12, 13. We also observe that in Hebrews 2:10, 11 the preacher established a bond between "the one who sanctifies and those who are sanctified." Because "all have one Father," the glorification of the one carries the promise of the glorification of the many. This archetypal image (the son of man) thus serves both protological and eschatological functions.

Equally strong, however, was another motive: the verse from the Psalm helped the homilist to distinguish the many from the one in such a way as to underscore the continuing dependence of the sanctified upon the one who has sanctified them. Because of Psalm 8, the moment of truth experienced in worship held two major components: recognition of unity with this Lord, first in the act of their creation, in their common subjection to angels, in their sharing of suffering and death; and second in their awe and reverence before the one who has already been crowned with glory and honor, the whole angelic world having been subjected to him.

The exegetical work of the preacher served to locate the worship of the listeners within the widest conceivable horizons of time and space. A shared vision enabled them to enter into a new calendar and a new geography. This was a vision of the Son of Man—"We see!"—subjected and glorified. It was simultaneously a vision of humanity, subjected but not yet glorified—"We do not yet see." The archetypal mythology of origins encouraged the homilist to be a realist, all the while the vision of glorified humanity gave worshipers an assurance of life in "the coming world" (Heb. 2:5). He would not let the worshipers forget their own Passion stories nor the Passion story of their *archegos*, but this memory was set within the wider context of communal memories as embodied in the words of the psalm and in the archetypal myths of creation and glorification.

All interpreters of the New Testament should aim at recovering "the experience of glory which lies at the heart of Christianity,"[7] but which has been all but forgotten by the church today. This recovery of glory would be "the greatest single contribution that a new theopoetic could make."[8] To be sure, the whole New Testament makes it clear that this glory is inconceivable apart from crucifixion. Its recovery therefore awaits the ability to "repossess the mystery of the cross and its glory in a way that would speak to all," an ability that would require a new fusion of theology and poetry, of vision and social ethics. There is no way by which "the seraphic joy of the church triumphant" can be apprehended except through a celebration of "the travail and triumph of the church militant." Believers become believers only by participating "in that divine operation in which evil is encountered and transmuted"; so also they discover the mystery of *Kreuzseligkeit*, cross-blessedness.[9]

How well, then, does the author of Hebrews exemplify these features of the religious imagination? From passages other than the homily of Hebrews 2:5–3:6 we learn that this community had earlier been "publicly exposed to abuse and affliction" (Heb. 10:32-36) and that the prospect of renewed persecution was even then testing its poise and confidence. The interpretation of Psalm 8 presupposes that situation; in fact, it was precisely this type of suffering that was identified with subjection to angels, that very subjection that bound these "human beings" to the "Son of Man." Familial connection, a common origin, sanctification, praise, trust, glory—each of these derives its force in this sermon from a shared Passion. All forms of travail seem to be summed up in the one phrase "the suffering of death," which defines both the subjection to angels and the glory and honor of which the psalm speaks. Death is what it is because it stands under the power of the devil; it is what it is because the key to this life-long bondage is human fears. Deliverance from those fears accomplishes the termination of bondage and the veritable destruction of the devil himself (Heb. 2:14-18). For this congregation those fears have therefore been the occasion for both temptation and sin. It was their impotence before the devil, in times of hazard and hostility, that gave ominous weight to the archetypal myth of Psalm 8 and prevented the interpretation of that hymn from becoming an idle exercise in aesthetic fancy. With the psalmist and with Jesus, the homilist had taken full account "of the radical jeopardies of the human lot"; he could therefore legitimately detect a universal significance in the liturgical myth. He had earned the right to speak of a glorious crown. Accordingly he safeguarded the ethical integrity of the gospel by linking the gift of glory to the rigorous self-discipline, to the confidence and pride demanded of those who were tempted (Heb. 2:18; 3:6-15). The communal worship by these "descendants of Abraham" provided an appropriate liturgical setting for this celebration of travail and triumph, but the travail itself was the nonliturgical substance of life in the world. The homilist was most deeply concerned with that substance, for it was that travail that prompted these recollections of Moses, Abraham, the Exodus years in the wilderness, the synagogue readings from Psalm 8, and the story of Jesus. *Kreuzseligkeit*, indeed!

Wilder is emphatic about one further feature in the religious imagination of biblical authors and therefore of their interpreters. The new calendars and geographies of early Christian thinking were oriented around their vivid testimonies to the resurrection of Jesus. Through this event God had brought into existence a new people and a new creation. Many current treatments of this event are shockingly deficient in theological and poetic imagination, and nowhere is this deficiency more stultifying than in their separation of the appearances of the risen Lord from "the horizons of world drama." Apocalyptic categories of thought provided early Christians with a symbolic language capable of articulating ultimate realities with visionary intensity. Having lost that intensity, many interpreters no longer can penetrate the pristine power of the language. No longer aware of the presence of Jesus standing among his brothers and sisters at worship, they make little sense of stories that celebrate "the imminent renewal of creation as a whole."

— 12 —
The Homeland
(Revelation)

It is inevitable that historical science should reflect the cosmological presuppositions of the historian's own age. Among these presuppositions, the most pervasive and influential in our time are basal attitudes toward space and time. These presuppositions thoroughly condition contemporary interpretations of biblical thought.

I began in hope of recovering John's conception of time and space, but I had not proceeded far before it became apparent that to concentrate upon this conception would distort his worldview. So I began to look for categories more native to his outlook and settled on the indigenous categories, heaven and earth. For John it was axiomatic that all earthly happenings, whether present or future, derive from what happens in heaven. For him, therefore, a vision of heaven was quite indispensable to the understanding of earthly events. A correct grasp of his conception of heaven and earth may lead us nearer to his attitudes toward what we call space and time. So the first question must be this: What perceptions of heaven and earth were essential to John's message?

We may glimpse some of the answers by a study of the opening verses of Revelation 21: "Then I saw a new heaven and a new earth; for the first heaven and the first earth had passed away, and the sea was no more. And I saw the holy city, the new Jerusalem, coming down out of heaven from God." To many readers it will seem wrongheaded to begin with John's final and climactic vision. Is not the whole of the Apocalypse an example of the most extreme futurist eschatology? Does not the closing vision lead our minds toward the most remotely future event of all? To this objection there are several answers. (1) Critical study of the final vision has revealed multiple correlations between it and all the earlier visions. Already in the letters to the seven churches (Rev. 2, 3) the prophet has anticipated the major themes of the concluding chapter. Neither the literary structure nor the thought structure of the Apocalypse justifies isolating the later from the earlier chapters. (2) In any effort to trace the morphology of the prophet's imagination, we are justified in beginning with the clearest expression of that imagination, providing we test our inferences by evidence provided by his total composition. (3) To reject this vision as in fact normative of the prophet's mind on the ground of its extreme futurity would be to make normative our own conceptions of time, our own tendency to segregate future realities from the present. As a matter of fact, the passage itself stresses future possibilities far less than present actualities. ("Then I saw . . . !")

Let us see then what inferences may be safely drawn from this passage. "The first heaven and the first earth had passed away." Immediately one axiom of the prophet's mind suggests itself. A heaven belongs inseparably to its earth, and vice versa. Together they constitute a single, interlocking reality. This conjunction of a heaven with its earth is a familiar element in biblical thinking. From this axiom, a hermeneutical principle should be drawn: Where either heaven or earth is mentioned in a text, one should ask whether the other is also present implicitly.

Another axiom is suggested by the common transiency of the first heaven and the first earth. This earth cannot pass away without its heaven. They have been created through God's will; they remain subordinated to it; their obsolescence is an expression of it. In this idea of an interdependent transiency, space and time coalesce. Space is not conceived as an unchanging frame within which time's changes proceed; nor is time visualized as an unchanging string along which spatial changes appear as separated beads. This heaven and this earth pass away together. Together they embrace all the first things, which pass away (Rev. 21:4).

The first things of the prophet's vision include, of course, more elements than celestial, terrestrial, and marine phenomena. Those are, throughout the prophet's vision, the backdrop for social history. John is more concerned with the mourning, crying, and death of the saints, and with the punishment of the liars, the cowards, the faithless, the fornicators, and the idolaters (Rev. 21:8). In fact when one tries to find a single category that will encompass the penalty of these sinners (murderers and liars), the trials for these saints (pain and death), and these cosmic phenomena (moon and rivers and sea), perhaps the term "the first things" is more adequate than the phrase "the first heaven and the first earth." That is to say, the adjective "first" is more definitive of the idea than the nouns "heaven" and "earth." They are more completely qualified by their firstness than this firstness is qualified by their status as heaven or earth. While for the prophet the latter phrase is entirely adequate, we should be warned that wherever he refers to the first heaven and the first earth we are dealing with a symbol that embraces the existence of all first things. And among these phenomena a central place must be given to the object and fact of human worship, the power that operates through human allegiances, the lords that provide the cohesion and ground of human communities. If we were to make these observations the basis of a hermeneutical principle, it would be this: The interpretation of all references to the first heaven or the first earth should seek to do full justice to the symbolic scope and meaning of the decisive adjective. This, however, cannot be done without giving careful consideration to its antonym.

"I saw a new heaven and a new earth." The passing away of the first things does not give way to a void, but to a new creation. The appearance of the new establishes the decisive frontier of the old. The passing away and the coming down are interlocked yet opposing movements. We must deal with not only one but two heavens and two earths.

We should note also that the new earth and the new heaven are components of a single reality. Neither could be conceived apart from the other. The new creation as a whole is the locus where all things are new (Rev. 21:5). The choice of the adjective is not fortuitous. If the relation of the new to the old were one of simple temporal succession, the use of the ordinal "the second" would be sufficient. The term *new* negates the idea of a continuing, and perhaps endless, series of heavens and earths. The new heaven-and-earth is not a phenomenon that can become old and pass away. The accent therefore falls not upon temporal novelty but upon qualitative newness. Temporal measurements of duration immediately lose their relevance. Throughout the New Testament the adjective *new* is an eschatological term, related to an eternal life in a Kingdom that has no end.

Precisely in the same way that the first things indicated the inclusive range of the first creation, so here all things new indicates the inclusive range of the new creation. What then does the prophet see as the decisive determinant of this newness? "The home [tabernacle] of God is among mortals. He will dwell with them as their God; they will be his peoples" (Rev. 21:3). It is this new situation that is the key to all the other symbols of newness: the holy city, the bride, the death of death, the water of life, the army of the conquerors. The changes in celestial and earthly phenomena are oriented toward the coming of this communion and community, this "Emmanuel." The celestial bodies, the sun and moon, are replaced by the glory of God (Rev. 21:23), yet the prophet continues to visualize this glory in terms of trees, streets, rivers, and a city. It is the city that binds this new heaven and its earth together, for it is the place where God dwells with his people. The strategic difference between the first and the new creation is thus defined by the community that dwells there. The mark of one community is idolatry (Rev. 21:8), the mark of the other is victorious faithfulness (Rev. 21:7). The interdependence of heaven and earth provides the inner structure of the human community that inhabits it.

These observations suggest another hermeneutical postulate dealing with either heaven or earth in either the first or the new creation: one must recognize the God-relatedness of the dwellers as the definitive factor. Let us then look more closely at those who dwell in the first heaven and the first earth, drawing into our analysis the earlier visions in the book. Those who dwell in the first heaven are described in varied colors. Their chief appears to be the dragon, Satan, the tempter. This beast can command an extensive cavalry of demonic forces. He operates through the prestige and power of Babylon. In depicting the celestial powers of evil, John draws upon an extensive gallery indeed.

The link that, as we have noted, joins the first heaven and the first earth is expressed by the interdependence of these lords and their servants. The unity of this creation is, in fact, quite inseparable from the relation of sovereignty and obedience that constitutes the covenant between the beast, the kings of the earth, the false prophets, and "all, both free and slave, both small and great" (Rev. 19:18). We must ask the exact reference of this word "all." How wide is its range? The answer, I am convinced, is: *all* the inhabitants of the first earth, but *only these*. This earth is the complement of this heaven; these servants are defined by their service to these lords. Nine times in the Apocalypse we find the phrase "the inhabitants of the earth" (Rev. 3:10; 6:10; 8:13; 11:10; 13:8, 12, 14; 17:2, 8). In every case these dwellers are servants of the evil powers of the first heaven. They have been so deluded that they worship the beast (Rev. 13:8, 12, 14); they constitute the citizenry of Babylon (Rev. 17:5). They are without exception the enemies of the saints and the prophets (Rev. 6:10; 11:10). Idolatry and fornication create their community.

In every vision the prophet sees this heaven and this earth as the home of these lords and their servants. But in every vision he also sees this home as a realm under attack, as a battlefield on which these lords and their servants are decisively defeated. "War broke out in heaven," and as a result no place is left in heaven for the devil and his angels (Rev. 12:7, 8). We must therefore see this heaven and earth as passing away because of the incursion of a powerful conqueror. The transience of the first is the measure of the power of the new. The aggressors are clearly identified: the declaration of war proceeded from God and from his throne. His emissary, who judged and fought in righteousness, was the Lamb that was slain. In the prosecution of his campaign he used his prophets and apostles, his kings and priests, his virgins and lampstands—the whole retinue of God's servants.

What marks the progress of this war? Divine judgment on the lords and on their servants. These lords and servants are so interdependent that every stage in the Messiah's attack affects both groups. They constitute a single unit in the execution of justice, although the processes of judgment can be described in a protean way. It is typical of the prophet, however, to describe judgment on this Satanic community by progressive recitals of plagues that fall alike on its heaven and earth, including the sea and rivers. Whatever the form of the plague (famine, pestilence, hail, earthquake, death), it normally affects first the heaven and then inevitably the earth. The blackened sun, the bloody moon, and the falling stars draw into their orbit of punishment the earth and all its dwellers. These descriptions of divine destruction convince us that this heaven and this earth are synonymous with the *first things* of Revelation 21. Thus the prophet forces us to include in this category three elements. The first heaven with its earth is a realm of idolatrous community; it is the realm under attack by God; it is the realm that is already passing away as a token of God's judgment.

We now turn to the question: How does the prophet visualize the heaven and earth that has initiated the attack on Satan and his idolatrous community? In our answer we may begin with the observation that John never describes the saints as earth-dwellers. As servants of him who makes all things new, they have a different residence. How can this be? What is the relationship to the first earth of God's witnesses if they do not dwell in it? The prophet explicitly assures his readers that the faithful are guarded from the hour of trial that confronts all earth-dwellers (Rev. 3:10). This earth cannot be plagued until the saints have been sealed as the servants of God (Rev. 7:3). Earth-dwellers have no such seal (Rev. 13:8); the two communities therefore do not share a common home (Rev. 9:4; cf. 7:3). The saints have been redeemed from this earth (Rev. 14:3); it is a habitation belonging solely to the destroyers (Rev. 11:18). In the idiom of the struggle between the dragon and the sun-clothed woman, the messianic people are located not on the earth but in a wilderness prepared by God (Rev. 12:6, 14). This image is clearly reminiscent of the Exodus wanderings of Israel and of the temptations of Jesus. The offspring of the woman are specifically excluded from "the whole earth" that follows the beast with wonder (Rev. 13:3, 8, 12, 14). They do not live on that earth whose fateful harvest is blood (Rev. 14:7-20). Consequently the destruction of this earth is no trial or punishment for the saints. To be sure, they need constant warnings. They must stay awake (Rev. 16:15). It is significant that in spite of the lurid sights and cacophonous sounds of earth-wide judgment, it was possible to slumber, quite unaware of the collision of the two creations. But as long as the saints stayed awake they were not implicated. Similar motifs appear in the depiction of Babylon. Citizens of Babylon and citizens of Jerusalem do not live on the same earth (Rev. 18:1–19:1). And in the presence of the great white throne the first heaven and earth flee away, for "no place was found for them" (Rev. 20:11). Although God could prepare a place for his new people in the wilderness, no place could be found in the new creation for the first heaven and earth. The apocalyptic vision of reality thus stresses in the most vivid way the incompatibility of the first and the new.

In one realm all creatures worship God and the Lamb; in the other all creatures give glory and power to the dragon. In one, the kings of the earth bring their glory into the virgin city; in the other, they commit fornication with Babylon.

The incompatibility of the two realms is most clearly revealed in the redemptive work of the Lamb. Of all creatures only he can open the seven-sealed book. The greatest conceivable importance attaches therefore to the question: What enables him to do this? The answer is definite: "You were slaughtered and by your blood you ransomed for God saints" (Rev. 5:9). His work of redemptive dying entitled him to open the scroll, to create a kingdom of priests from every tribe and tongue and people and nation. Obviously this death and its corresponding witness were conditioned by time and space, for it happened at one place and moment. Yet this temporal victory constitutes the theme of the heavenly and earthly choirs.

It is the nature of this sacrifice-victory that explains the radical incompatibility between the realm of crown-casters and the realm of drunken idolaters. But this event also makes clear that the two realms do actually meet. Apart from their coexistence, their mutual exclusiveness would not be disclosed. They separate at the point of collision. This point of collision is the slaying of the Lamb. But it is also the place where the Lamb's servants give their testimony (Rev. 12:10-12). This point can be located on the map in such places as Jerusalem, Smyrna, and Egypt. It can also be dated on the calendar. Where this is so, *we* would immediately place the antagonists on the same earth, but the prophet did not see things that way. Not only does he refuse to describe saints as earth-dwellers, he also insists upon their status as heaven-dwellers (Rev. 5:9-13; 12:12; 13:6). They have new names written in the Lamb's book of life from before the world's foundation (Rev. 2:17; 3:12). They sing a new song (Rev. 5:9; 14:3) as citizens of the new Jerusalem. As congregations their lampstands are in heaven (Rev. 1:20). Their prayers arise as incense before the throne. They are permanent pillars in the Temple, wearing the blood-white clothing of virgins. Day and night they serve God, acknowledging his salvation (Rev. 7:10-15). Their existence is wholly oriented toward the throne before which they cast the crowns of life they have received.

This heavenly home was, however, no measurable distance from the place where they gave their Christian testimony. It was here that God had descended to dwell with them. In this descent God did not leave his throne, any more than the cross and the throne of the Lamb could be separated. God makes his dwelling among them. In the new Jerusalem they are God's people. His throne is the source of the river of life for this city. It could not be otherwise if the Lamb's sacrifice is to provide the liturgy of this temple. In the community that was realized in and through the Lamb, God dwells on the new earth, and they are made citizens of the new heaven. It is this inversion of things which plays havoc with temporal and spatial calculations.

The character of the new creation suggests the relevance of a third use of the term *heaven* in the Apocalypse: it designates the throne-heaven from which the new heaven descends. "I saw the holy city . . . coming down *out of heaven* from God" (Rev. 21:2, emphasis added). Which heaven is this? It is possible to think of it as the new heaven from which the new Jerusalem descends to the new earth. But it is also possible to think of it as the ultimate source of the new creation, which descends from God. In this case we are dealing with the source of all God's creative acts. The phrase "from God" would seem to underscore the ontological ultimacy of this heaven. So conceived, this heaven (it would be wrong to use the term "third heaven," with its suggestion of a Gnostic ladder) has no satellite in the form of an earth. The only distinctions allowed are that which can be drawn between this heaven as the source of all God's action, on the one hand, and both the first and the new creations on the other. As such, we find here not the simple category of the above, but the more complex notion of what is above the above. As the throne-heaven from which the Most High speaks and from which eternal life flows (Rev. 21:5, 6), it is a symbol of unconditioned primacy. As the sphere of God's glory (Rev. 21:11, 23), it is the source of the light that needs no darkness for its definition (Rev. 21:24, 25). If this exegesis be permitted, the text reminds us that the prophet was aware of the danger of absolutizing the relative and of diminishing the inexpressible transcendence of God to the dimensions of creation. If we ignore this distinction we may easily underestimate his stature as a metaphysical theologian.

In any case, to the prophet the advent of the new Jerusalem is a con-descension by God, not an ascent by mortals. The new city continues to bear the marks of its place of origin. God has come with his eternal glory, so there is no need for sun or stars. Yet he remains God, the sole ruler of this city. God dwells with his people, but God's government does not resemble an ecclesiastical oligarchy or a town-meeting democracy. The throne, the center of everything, remains the symbol of eternal tran-scendence, even over the city itself. Creation proceeds outward and downward from this invisible center; toward it the life of the new cre-ation is oriented upward and forward.

From these visions of the Apocalypse can any systematic cosmology be derived? Any analysis is bound to distort the worldview of the prophet, because the conventions and traditions of this medium are not deduced from maps or timetables. The sharpest distinction seems to be observable in the contradiction between the first heaven-and-earth and the new heaven-and-earth. This contradiction seems to require an *infinite qualita-tive distinction* between the two, yet there is abundant evidence that the two do meet in place and time. The first heaven-and-earth, analyzed in terms of its effective sovereignty, is one interdependent realm. So, too, the new heaven-and-earth. But when the two are analyzed in terms of competing power structures they collide at every point. The citizens of the two earths met daily in the streets of Philadelphia and Pergamum, yet they did not dwell on the same earth, although in their hearts as well as in their behavior the forces of the two met in decisive combat. The prophet was firmly convinced that these citizens would understand their meeting on the streets of Smyrna only if they understood what was happening in the conflict between heavenly forces. It was his function as prophet to guide them to this understanding.

Just as the new creation has dimensions that transcend space-time conceptions, so, too, the throne-heaven of the Most High transcends all creations. The prophet John preserved this final mystery even in the face of pressures from his church to know "how long." By the image of the throne he joined in praising a God whose sovereignty had been fully embodied in events, in persons, in community, in fateful decisions, in transiency and duration, in successiveness and simultaneity.

If this comprehension of John's use of the category of heaven and earth is near the mark, then certain hermeneutical procedures must be judged as quite ineffective in dealing with such an outlook. Because these three heavens are not visualized in terms of a hierarchy of aeons separating earth from the highest heaven, the Gnostic type of celestial astronomy must be excluded. Mediation between God and the earth proceeds not through intervening heights but through a Lamb who is King of Kings. Similarly ineffective are millennial speculations regarding the date, on a supposedly permanent timeline, of a future event. The two creations are everywhere juxtaposed, yet only the saint can become aware of their meeting place and time; and such awareness springs from present choices and not from calendrical studies. Ineffective also, I believe, are the two opposing caricatures of hellenistic and biblical thought. On the one hand the boundary between the two creations does not follow the line between time and the timeless (the caricature of the Platonic). On the other hand, the eternal life of the new Jerusalem cannot be equated with the total span of an endless timeline (the caricature of the biblical). The shift in vision, produced by the prophet's own struggle of faith, produced a permanent negation alike of timelessness and of endless time. It is wrong for a nonprophetic writer to classify the prophet John according to a scheme that gives to the scholar's presuppositions regarding space and time genuinely arbitrary precedence over the prophet's own presuppositions. None of these solutions to the time-space problem does justice to (1) the integrity of heaven and earth in each of the two creations, (2) the radical warfare between the two creations as waged by the slain Lamb, or (3) the ultimate transcendence of the throne-heaven, which gives to existence within space and time a final and indestructible meaning.

— 13 —
The Bond
(2 Corinthians)

T

In various respects modern students know more about Paul than did students in earlier centuries, yet an understanding of Paul himself has been steadily diminishing. We feel little kinship with his dramatic conversion and his tumultuous career. His battles with Christian adversaries, no less than his inner conflicts, seem increasingly unreal. The compulsions of his vocation, the basic perceptions of reality, the skeletal cohesion of his thought—all these seem to recede steadily into the distance. He has lost the power to disclose those universals of Christian existence that once made his writings such compelling mirrors of self-knowledge. There was once a time when his grasp of the elementals could shake us loose from preoccupation with the superficials—no longer. His letters, of course, have not changed, but a sound-proof curtain has fallen between them and us.

Among the elementals and the universals that magnetized Paul's thinking were his varied notions of death and dying. Touch the Epistles at any point, examine the dynamics of his mission, overhear the line of argument in any debate, and you will encounter a reference to some form of dying. Yet in the current flurry of discussions of death, our most influential savants seldom have recourse to those letters. Presumably Paul has little to contribute to current reflection. Yet the very foreignness of his perspective may make his remarks about dying more provocative than the penetrating insights of a psychiatrist or a poet. Consider, for instance, the tapestry of ideas in Romans 14:7-9:

> We do not live to ourselves,
> and we do not die to ourselves.

If we live, we live to the Lord,
and if we die, we die to the Lord;
so then, whether we live or whether we die,
we are the Lord's.
For to this end Christ died and lived again,
so that he might be Lord of both the dead and the living.

The parallel structure of these lines reveals some features and accents typical of Paul. His thought focuses on the shared experience of those who belong to Christ. Life and death are accepted as opposites in an ordinary human way, yet both are viewed from a vantage point that includes but transcends both. Life and death are conceived not in impersonal but in fully personal terms; that is, Paul thinks not of death but of the dead, not of life but of the living. Moreover, the decisive question is not the matter of dying in itself, but *to whom* a person dies. The noun is defined by the prepositional phrase. No longer do we measure our own end by reference to our own interests; our rights have been replaced by the rights of the Lord to whom we belong. The story of this Lord has produced a vast change in the significance of both living and dying; Christ's death and life become the standard by which the boundaries are marked off. In consequence, death is no longer defined by medical proofs but by vocational tests: by the human beings who die, by the Lord to whom they die, by the living and dying of that Lord, and by his lordship over the dead and the living.

We can now expand this preliminary sketch of Paul's attitudes by distinguishing seven basic connotations for the term death. These seven connotations will provide points of reference for the subsequent discussion.

(1) There is the use of death in the ordinary sense to refer to the moment when a person's life is terminated (e.g., Rom. 7:2). We may dub this use *death as a medical fact*. Only in a minority of cases does Paul employ this connotation, and, when he does use it, he often plays down its importance: "dying is gain" (Phil. 1:21). At times he avoids employing the word with this meaning (though never because of a desire to hide the brutal reality with a euphemism). In 2 Corinthians, for example, he contrasts the time when he is "at home in the body" to the time when he will be "away from the body and at home with the Lord" (2 Cor. 5:6-8).

(2) Paul displays more frequent and greater concern over that form of dying that takes place when a person sins. Romans 7 provides two examples: "Sin revived and I died"; "Sin . . . deceived me and . . . killed me"

(Rom. 7:9-10, 11). We will dub this use *death in sin*. Here sin is viewed as an enemy, a murderer using deceit to trap the sinner. Through the sinner's own choice, life is forfeited. We should note that this death is not postponed to some later penalty, but is viewed as an immediate though perhaps unwitting consequence of a person's choice.

(3) Paul was inclined to link all instances of death-in-sin to *death-in-Adam*. "Sin came into the world through one man, and death came through sin, and so death spread to all because all have sinned" (Rom. 5:12). This death of Adam is seen as an archetype that is applicable to humanity as a whole. By sharing this death, all persons become equal, and equally bound to one another.

(4) Because of the inclusiveness of death-in-sin and death-in-Adam, Paul viewed death as one of the invisible spiritual powers that tyrannize the human race. Wherever sin reigns one may discern also the sovereignty of *Death as the last enemy*. This tyrant governs a tightly organized realm in which people obey its orders, all the while yearning for deliverance. That realm can be spoken of as "the body of death," or as a world (*kosmos*) or age (*aion*) that is constituted by Satan's rebellion against God's life-giving power.

(5) Through his faith Paul was enabled to see an alternative beginning and ending of the human story in the death and resurrection of Jesus, who exercised power sufficient to subjugate the last enemy and to create a body capable of displacing the body of sin. God gave him authority to become Lord of the dead and of the living, a power manifested wherever people overcame the death-in-sin to which they had become habituated. By sharing his freedom and life with others, Jesus redefined both dying and living, and drew a new set of boundaries between them. The death of God's Son becomes the new starting point for all thinking about the dying of others.

(6) A comprehension of these boundaries came to Paul by way of his being crucified with Christ (Gal. 6:14), by way of continued sharing in Christ's death (Phil. 3:10). Baptism symbolized this sharing (Rom. 6:1-11). Such baptism could be described as a dying with Christ to the self (Rom. 6:6), to the flesh (Gal. 5:24), to the law (Gal. 2:19, 20), to the world (Gal. 6:14), to the elemental spirits (Col. 2:20), and to the body of sin and death (Rom. 6:2, 10). A shorthand expression for this multiple transition is *death-in-baptism*.

(7) For Paul, the witness to the dying and rising of Christ took the form of dying daily (1 Cor. 15:31). Such an extension of the term death

was not as hyperbolic as it may sound, since this dying took the form of accepting violent persecution and the daily risk of assassination. Prison sentences and mob actions recurred often. Paul thought of himself as sharing the sufferings of Christ (Col. 1:24), as bearing in his body the *stigmata* (Gal. 6:17), as accepting death as a constant companion, and as being changed into the likeness of the risen Christ "from one degree of glory to another" (2 Cor. 3:18). Constant change took place not only in the apostle himself but, more important, in those for whom he died: "death is at work in us, but life in you" (2 Cor. 4:12). Thus we must keep in mind that for each of the seven connotations of death, Paul had a corresponding way to speak of life.

Having sketched these typical ways in which Paul spoke of death, let us examine a single confession in which some of these accents recur and other nuances come to the surface. This statement provides one of the most succinct and luminous glimpses of resurrection faith to be found in the scriptures:

> For the love of Christ urges us on, because we are convinced that one has died for all; therefore all have died. And he died for all, so that those who live might live no longer for themselves, but for him who died and was raised for them. (2 Cor. 5:14, 15 [The Greek text has only one sentence.])

Before proceeding to analyze this sentence, we should remind ourselves of one danger facing all interpreters. Because we are usually concerned with the substance of Paul's ideas, we may treat the apostle primarily as a great theologian, whose chief value to us is the verbal precision he gave to certain doctrinal convictions. But, as a matter of fact, he was fighting with a very specific and a very able group of adversaries; he was primarily concerned with choosing weapons that would be effective in that battle. The letter gives firsthand evidence that this debate was packed with tension, seething with venomous recriminations and counterattacks. To be sure, we have access only to Paul's side of the controversy, but we should take into account his preoccupation with the need to refute these opponents.

We cannot detail here the full story of the conflict, but we must be alert to the bitterness of the attacks on Paul and to the shrewdness of Paul's partisan responses. *Superfine apostles* (cf. 2 Cor. 11:13) had persuaded Paul's own converts to repudiate his authority. They accused him of exercising earthly wisdom (2 Cor. 1:12), of shaping his policies to take advantage of prevailing winds (2 Cor. 1:17), and of claiming dictatorial power over the church in matters of discipline (2 Cor. 1:24; 3:1). He was said to have exploited the congregation for his own personal and financial profit, hiding fraud behind a facade of piety. Even his sanity had been challenged. As a result, any statement made in his own defense could be misinterpreted as proof of mental instability (2 Cor. 5:13) or of personal vanity (2 Cor. 5:12). Any intervention on his part might be counterproductive. So tense was the situation that Paul had stayed away from the battle zone, sending Titus to reconnoiter and to report back the latest developments (2 Cor. 1:23–2:4). When Paul wrote this letter, Titus's report was in hand, and it was a better report than Paul had dared hope (2 Cor. 7:5-16). Even so, every line in the letter had to be carefully phrased if further explosions in Corinth were to be avoided.

One of Paul's objectives was to re-establish common ground with his adversaries, to capitalize on their shared memories and loyalties. Could he advance a basis for unity that would be deeper and stronger than their animosities? At the risk of kindling new fires of hostility, he had to set the record straight and correct false charges against himself. Because his authority as an apostle had been undermined by attacks on his personal integrity, he had to defend both. At the same time, those attacks impelled Paul to examine his own motives and methods. Why could he, why did he, speak with such boldness as to create resentment? Had his earlier self-defense actually been a subtle form of pride and injured dignity? What kinds of self-defense would be consistent with his apostolic vocation, and what kinds of defense would contradict that vocation?

Different questions provoked different answers. What kind of credentials count most? Not formal letters of recommendation, but only the kind of letters that are written on human hearts, sent from Christ though "prepared by us" (2 Cor. 3:1-3). What is a legitimate source of boldness? Not any competence of one's own, but only the persuasive presence of the Spirit (2 Cor. 3:4-6). What can destroy one's fear of others, one's craven bondage to the demands of "public relations"? Only the fear of God, whose verdict is to be delivered before the judgment seat of Christ (2 Cor. 5:6-11). What kind of weapons can an apostle legitimately use? For the right hand, such weapons as the endurance, without complaint, of hardships, labors, and calamities. For the left hand, such weapons as honesty, kindness, purity, and forbearance (2 Cor. 6:3-7). Loyalty to the gospel placed reliable ministers at the meeting-point of many paradoxes: "We are treated as impostors, and yet are true . . . as dying, and see . . . we are alive" (2 Cor. 6:8-10). Paul wrote this entire letter from the point of maximum tension as expressed by such paradoxes: "as poor, yet making many rich."[1] It is from this vantage point that he defended his own role in Corinth and appealed to his adversaries to meet him at that particular point. As we shall see, both that defense and that appeal were implicit in the two verses we have chosen to analyze.

We return, then, to the thought-complex of 2 Corinthians 5:14, 15 (see p. 168). It is clear that the entire complex is anchored in the event of the death and resurrection of Jesus (connotation no. 5). In these two verses, Jesus' death is mentioned three times, his resurrection once. Every change in the human situation is traced to that twin event. It is also clear that this event is defined and qualified by decisive prepositional phrases: "for all," "for them." Motive and event are inseparable, each drawing its basic significance from the other. To express this integrity we need not three words but one: "death-for-all." In fact, Jesus' love could be called the ultimate reality because it produced the event of the crucifixion, with all its consequences. Among these consequences is the emergence of love among those for whom Jesus died and rose (the Greek syntax indicates that resurrection as well as death took place for their sake). Disciples witness to Jesus' death by the fact that they no longer live for themselves; such a change in motivation marks their participation in his death (connotation no. 5). The fact that they live now "for him" points also to participation in his resurrection; their love, which now animates their lives, effectively witnesses to the truth that God has raised Jesus from the dead. As his love now exhibits a *post mortem* power, so their living for him, made possible by dying to themselves, exhibits a *post mortem* life. Implicit in the whole confession is Paul's effort to explain and to defend himself: "the love of Christ urges us," though the unfriendly reader may detect in that defense a contradiction of the idea of death to the self. Implicit in the confession also is an appeal to his adversaries: "Be reconciled to God" (2 Cor. 5:20).

Before pursuing those implications, let us now raise a further question concerning this thought-complex, a question concerning Paul's intention in the clause: "one has died for all; therefore all have died." How many people are covered by that second *all*? It is clear that, at the least, Paul included all believers who were convinced that Christ had died for all, those who therefore no longer live for themselves. But did he also intend to include a wider circle, all human beings, in fact? And if so, does this conception become so essential to the structure of thought that without it the structure would collapse? Our initial reaction may well be negative. It is difficult enough to make the clause apply to those who have died to themselves (connotation no. 6). Why compound the difficulty by considering a wider reference?

There is considerable evidence, however, for such an extension. For instance, we should note that the word *all* appears three times in the same sentence, and in the other occurrences we cannot doubt an inclusive intention. Where two references are inclusive, we must expect the third to be inclusive as well. Supporting evidence may be found by considering Paul's own story. He believed that Christ had died for him while he was yet an enemy (Rom. 5:6-11). To be sure, Paul had become aware of that fact only later, but he never confused his act of faith with the prior events on which his faith rested. He would surely have applied to others what he recognized as true for himself. He had died before he became aware of it. A third line of evidence emerges in the subsequent paragraph. One corollary of the conviction that all had died was Paul's change in attitude toward all other people, believers and nonbelievers alike: "We regard no one from a human point of view." When the change takes place in the believer, that change affects the believer's judgment of all other people. Believers now look on others as having died. Another corollary emerges in the assertion: "In Christ God was reconciling the world to himself" (2 Cor. 5:19). The message of reconciliation is important, as is the mission; but the message announces what God has already done, and the mission is to persuade people that the *kosmos* has been changed. If all have died, the primary evidence is provided not by their own awareness of it, but by God's purposes as disclosed in Christ's death.

This is to say that only a profoundly theocentric view of things can make sense of such an assertion. But, of course, Paul's mentality was controlled by that view. Since God is the creator and sustainer of all things, any action by God is bound to have immediate and important implications for creation as a whole. He alone sees the end from the beginning. Everything comes from him and moves toward him. If the dying and living of Jesus serve to reveal his will, those events throw light upon an unlimited range of human experience. As Paul saw it, the Passion story of Jesus could be no less universal in its scope than the death of Adam, especially since Jesus' self-sacrifice had demonstrated power to overcome death-as-last-enemy (connotation no. 4). In other words, it is a basic assumption of Paul, and presumably of his adversaries as well, that if God's will was fulfilled in Jesus' death and resurrection, then that twin event expressed final judgment and final mercy for *all*.

171

Of Jesus' centrality in God's design, Paul could have no doubt. Jesus' love, impelling him to die for all, was God's love in action. Christ was, in fact, one through whom and for whom all things were made (1 Cor. 8:6). His taking the form of a servant, his humbling of himself in death on a cross, his being exalted to a throne before which every knee bows—the whole story reveals his pre-existence with God (Phil. 2:1-11). With such a perception of the ontological roots of these historical events, it would have been entirely consistent for Paul to have believed that all had died in the death of Jesus for all. It was no more difficult to accept this archetypal conviction than to believe "dying yet behold *he* lives" or to share in that miracle: "dying yet behold *we* live."

Of course, this concept of the death of all in Christ's death represents a quite unusual way of thinking about death. What makes it difficult for us to grasp is our own prior conceptions of death and life, conceptions in which the first connotation provides the core ingredient. But Paul had experienced an upheaval in prior understandings of that sort. To his mind as a Pharisee, the death of Jesus had at first conveyed a cluster of meanings that made it quite impossible for Jesus to be the Messiah. A wholly different cluster emerged from Paul's encounter with the risen Lord. Basic attitudes toward both death and life, and toward the boundary and transition between them, were now thoroughly controlled by his experience of the love of God as mediated by the crucified Messiah. It became entirely intelligible for him to think of all people as having died in the death of Jesus for all.

"One has died for all; therefore all have died" *(ara apethanon)*. *Ara* is an inferential particle, used here in the sense of *therefore, consequently,* or *as a result.* The clause stresses the result of Jesus' death, a result in which there is a sharp polarity between the death of *one* man and the death of *all.* How are we to think of the causal relationship between these two deaths? Two options appear. The first possibility is to view the death of all, in this clause, as equivalent to the death (in the second clause) of those who no longer live for themselves. These are followers who have died with Christ and who subsequently live with Christ (connotation no. 6). Their death is linked to Christ's death-for-all in becoming, like his, intercessory in character. I find certain difficulties with this solution of the puzzle. Such a meaning could hardly be predicated of *all* in the sense of present actuality, though it might be conceived as the anticipated destiny of all. However, even the latter is not entirely cogent when we consider the use of the punctiliar aorist *(apethanon)*, or when we perceive a shift in thought from *all* in this clause to the more restricted "those who live" in the subsequent clause, or when we recall the polemical situation with which Paul was dealing.

We therefore opt for a second conception of "all died." By dying alone, rejected by all, Jesus demonstrated the alienation from God of all who live for themselves, in slavery to self-love. I sense the presence of an intended contrast between Jesus' death *for* all (connotation no. 5) and the death *of* all (connotation no. 4). That contrast constitutes God's judgment on all, his declaration that they are all in bondage to the body of sin and death. Jesus' intercession shows that all people, both Jews and Greeks, are under the power of sin (Rom. 3:9). All have died in the sense of Romans 11:32: "God has imprisoned all in disobedience so that he may be merciful to all."

This option has several advantages. It preserves a distinction between the death-in-sin of all and the death-to-sin of those who no longer live for themselves. Moreover, it preserves a grammatical and logical distinction between the two clauses, one of result and the other of purpose. Indeed, the repetition of the phrase "he died for all" in 2 Corinthians 5:15 suggests the presence of such a distinction. The *ara* ("therefore") clause stresses result: "[he] died for all; therefore all have died." The action is described in such a way as to be neither intentional on Jesus' part nor voluntary on the part of *all*. Jesus' act of intercession results in God's judgment on the whole realm of death in which people are trapped by living for themselves (connotation no. 4). By contrast, the *hina* ("in order that") clause expresses purpose: "he died for all in order that those who live might live no longer for themselves but for him." In the death and resurrection God had purposed this human response, though this response must stand as a voluntary one. To preserve the contrast between result and purpose does greater justice to the eschatological miracle that enabled believers and lovers to escape from one death to the other. Moreover, this reading enables us to see how the sentence exerted subtle pressures on the readers in Corinth to identify themselves with the three *alls* as prelude to a new resolve to live by the criteria provided by the dying of Jesus. By implication, the purpose clause exhorts them, "you should live no longer . . . but . . ."; yet that exhortation carries more weight following the clearcut indicative "all have died." From bondage to death-in-sin, they can be freed by Christ's death for them. Such a movement of thought also makes more hortatory sense of 2 Corinthians 5:21: "For our sake he made him to be sin who knew no sin," and it makes more evocative sense of the idea of "new creation."

We venture, then, to suggest the following resolution of the puzzle of 2 Corinthians 5:14, 15. Christ's death for all was an expression of his love for all; it was vindicated by God's act in raising him from the dead (connotation no. 5, with connotation no. 1 as an essential element). That vicarious and voluntary act of Christ resulted in the death of all as God's judgment on their self-centered existence (connotations no. 2, 3, 4). The purpose of Christ's death is that those who have been living for themselves and who now accept God's judgment on themselves are enabled to become "a new creation," reconciled to God and controlled by the love of Christ (connotations no. 6, 7). That control transforms their ways of judging life and death (2 Cor. 5:16), for they have become ministers of reconciliation in a *kosmos* that is itself reconciled to God. The love of God and the love of Christ unite all seven connotations of death into a consistent pattern. That same love constrains the apostle to use both types of weapons (2 Cor. 6:4-7) and to accept existence in terms of the paradoxes (2 Cor. 6:8-10) as ordinary Christian common sense (e.g., "dying, and see—we are alive").

We return now to the battle zone in Corinth at the time when Paul wrote these lines, and we recall the tangle of personal, practical, and theoretical issues that had set various leaders at each other's throats. Paul's interest was not so much in formulating correct theological doctrine for the benefit of later generations as in coming to better terms with his own suspicious and angry opponents. To do this, he attempted to shift the debate from its turbulent *you-versus-me* axis to a *Christ-versus-us* axis. He tried to focus attention upon the cardinal convictions of the gospel, with its message concerning what God has done in the cross of Jesus. He wanted to subordinate issues of leadership roles and personal integrity to more ultimate matters of life and death, or rather, to the issues of competing perceptions of various kinds of living and corresponding kinds of dying.

In this complicated and contorted situation it is altogether likely that Paul himself was not wholly controlled by Christ's love. In his letter it is possible to discern innuendoes that represent the back-spin of hurt vanity and resentment over lost dignity. It is also possible to detect a stubborn tendency to impugn his opponents' motives and to deny to them the integrity he claims for himself. His adversaries probably had more justification for their attacks on him than saint-worshipers are ready to grant. The situation is too remote from us and the evidence at hand is too ambiguous for us to rely upon modern verdicts, including the one expounded here. On several occasions Paul came close to admitting that his efforts to defend himself had involved him in betrayal of the gospel. But human failings on his part need not invalidate his confession concerning the multiple effects of Christ's death for all. Faith rests not on Paul as sinless but on Christ as sin-bearer (2 Cor. 5:21). Paul himself recognized that fact with complete candor and clarity. That recognition qualifies him to remind us of the primal and final horizons of life in Christ, of the beginnings of that life in death and resurrection, and the ending of that life when we are all "away from the body and at home with the Lord."

— 14 —
The Peace
(The New Testament)[1]

The unabridged *Random House Dictionary* contains sixteen various denotations of the word *peace*, but not one of them coincides with its primary use in the New Testament. The contrast is, of course, not absolute. One can find a few instances of agreement. *Random House Dictionary* accords first place to the definition of peace as the normal, nonwarring condition of a nation or group of nations. So far as I can tell, that conception plays no role in early Christian thought. But there is greater agreement on a second definition: peace as an agreement among antagonistic nations to end hostilities. The book of Acts tells of an embassy sent from Tyre and Sidon to ask for peace, because that region was dependent on Herod for its supply of food. In this story the notion of peace was present, but it was of no interest to Christians.

A similar conception of peace appeared in a parable of Jesus. A king began war on another king but found too late that his enemy's army was twice as large as his own, so he was forced to "[ask] for the terms of peace" (Luke 14:31-35). Why was this story told? Not as a lesson for kings, but to warn potential disciples not to commit themselves to Jesus unless they had given up all their possessions. The meaning of the term *peace* is clear, but its importance is marginal.

According to the dictionary, peace may mean freedom from civil disorders. This notion appears in the account of one of Paul's trials. The prosecuting attorney began his case against the apostle by flattering the judge. "Your Excellency, because of you we have long enjoyed peace" (Acts 24:2). But such preservation of social order was of no concern to

Paul. The peace of which the Scriptures speak is indigenous to a very different thought world. To understand it, we must first enter "that strange new world in the Bible" (K. Barth).

GOD'S PEACE

The difference between the New Testament notion of peace and the definitions from our modern dictionaries is the essential linkage of peace to the deity. Peace points to a specific human relationship to a very specific God. This is what one should expect among a people for whom the love of God is the greatest commandment. Where that is true, the relation to God can spell the greatest good, while a broken bond spells the greatest dereliction. Every change in thinking about this God is bound to affect the entire world of thought. It is God who determines and defines the true meaning of peace.

This primacy is reflected in the greetings typical of early Christian letters. "Grace to you and peace from God our Father" (Rom. 1:7). Many inferences may be drawn from this greeting, which appears at least eighteen times. This peace is known by its source: the Father's gift to his children, forming a firm intimate bond with every member of a specific family of believers. These persons recall a time when they had known nothing of such peace, and a later time when they had first experienced it. The idea of peace was as different from other ideas as the idea of God was different from other ideas. The word telescopes all that the good news of God's grace had brought to them, in contrast to previous isolation and ignorance. So the word became one of the boundary posts, separating the time before and the time after. The writer of each epistle was bound to each reader by this peace, both of them conscious of forming one family with the Father.

Before saying "peace," think of this God, this Father.

Letters that began with this greeting often closed with this farewell: "The God of peace be with all of you" (Rom. 15:33). In other words, this peace helps to distinguish this God from all others. He and his peace are inseparable; that is why recipients call him Father. Whenever this family gathers, it can say, "The God of peace is with us." More than the source of peace, God's presence is that peace. God himself is as present or as absent as his peace; this presence creates the cohesion, the solidarity of his family.

Before using the word "peace," think of this presence.

We may now extend the orbit of thought by completing the greeting: "Grace to you and peace from God our Father and the Lord Jesus Christ" (Rom. 1:7). That last phrase is essential. This Lord is the source of this peace; the gift is simultaneously his and his Father's. As Peter phrased it in his first sermon to Gentiles, "You know the message [God] sent to the people of Israel, preaching peace by Jesus Christ—he is Lord of all" (Acts 10:36). Or as Paul put it in his greeting to the Galatians, "Peace from . . . the Lord Jesus Christ, who gave himself for our sins to set us free from the present evil age" (Gal. 1:3-4; also Rev. 1:5, 6). Just as the Father/Son image dominates the relationship to God, so the Lord/slave image dominates the relationship to Christ. It was through the life-death-life of this Son that the peace of God came to all brothers and sisters in Christ. As they responded to the story of what Jesus had done, that story revolutionized their God-relation, their God-thoughts, their God-talk—and thereby their peace-talk. The measure of this revolution is suggested by Paul when he wrote, "May I never boast of anything except the cross of our Lord Jesus Christ, by which the world has been crucified to me, and I to the world" (Gal. 6:14-16). For Paul, peace came on the far side of that triple crucifixion.

When you say "peace," recall Jesus' entire story.

We may now estimate the range and depth of that peace by noting some of its specific results. For Paul, to believe in Christ is to be *in* Christ. To be in Christ means belonging to a new creation where everything old has passed away and all things have become new (2 Cor. 5:17). Paul believed himself to live under a new government in which every Christian is under new orders. "Let the peace of Christ *rule* in your hearts" (Col. 3:15). Relevant to every congregation is the prayer, "May the Lord of peace himself give you peace at all times in all ways" (2 Thess. 3:16). So we ask, what are some of those ways?

For one thing, the inner world of the heart is transformed. "We have peace with God through our Lord Jesus Christ" (Rom. 5:1). The context of that assertion in Romans spells out some of the components of that peace. No longer does the memory of sins against God guarantee the wrath of God. Paul had been weak, ungodly, an enemy of God. No longer. Anxiety about the future had spawned despair. No longer. Once suffering had prompted resentment and fear. No longer. Now intensified, suffering and danger produced hope. Now the love of God, poured into the heart, gave birth to forgiveness, trust, hope, and even the love of persecutors.

When saying "peace," think of those changes.

But there were broader social results as well. A radical change had taken place in the human habit of dividing all humanity into two segments, Jew and Gentile. As a Jew, Paul had belonged to the first type. With other Jews he had considered all Gentiles to be "far off." Now he believed that through Christ's death they had been brought near. Christ had made peace between them by creating in himself one new humanity, the new Adam. Centuries of alienation had ended. High and thick walls had crumbled. A new habitat for God had been created where he is now seen to dwell in the Spirit (Eph. 2:13-18). He had made obsolete economic, sexual, and cultural distinctions: slave and free, male and female, wise and foolish.

Before saying "peace," think of the demolition of those walls.

Our own resistance to such a revolution is as nothing compared to the resistance on the part of ancient Jews and Gentiles. Could they now eat together, the clean and the polluted? Could they agree to defy God's earlier commands for circumcision? Could they worship together, ignoring the laws of the Sabbath and accepting the hatred of the synagogue? Jewish antipathies to unclean Gentiles could not easily be jettisoned, nor Gentile scorn of the fastidious conscience of Jews. What did "peace in the Holy Spirit" mean in polyglot congregations? The apostles answered: mutual acceptance and forbearance; refusal to condemn the immoral freedom of some, or the moral caution of others; absolute priority for the demands of love; and readiness to let God be the judge. The peace of God was designed to produce peacemakers. The communal infrastructure became a fabric woven of mutual care and concern, self-discipline and self-sacrifice, the practice of returning good for evil, and complete honesty in speech (1 Pet. 3:8-10).

Before saying "peace," think of these forms of peacemaking.

In the church at Corinth some of the greatest threats to peace erupted during moments when worship reached a peak of emotional intensity. Charismatic speech produced pandemonium. Many prophets wanted to reveal God's will at the same moment, and each revelation seemed too important to permit delay. The apostle felt obliged to call the meeting to order and to remind all the charismatics that their God was "a God not of disorder but of peace" (1 Cor. 14:33).

We should not overlook the situations faced by wandering apostles as they carried the news from town to town. They had been charged to travel fast and light, with neither a picnic basket nor traveler's checks, wholly dependent on hospitality given by strangers. Often they were followed by truth squads who alerted synagogues to the arrival of troublemakers. The rules to be followed by Jesus' messengers were quite specific: "Carry no purse, no bag, no sandals. . . . Whatever house you enter, first say 'Peace to this house!' And if anyone is there who shares in peace [a son of peace], your peace will rest on that person; but if not, it will return to you" (Luke 10:4-12; Matt. 10:11-14). This was a dangerous calling. Each house needed to test the legitimacy of each visitor; each visitor, in turn, needed to judge the sincerity of a welcome, from one bed and breakfast stop to the next. Each potential guest brought responsibility and risk, for the host became accountable for the guest's deeds, whether good or bad (2 John 11; Acts 17: 5-9). Both hosts and guests were sons or daughters of peace who, after meeting each other, shared the same peace.

GOD'S WAR

We have examined the roots and fruits of God's peace but have thus far overlooked evidence that contradicts the picture of Jesus as a dispenser of peace. Consider, for example, this warning that he addressed to his closest companions. "Do not think that I have come to bring peace to the earth. I did not come to bring peace, but a sword" (Matt. 10:34). What is this sword? And how is it related to peace? In any modern language the two are mutually exclusive—peace is possible only after hostilities cease—but in early Christian language, the two seem interdependent. This interdependence is reflected in the prophet's picture of the sword coming from the mouth of the victorious Lamb, as well as in the command issued from that Lamb to the four horsemen to "take peace from the earth" (Rev. 6:4; 19:15, 21).

What, then is this sword? Jesus spoke most directly of the divisions within families that would be caused by his call for followers. "Five in one household will be divided, three against two . . . father against son . . . mother against daughter" (Luke 12:52-53; Matt. 10:34-39). This definition of the sword might be readily intelligible if it meant simply that loyalty to Jesus would create family dissension as a regrettable by-product. But the sword cut deeper than that. "I have not come to bring peace, but a sword." His work and word were designed to arouse hostility as essential to the success of the mission—no less essential than Jesus' own cross. In reacting to this insistence interpreters look desperately for euphemisms to hide the scandal, but Jesus resisted such euphemisms. "Brother will betray brother to death, and a father his child" (Matt. 10:21). Disciples would be murdered by their own parents. And Jesus' mission was designed to produce such murders!

Moreover, the same sword cut through other circles than the family. Followers would be ostracized from their religious home, the synagogue. They would be publicly flogged by their neighbors. Hounded out of one town, they would be followed to the next. Haled before courts responsible for adjudicating conflict, they would be condemned as enemies of Israel. Handed over to Gentile governors, penalties would be inflicted by aliens who cared nothing about Israel's God. "You will be hated by all because of my name" (Matt. 10:22). That is the sword Jesus came to bring.

Before saying "peace," remember this sword.

One further aspect of this warfare should be noted. The dangerous mission of the lambs was motivated by concern for their enemies, the wolves. It was a sign of God's love for those wolves. Only by bringing his peace to those enemies could disciples become sons and daughters of this Father (Matt. 5:38-48). The example of Paul in changing from a persecutor to a victim of persecution was typical. This peace was very unusual in that it seemed to grow with the intensity of the warfare. How can one make intelligible, not to say credible, a mission to bring peace to enemies by inciting them to murder the missioners (for example, Stephen, James, Peter, and Paul—as well as the archetype for such missioners, Jesus himself)?

A further dimension should be added. This warfare was not limited to strife within families, synagogues, and civil courts. It became visible there, but its origin lay in an invisible conflict between God and Satan that spanned all times and places. That conflict had first been fought and won in heaven, from which Jesus had seen Satan fall (Luke 10:18; Rev. 12:7-9). His eviction had enabled Jesus to defeat Satan's most deceptive attacks on earth, including his mastery over demons. The same struggle pervaded the decisions of the early church (Eph. 6:10-17), which was sustained by the promise that "the God of peace will shortly crush Satan under your feet" (Rom. 16:20). Satan's power was the power of self-love; God's power was the power of enemy-love. The internal battles between these two loves were mirror reflections of the battle in heaven between God and Satan.

Before saying "peace," think about this heavenly warfare.

THE BENEDICTIONS

The implications of this peace may become clearer when we examine three benedictions in which participation in this cosmic warfare was seen as central to the Christian vocation. The first of these benedictions comes from Paul's letter to the Philippians. "The peace of God, which surpasses all understanding, will guard your hearts and your minds in Christ Jesus" (Phil. 4:7). This text sounds altogether too banal until we recall the original setting. Paul was writing from jail, where the sentence of death was possible, and even probable (Phil. 1:19-26). Such a sentence, then as now, carried with it disgrace, futility, the vindication of enemies, danger to friends, and the possible destruction of the church. Paul was writing to a tiny new commune that was decidedly poor, unpopular, and subject to violence from both Jews and Gentiles. It had already survived one pogrom and, by sending help to Paul, had risked another. It was in turmoil over what strategy to adopt toward its adversaries. Some leaders were taking advantage of Paul's situation to argue for appeasing those adversaries. When Paul was writing, it appeared that those leaders might win. He called them "enemies of the cross of Christ" (Phil. 3:18).

Now set this mild benediction against that background. Notice the verb: the peace of God will *guard*. The related noun *phroura* usually denoted a guard posted at the door of a prison. For a prisoner to use this verb in a benediction was far from accidental. He was being guarded. And by what? By peace. He viewed God's peace as an active force, capable of standing guard over prisoners. And what, in this case, was being protected? Hearts and minds. For a prisoner facing death, what was more vulnerable than heart and mind?

This benediction also has a relative clause: "the peace . . . which surpasses all understanding." That translation is too vague. Of course, the peace that enables a martyr to accept death does transcend normal understanding. But something more is suggested by the Greek *hyperechomai,* translated "surpasses." That verb belongs to a situation where two forces are in sharp conflict and one of them establishes mastery over its rival. In this case, presumably, one force is God's peace. Its rival is the human desire for self-preservation. God's peace is strong enough to establish mastery over every contrary desire and temptation, including the devil's most deceptive seduction.

Now we should note that this benediction is really a promise: God's peace will guard your hearts. As a promise it is based on meeting certain conditions. If you do these things, that peace will stand guard: if you are fearless, stand firm, rejoice in your sufferings, give thanks, and rely on Jesus' power "to subject all things to himself." Do these things, and God's peace will post a guard over your prison to protect your minds and hearts. Understood in this way, the benediction is a martyr's farewell to potential martyrs, promising them the same peace that guards him in his prison as he faces death.

The second benediction is provided by John's account of Jesus' farewell to his disciples immediately before his arrest:

> The hour is coming, indeed it has come, when you will be scattered, each one to his home, and you will leave me alone. Yet I am not alone because the Father is with me. I have said this to you, so that in me you may have peace. In the world you face persecution. But take courage; I have conquered the world. (John 16:32-33)

Among many possible inferences from this text, these bear on the idea of peace:

- The hour that has come is the hour of Jesus' martyrdom.
- He faces that hour alone except for the presence of his Father. It is by accepting death from the world that he has conquered that world.
- The same hour has not yet come to his disciples. At his arrest they will scatter in panic, unaware of God's presence and unaware of Jesus' victory; therefore they will be strangers to his courageous peace.
- Their own hour, however, will come later, when they face persecution from the same enemy. Through their new courage they will then receive his gift of peace. In the world—there will be persecution; "in me—peace."
- The warfare continues in which God's love for his enemies (the world) and Jesus' love for his enemies will be continued in the disciples' love for their enemies, producing both apparent defeat and this mysterious and miraculous peace.

We find a third benediction in the Epistle to the Hebrews. Here an author addressed a church that had suffered greatly from earlier pogroms and was threatened by a violent recurrence. Some of its members were in prison; to visit them placed the other members at great risk.

> Now may the God of peace, who brought back from the dead our Lord Jesus, the great shepherd of the sheep, by the blood of the eternal covenant, make you complete in everything good so that you may do his will, working among us that which is pleasing in his sight, through Jesus Christ, to whom be the glory forever and ever. (Heb. 13:20-21)

The pattern of thought is complex. The final appeal is to the God of peace, whose peace comes through the sealing of an eternal covenant with his people through the death and resurrection of the Good Shepherd. All things are subjected to this Lord's transcendent glory. God's purpose is this: "that you may do his will." But such obedience is itself evidence that God is "working among us that which is pleasing in his sight." When human wills coincide with God's working, then the gift of God's peace arrives.

The author of Hebrews specifies the kind of actions that proceed from this convergence of human and divine wills. The faithful go outside the holy city, beyond its gates and protective walls, to the profane place where Jesus suffered. There they share his abuse. In doing this they look to him as the pioneer and perfecter of their faith. They welcome this discipline that the Father inflicts on all his children (Heb. 12:6). Receiving his peace, they "pursue peace with everyone" (Heb. 12:14). So in Christian parlance the word peace comes to include all those individual and communal actions by which God produces "that which is pleasing in his sight, through Jesus Christ."

When we ponder the mystery of how all these separate wills can become a single will within the orbit of ordinary human living, we begin to realize that previous ideas about God, about the self, about such a community as the church, about the invisible realm out of which desires emerge and actions are born—all these ideas have to be radically revised. They begin to make sense in a world of thought where old words are being used to point to new relationships. Peace is one of those homespun words that can be used as a key to this new language and to life in this new world. In this new creation, peace refers primarily to the occasions when the divine takes over the control center of the individual heart and when the Father, in being worshiped, takes over the control center of his worshiping family. This peace is not a condition to be described simply in psychological terms, nor is it something whose effects can be measured simply in sociological terms. It comes, as the benedictions imply, when crucifixion-like events are transformed through Jesus Christ into resurrection-like fulfillments.

This world of thought is alien to most modern people. And it is true that early in its history the Christian church found other outlooks more conducive to its safety, popularity, and growth. Martyrdom becomes the price of sharing in God's peace and martyrs die for the sake of enemies who kill them in the name of the martyrs' own God. Not many will be found to accept a God of peace who links discipleship to such demands. What, then, can be done with the universe of thought in which peace plays this role?

For those historians, who by nature and professional training are inclined to have recourse to philosophical relativism, this biblical world-view is strictly relative to the conditions that spawned it. Like all other ancient worldviews for the historian, this biblical worldview may be interesting, and all the more interesting as it is esoteric and unique. But authoritative? No. At least not for an historian who wishes to remain credible as an historian.

Scholars whose thinking follows the rubrics of sociological analysis give a different answer. For them, such a worldview must be judged in terms of the social structures of the ancient Roman world. It reflects the conflicts between rural and urban cultures, or between the rich and the poor, the powerful and the powerless. Prophets and apostles spoke for a tiny religious minority that was under deadly attack from a threatened religious establishment, a minority that projected its defensive mechanisms on a cosmic screen. As a weapon of defensive warfare, this perspective enabled the defeated to claim an illusory victory against their enemies. Like all other ideas, the idea of peace was a result of the complex interplay of economic and social forces.

Another method of dealing with the ancient worldview is adopted by many church leaders, who have been convinced that the relevance of any religion must be demonstrated by its contribution to current desires for a more peaceful world. Professional credentials depend on offering the kinds of peace that the world seeks. The New Testament pictures of a peace that the world cannot give, a peace won by using Christ's sword—such pictures have little to offer to contemporary movements, whether left wing or right wing. Unwittingly, these leaders reflect their kinship to the adversaries of Jesus, Peter, and Paul. The very unanimity with which academics and clerics reject the early Christian perspectives should tell us something. At least it gives a negative testimony to the uniqueness and potential importance of these churchly perspectives.

What can be done with the New Testament conceptions of peace?

Instead of giving yet another answer, let me suggest a still more trouble-some question. The question grows out of a recognition that early Christian thought centered in a revelation of God as a God of peace. The ultimate issue is this: Does that God exist? Is this the true God? If the answer is no, then none of the correlative attitudes toward peace is worth salvaging. For many, that no is the only honest answer.

But what if the honest answer is yes? What if the God of peace is the only true God? If this God of peace is truly God, then he exerts an authority independent of succeeding changes in social crises, cultural developments, or philosophical systems. If the God of peace is truly God, his authority is quite independent of alternative ways of measuring wisdom, power, or relevance. The ultimate issue is not the idea of peace, but how we are to think about this God of peace and, what is more important, how to enter the realm that is created by his "grace and peace."

— 15 —
The Hope
(1 Peter)

The background for this chapter is the late twentieth-century proliferation of contextual theologies—African, Asian, liberationist, feminist—each with its own motivation and method for doing theology. One result has been an exciting but bewildering variety of ideas that threatens at times to sever all ties to the gospel. The World Council of Churches convoked three consultations during the last half of the last century to assess the confused situation: Are we still united by one hope, or do our ways of doing theology betray it? The following chapter represents my participation at the third of these consultations. This chapter provides a fitting conclusion to part 3, with its emphasis on the variety of New Testament contexts, and the ultimate context provided by the Messiah's presence with the churches.

Let me first call to the stand three contemporary witnesses who have something to teach us about hope and about doing theology. The first of these is Jacques Ellul, who began his book *Hope in Time of Abandonment* by observing the truth of Castelli's quip: "Much has been written about hope, almost always in a hopeless manner."[1] He confessed his own vulnerability to that charge in that his own earlier theologizing about hope had proved "worthless." During the experience of a severe psychic storm he found that his former theological ideas had so far lost their force that he had been obliged to call everything into question. When hope again emerged, it came as a mysterious and miraculous gift, not as a result of theological cogitation, hermeneutical recipe, or religious activity. He learned that the actuality of hope precedes mental reflection and verbal accountings, and that such theological activity is often self-defeating.

"There is an intellectual formalism which, in the very act of communicating the word richest in meaning empties it of its meaning."[2]

Ellul's confession represents a broad segment of Western theology today. "Western man distrusts high-sounding words, especially those borrowed from religious terminology. . . . The word 'God' has been misused and cheapened, harnessed to every conceivable purpose." Where the word "God" has been so polluted by theologians, can the word hope remain uncorrupted?

Next let me call to the stand a British missionary-theologian, John V. Taylor, whose book *The Go-Between God* presents a persuasive picture of the New Testament prophets, whose ways of doing theology did not empty the essential Christian words of their weighty cargoes. As Taylor describes their work, these prophets practiced "a true situation ethic," and their power as theologians stemmed from that practice. Each successive situation (*nota bene*) confronted God's people with the unmediated presence of God himself, which conveyed to them the pain of final judgment and the gift of miraculous mercy. The future was so vividly embodied in present promise and hope, God's power was so amazingly perfected in human impotence, that liberation was experienced and theological reflection was triggered by that experience. The future and the present, the eternal and the temporal, heaven and earth, were no longer separated from each other, but were "superimposed in one single image of reality."[3] Theologians should take as a model of doing theology the prophetic vocation of disclosing God's presence in a given situation in such a way as to convey a message from God to his people, a message that elicits hope at the innermost core of their consciousness.

Our third contemporary witness is a Swiss pastor, Roland de Pury, whose book *Journal from My Cell* is a good example of situational theology. This journal was written on contraband scraps of paper, smuggled in during his imprisonment in Paris under Nazi occupation in 1944. That period, including seventy-five days of solitary confinement, represented a continuing battle between despair and hope, during which de Pury, like Ellul, experienced the futility of formal and verbal theological resources. Each day the battle was renewed against the cell's stench, its bugs, its food, and its loneliness. Struggling to maintain sanity in this "abode of the dead," de Pury learned that "spiritual struggle is fiercer than mortal combat,"[4] that he was subject to sudden and sly attacks from the devil, as crafty and ferocious as the lion of 1 Peter 5:8. He was able to survive only by recognizing the identity between "the place of our captivity" and "the spot where Jesus prayed at Gethsemane,"[5] and by tasting in the daily food the flavor of God's grace. He discovered that "the presence of Christ and the expectation of Christ are one,"[6] and that the experience of the presence of Christ in the midst of suffering conveys a liberation and a hope that constitute "the whole meaning of the Church on earth."

This experience of hope in suffering was, for de Pury, simultaneously an experience of Christian community in the conditions of solitary confinement. The walls did not shut out the prayers of supplication and intercession; in fact, those prayers demonstrated the tensile strength of the fabric of community. The prisoner became acutely conscious of his bonds to kinfolk, to parishioners, and even to the obscure brothers and sisters greeted in the New Testament Epistles—bonds that spanned the centuries and broke through prison walls. So he wrote: "The Church was well founded on the joy human beings take in sharing their hope."[7]

Contemporary theology presents us not simply with a condition of diversity, but rather with strident anarchy and abrasive turmoil. If there must be a tolerance for diversity, there must also be candor in recognizing the current demoralization and fragmentation of the theological enterprise. At least in Europe and America the scene is one of almost unrelieved confusion. We seem to have lost both compass and map. Historical disciplines have become fragmented, trivialized, and disjointed from ecclesiology or dogmatic concerns. Theological disciplines have become diffused, amorphous, one-dimensional, and reduced to superficial anthropology and sociology. There is no longer a common set of objectives, agreed-upon methodologies, or accepted language. Our linguistic and procedural habits abort rather than facilitate mutual understandings. Each of us chooses a vocabulary that seems appropriate to his or her own mental history, yet one that marks me as an alien to you, my colleagues.

The New Testament readily becomes a casualty of this internecine conflict. It becomes a weapon in the hands of sectarians who, if they use it at all, find in it support for their own linguistic formulations or project upon it their own paradigms of the modern situation. Whenever theologians are at odds among themselves they tend to discern the same kind and degree of anarchies among the New Testament apostles. What fellowship could Paul have had with Luke, since they used such different vocabularies and visualized the human situation in such antithetical ways? Contemporary scholars visualize the apostles as caught up in intramural polemics in which their thought was dominated by an "anti" of some sort: anti-Gnosticism, anti-Judaism, anti-Romanism, anti-spiritism, and so forth. Then, as now, we suppose that each Christian thinker must have chosen an identity with some *Tendenz* that alienated him or her from other Christians. Peering into the New Testament mirror the sectarian theologian is unable to see a catholic theologian looking out.

For almost three centuries now it has been our practice to treat the New Testament in the same way that we treat any other ancient document. That has come to mean treating each writer as representing simply one stage in the long complex history of theology, subject to all the foibles and fashions of that craft. There is much, of course, to commend that treatment. We too easily forget, however, that for eighteen centuries Christians were acutely aware of grounds for a very different appraisal. They believed that the New Testament writings belonged by right to a class by themselves carrying a high degree of authority as inspired fruits of prophetic or apostolic vocation. I want, therefore, to voice my conviction that the New Testament writers have much to teach us concerning the theologian's vocation and that we should accord to them greater authority than is customary, precisely at the point of methodology *vis-á-vis* our discussions of hope.

There is an illustrative case to be made by examining the literary and theological context of 1 Peter 3:8-18. First, let us listen to the *literary* context for implications concerning the author's idea of an accounting for hope:

> Finally, all of you, have unity of spirit, sympathy, love for one another, a tender heart, and a humble mind. Do not repay evil for evil or abuse for abuse; but, on the contrary, repay with a blessing. It is for this that you were called—that you might inherit a blessing. . . . Now who will harm you if you are eager to do what is good? But even if you do suffer for doing what is right, you are blessed. Do not fear what they fear, and do not be intimidated, but in your hearts sanctify Christ as Lord. *Always be ready to make your defense to anyone who demands from you an accounting for the hope that is in you;* yet do it with gentleness and reverence. Keep your conscience clear, so that, when you are maligned, those who abuse you for your good conduct in Christ may be put to shame. For it is better to suffer for doing good, if suffering should be God's will, than to suffer for doing evil. For Christ also suffered for sins once for all, the righteous for the unrighteous, in order to bring you to God. He was put to death in the flesh, but made alive in the spirit. (1 Pet. 3:8-9, 13-18, emphasis added)

This passage bristles with implications for our project. I have already mentioned the fact that this hope exists prior to the accounting and is therefore independent of that verbal exercise. Limitation of space forces me simply to list other implications, each of which merits much expansion:

- The defense is presumably given to outside adversaries who have haled believers before the courts.
- The defense is given by an individual, but the hope for which this individual accounts is a corporate possession (the *you* of 1 Pet. 3:15 is plural).
- The hope is of such a nature that gentleness should characterize its presentation.
- The verbal defense given before a court is an audible expression of inaudible reverence for Christ as the ruler of hearts (1 Pet. 3:14).
- This hope and this reverence are correlated to a way of life in which the righteous, following their ruler, sacrifice themselves for the unrighteous. The hope is thus a mode of existence oriented toward the unrighteous opponents (1 Pet. 3:18).
- So prominent is this motivation for giving the account that the *one who hopes* returns good for the evil done by those opponents (1 Pet. 3:9).
- This aim includes the desire to bring those adversaries to shame (1 Pet. 3:16) and thereby to God (1 Pet. 3:18). The suffering that has been occasioned by Christian loyalty is thus transformed into an occasion for Christian mission to the persecutors.
- This hope is grounded in the conviction that the persecuted cannot be harmed by their persecutors so long as their hearts are right and their consciences clean. Hope thus becomes a corollary of fearlessness and trust (1 Pet. 3:13, 14).
- To speak of the hope of the community is one way of articulating a communal ethos pervaded by unity, sympathy, humility, and love (1 Pet. 3:13). It is assumed that the refusal to give an account (1 Pet. 3:12) would seriously contradict and undermine that ethos.
- The whole situation is seen to be a result of the calling of this community (1 Pet. 3:9), a result that offers the opportunity for the fulfillment of that vocation.

There are other corollaries, but these may be sufficient to indicate the character of the community that is embodied in the struggle between despair and hope (*a la* de Pury), and also to indicate the way in which this author could speak of hope without emptying that word of its rich penumbra of connotations (*a la* Ellul). What we are privileged to observe in this fragment of conversation is not a dogmatician devising a web of doctrines about hope so much as a charismatic leader disclosing the hidden structures of a communal vocation by relating its situation of persecution to the revelation of God's will (1 Pet. 3:17) in the death and resurrection of Christ.

When we now ask how this author was doing theology, we answer by using the context of ideas furnished by the Epistle as a whole. What is the inner configuration of the forces that produce the hope of 1 Peter 3:15? We may distinguish six structural features:

(1) The ultimate source and ground of hope is the God who has chosen this community and has sealed a distinctive covenant with it. Its hope is a corollary of its vocation; both hope and vocation are communicated through the miracle of new birth and are signs of constant protection by God's power (1:2-5). Apart from God's action, this hope could neither exist nor perdure. What distinguishes this hope is its *in-God-ness* (1 Pet. 1:21).

(2) The inner structure of this hope is also defined by the unique relation of hope "to be obedient to Jesus Christ" and "to be sprinkled with his blood" (1 Pet. 1:2). His resurrection has been the means of new birth (1 Pet. 1:3). His death has formed the paradigm for the church's vocation of suffering (1 Pet. 3:18–4:2). Hope therefore becomes an expression of reverence for him "in your hearts" (1 Pet. 3:15). Hope is a form of coming to him, of being built up in him, of offering sacrifice to God through him (1 Pet. 2:4, 5). The in-God-ness of hope is identical with its *through-Christ-ness* (1 Pet. 1:21).

(3) The appearance of hope in the hearts of this community is the seal of sanctification by the Spirit, the same Spirit that in the prophets had predicted the sufferings and glory of Christ and that had become the mediator of heavenly life (1 Pet. 1:2, 11, 12). It is in and through the Spirit that the church discovers in the sufferings and glory of Christ its bond both to earlier revelations and to the last things. The realm of the Spirit's activity is coextensive with the realm of hope. Where hope is, there too is the Spirit.

(4) The phrase "the hope that is in you" brings together a noun in the singular and a pronoun in the plural. One hope, many persons. Integral to this hope is its communal anchorage. The Epistle is replete with images that articulate the vocation and the life-story of this community: exiles, dispersion, children, temple, priesthood, race, nation, people, and flock. As a word, hope points to the cohesive forces that enable each of these images to express a corporate totality, without blurring the fact that

each individual member becomes a steward of a particular grace (1 Pet. 3:8-12; 4:9-11).

(5) Hope as a "mode of being in the world" comes to expression in a "fiery ordeal" (1 Pet. 4:12) that appears to defeat the unique vocation of the church, but actually vindicates that vocation. Although the ordeal has been precipitated by that vocation ("your good conduct in Christ," 1 Pet. 3:16), the ordeal could be viewed as a disproof of the gospel. Rather, it must be seen as offering a necessary and blessed way of sharing in Christ's sufferings, a sign of the approaching judgment, and an opportunity to fulfill the vocation as a witness, a worshiper, and a self-sacrificing priest.

(6) The situation in which hope fulfills its assigned task is a situation in which the momentary ordeal is transfigured and transcended by God's powerful presence. Hope links accused criminals to the victor over "angels, authorities, and powers" (1 Pet. 3:22). Facing death, prisoners are freed from fear of death (1 Pet. 3:14) and their fate is embraced within the grace promised to the prophets and realized in Christ. By being faithful in their immediate testimony both to believers and to enemies, their life and death now point to realities that connect "the foundation of the world" to "the end of the ages" (1 Pet. 1:20). In hope *this* present and *this* eternal are fused. Hope is this community's participation in primordial and eschatological realities.

Thus far we have looked only at 1 Peter. The reader may well ask: But is this epistle typical of the New Testament as a whole? Can we rely on it as representing a consensus of early Christian thought? So accustomed are we to expect radical diversity, if not acute conflict, among early Christian authors that anyone who claims to have found a normative consensus must defend his conclusion with a full arsenal of scriptural evidence and scholarly argument. It must, of course, be granted that the New Testament covers a broad spectrum of attitudes toward hope. Such variety can be illustrated by six key passages from as many authors: Romans 4–8; John 13–17; Revelation 1–7; Hebrews 10–12; Acts 2–3; and Ephesians 1–4. I have no desire to minimize their variety. And yet those same passages demonstrate an undeniable kinship. All six authors would find entirely acceptable the basic affirmation of Ephesians 4:4, "You were called to the one hope of your calling." That affirmation fuses three convictions: there is one hope; there is one vocation; the two are inseparable and interdependent. The immediate implication is this: theologians who wish to explore the character of the one hope may well concentrate on the character of their own vocation. If as theologians we are united in the same calling, we are also united in the hope that belongs to that calling. If this is true, the pandemonium of voices to which we earlier called attention is relative and not absolute. If untrue, there is nothing that can restore unity to our discordant voices. The prior question does not concern how to *do* theology—but how to *be* a *called* theologian. The first is a matter of profession; the second is a matter of vocation.

These two terms have long histories, of course, and convey wide ranges of meaning, so it is well to clarify the sense in which we use them. Although the two overlap, we can at the outset distinguish several contrasts. The choice of a profession is self-initiated; in the case of a vocation, a person responds to the call of Another. The former is a sociological category, the latter a theological. In the former, society as a whole serves as the authorizing and licensing agent, establishing the criteria for admission and advancement. It regulates financial and social sanctions to be applied to the successful or unsuccessful. As professionals, theologians accept certain academic standards and serve a specific academic clientele. Their audience goes with the job. This audience is usually one that places a premium on universality, on objectivity, on working within the prevailing assumptions concerning time and space, nature and history, systems of value, and cultural goals.

Vocation, as a theological category, brings into play a quite different cluster of associations. The theological vocation binds one to a religious community where all members to some degree have received the same calling, and where a unique covenant conveys a special mission to the larger society. It has its own sense of time and space, its own map of cosmic and ontic reality, its own ceiling and horizon, springing from its specific origin and *telos*. This vocation antedates and transcends any thought of salary, excludes notions of status and superiority, and therefore taps quite distinctive reservoirs of energy and motivation. It begins with a separation from the world that is an offense to the world, and moves toward an inclusive goal that is equally offensive. It is impossible to say of any profession that only one hope belongs to it; but of this vocation it is *necessary* to say just that. Every person called to be a theologian is called to this one calling and its hope.

This preliminary exploration of contrasts between the vocation of which 1 Peter speaks and the profession of theology in the modern university forces us to reckon with this possibility: the greater the distance between this profession and this vocation, the more alienated we are from the hope that inheres in that vocation, and the less qualified to do a theology of hope. Let us ponder that possibility, free from any subjective inclination either to attack or to defend our chosen profession.

First of all, we must be wary of certain dangers in hasty correlations between ancient and modern situations. The New Testament was never intended to serve as a norm for all Christian activities in all later periods. In the initial period there was nothing comparable to the modern theological profession. Moreover, none of the forms of leadership in the early church—apostle, prophet, teacher, and so forth—has survived unchanged to the modern day. It is therefore wrong to attempt any detailed correlation between the gifts of the Spirit, as spelled out in 1 Corinthians or 1 Peter, and the range of occupations within the modern church.

On the other hand, it must be granted that the original Christian vocation has become radically professionalized and that one result is the obscuring of the one hope of which Peter spoke. None can challenge the fact that the standards that govern the theologian's work are now set by the state and the university more than by the church. In many cases, those standards do *not* include the scholars' acceptance of the church's vocation. They may of course accept that vocation, and the church may recognize them as truly called, but standing within the profession does not depend on such factors. The process of professionalization of the vocation goes forward with increasing acceleration and momentum, and we should candidly recognize some of the results. I have in mind the following, stated all too briefly and arbitrarily:

(1) In a professionalized vocation, the role of the three Persons of the Trinity in educing both the vocation and its one hope becomes steadily more problematic and expendable. In this respect the theological girders in the thinking of 1 Peter become extrinsic rather than intrinsic, marginal rather than central, and for many scholars even unintelligible.

(2) The professionalization of the vocation alters the locus and character of the community to which the theologian feels primarily responsible. An individual covenant with the academic community tends to displace the corporate covenant between the church and the God of Abraham, Isaac, and Jacob. The audience is defined in university terms more than church terms. Daily hopes are those of academic colleagues rather than those of prophets, saints, and martyrs.

(3) Because the theologian's situation is now professionalized, the definition of theology suffers a radical change. It is no longer defined by the situation of 1 Peter. More effective in defining the situation are students,

university colleagues, or the daily newspaper. That situation is no longer seen as an episode in the battle between God and Satan, or as a collision between "God's people" and "the world," but rather as a problem posed for consultation with the psychologist, social worker, political scientist, or philosopher of history.

(4) To the degree that the theologian's vocation has become professionalized, the theologian tends to lose the perspective of seeing all things in the light of Christ, of viewing all nature and history afresh according to the revelation of God's wisdom and power in the death and resurrection of Jesus. It could be said in this regard that professions are equipped to deal with the old age (or the humanity of the first Adam, or the world of sin and death) in categories indigenous to that age. The one vocation, with its gift of hope, is the sign that God is making all things new; but the professionalization of that vocation marks an insistent tendency to revert to the *status quo ante*.

(5) One result is an altered relation of the theological vocation to the *charismata*. In the earlier period, those who received the calling also received the requisite gifts of the Spirit, among which the gifts of prophecy and the interpretation of prophecy were central. Professionalized theology is de-charismatized theology. When the gift of prophecy ceases, what happens to the gift of hope, of which the prophet was both recipient and channel? Today when theologians are praised as "gifted," the gifts are quite different.

When we weigh the cumulative force of these observations, we may be in a better position to appraise the dilemmas faced by theology as an academic discipline. Is the anarchy and demoralization of that discipline so surprising after all? Is it strange that there is no agreement on how to do theology? Can we expect anything other than a kaleidoscope of changing theologies, an endless proliferation of hopes? Should we continue to defend the legitimacy of theology as a professional discipline within the curriculum of a secular university? Certainly the conditions that originally produced the one vocation and the one hope no longer pertain in our academic departments.

It might be assumed from the preceding observations that we should try to reverse the process of professionalization. I do not want to support such a program. It seems neither feasible nor even possible to vocationalize the profession in the direction of recovering New Testament models. Any systematic effort to convert an academic discipline into a charismatic vocation would simply multiply anomalies and confuse the gifts of the Spirit with institutional atavism. Even though it seems that the church lacks the guidance of inspired prophet-revealers, it would be futile to force modern scholarship into ancient ministerial molds. To the degree that theology has become a professional discipline, comparable to law and medicine—to that degree the New Testament has virtually nothing to contribute to the problem of *how to do* theology.

That is not to say, however, that scripture has little to contribute to *theologians* as heirs of the one vocation. Nothing prevents us from reliance on and responsiveness to such charismatic gifts as prophecy and teaching. We can permit our perspectives of thought and action to be controlled by the revelation of God's ultimate judgment and mercy in the death and resurrection of Jesus Christ. We can develop a situational theology more akin to 1 Peter than to that of our secular colleagues. We can discover the one hope that is anchored in the work of the Triune God. At all these points the New Testament would contribute to our ability *to be* Christian theologians and to give a faithful accounting of the one hope that inheres in our vocation.

Is there deep tension between vocation and profession? Of course there is, as in every other profession. The theologian should expect no immunity to the eschatological struggles that pervade creation (Rom. 8). The Christian vocation belongs to that very battlefield. Should the profession be one of the institutional features inherent in the "old age," so much the more does it become a place destined for redemption.

The professionalization of the Christian vocation is a form of blindness and slavery, but the renewal of vocation may bring vision and liberation to theologians. When that happens, they can join Ellul, Taylor, and de Pury in the one hope that belongs to their calling.

ADDENDUM

The following resources by the author are also relevant to those issues in biblical theology addressed in part 3:

"Paul's Apostolic Call," in *Theology in Scotland*, 6 (1999): 5-31.

"The Death of Death," in *The Contribution of Carl Michalson to Modern Theology*, ed. H. O. Thompson (Lewiston: Edward Mellen, 1991), 245-258.

"Adam and the Educator," in *The Christian Scholar*, 39 (1956): 6-18.

"Holy People, Holy Land, Holy City," in *Interpretation*, 37 (1983): 18-31.

PART IV

The Messiah's Gifts, The Churches' Gratitude

Introduction to
PART IV

The Lord demonstrated his presence among the churches by making diverse gifts "to his own." Some of these were so visible as to create quick disbelief and hostility, or amazed faith. The more decisive gifts, however, remained invisible to outsiders even where they were most compelling to recipients, a contrast not surprising in view of the word of the risen Messiah to Paul: "Power is made perfect in weakness" (2 Cor. 12:9). Such gifts do not often weigh heavily on the scales of the historian. In the chapters that follow we probe the nature of some of these gifts. One example is the gift of the Spirit that comes to his aid when an apostle does not know how to pray, or what to say before hostile judges (chapter 16). Another such gift is the experience of being crucified with Christ to the world, along with the freedoms thus released (chapter 17). Gifts, too, are the exorbitant and even impossible promises made by the Lord to his disciples, promises both made and kept (chapter 18).

As the New Testament records make clear, believers were grateful also for gifts of welcome into the new heaven with its new earth, and for the new self, an essential part of the new creation (chapter 19). Recipients of these gifts discovered that there was no better way of expressing their gratitude than by carrying on a self-denying mission in the name of their new Lord (chapter 20). So, too, in grateful response they sang hymns in praise to the "Lamb that was slain," thus initiating an endless chain of Magnificats and Passions, like those of Johann Sebastian Bach (chapter 21).

These chapters do not pose the same kind of problems for the historian as earlier ones, but there are problems here nevertheless. Together these six final chapters constitute an implicit, cumulative challenge that calls to mind the ancient Latin proverb, *ex nihilo nihil fit.* Weigh again, historian, the presence of the Spirit in unspectacular but powerful ways, though unseen. Weigh again the following evidence, historian: being crucified with Christ produced new ways of viewing all people, eliminating distinctions between sexes, classes, and religions. Listen again to the prayers of gratitude at all times for everything, even to the hymns of joy resounding from Roman prisons. Such things do not emerge *ex nihilo.* With all other readers, historians must also answer, and not simply ask, questions about the source of such gifts.

— 16 —
The Spirit
(Romans, Luke, Mark, and Revelation)

In a symposium on the Holy Spirit I was once asked as a New Testament scholar and as a Protestant who has been active in the ecumenical movement to speak on the work of the Holy Spirit. So the first question for me, as historian and biblical theologian, was this: For what signs should a person look to detect such work? One answer is this: Signs that God is in action in human life.

When I think in terms as broad as those, I am impelled to say that I have witnessed the hidden presence of the Spirit at so many times, in so many places, in so many diverse modes of activity, and among so many types of people that I have been quite overwhelmed. So overwhelmed, in fact, as to be convinced of the inadequacy of any dogmatic formula or any psychological description. Congenitally inclined, as I am, to be skeptical of all claims to Spirit possession, my experience, over and over again, has made me even more skeptical of my own skepticism. The cumulative effects of biblical study, of ecumenical worship and dialogue, and of life inside and outside Christian institutions—all have made me confident of the power of the Spirit, even as they have made me aware of the Spirit's proclivity for hiding within the seemingly routine life of individuals and communities. In order not to take refuge in vague generalizations, I have constantly tried to visualize specific experiences: a Roman Catholic Mass and a Pentecostal dance in Accra, Ghana; a Thanksgiving Mass in a Benedictine Abbey in Minnesota; a Friends Meeting in Radnor, Pennsylvania; the ordination of deacons in the leper colony on Molokai; and an Easter service in the unfinished buildings of the Ecumenical

Institute in Jerusalem. Though I shall keep these and other experiences in mind, the main source for what follows is the New Testament.

Forty-five years of teaching that Testament have impressed me with the impossibility of reducing the wealth of biblical images of the Spirit to a single master-image. What is it that the Bible compares both to inexhaustible fountains of water and to flames of unquenchable fire? What is it that operates both as a warm moist breath that a person inhales and as the gale-force wind accompanying hurricanes and earthquakes? What is it that simultaneously produces both fear and courage? What is it that brings order out of cosmic chaos and yet also conceives a human embryo?

Wielding the power of the finger on God's right hand, it drives demons from their homes. It is a sword used by Christians in mortal combat, as well as the pen with which Christ writes a letter on human hearts. It comes down from heaven like a dove, and it is the oil with which prophets and kings are anointed. It is the early light that promises the dawn, the first gathering of the summer's fruit, the down-payment on a coming inheritance. It is the control tower guiding apostles and missionaries from one destination to another. Such profusion should remind us that we are dealing with a vast mystery that no net of words can capture. More important than the images themselves are the verbs that suggest the activity of the Spirit. The Spirit falls on people, fills and anoints them, blesses and judges them, hardens and softens hearts, builds up and destroys communities, makes them drunk and gives them peace. Human responses to the Spirit reflect similar variety: people resist or receive, ignore or hear, quench or obey, betray or please, and lie to or have fellowship in the Spirit. These verbs intimate that the Spirit, when it comes, requires an immediate response. That response, in turn, places the moment of decision within the horizons of ultimate significance. Unbelievers must be baffled by such language, but believers are humbled in awe before the *mysterium tremendum*.

I have been stressing this diversity of images because I believe that just here the ecumenical movement can reaffirm the wisdom of the Bible and can contribute to our thinking. Many churches have profited from studying the multiple images of the church in the New Testament.[1] A comparable benefit is available through a study of the images of the Spirit. Such study shows that our separate traditions have all been seriously deficient both in the experience and in the doctrine of the Spirit. The diversity of images also alerts us to the presence of the Spirit in unsuspected places, even at points where our most cherished traditions seem to be threatened.

For most church men and women, to mention the profusion of gifts is to call to mind the catalog of ministries, as found in 1 Corinthians 12–14: apostles, prophets, teachers, and so forth. Our minds turn first in this direction in part because these activities have been institutionalized, because we ourselves represent these ministries and because so much interchurch rivalry has focused on these offices. In identifying these ancient gifts with our own ecclesiastical offices, the poisons of egocentricity are often at work. These poisons may be communal rather than personal; we defend our church because it has preserved in its ordinations the authenticity of the original gifts. But ecumenical activity joins us to churches that have preserved other gifts; it thus tends to relativize our own institutionalization of those gifts. This has been as true for the Society of Friends as for the Roman Catholic Church, for Pentecostals as for Greek Orthodoxy. None of our churches has preserved intact the whole range of ministerial gifts as found in the earliest churches. In fact, all of those early gifts resist institutionalization more successfully than we may have supposed.

Ecumenical activity reinforces another biblical insight concerning spiritual gifts. It focuses attention upon a basic gift that is common to all Christians: "No one can say 'Jesus is Lord' except by the Holy Spirit" (1 Cor. 12:3). If we denigrate this initial gift, we blaspheme the Spirit. If we treat subsequent gifts as more important, we deny by implication the decisive significance of rebirth through the Spirit. It is this gift that requires the greatest sacrifice: nothing less than the crucifixion of the flesh with its passions and desires, including the stubborn wish to become number one among disciples of Christ. It is a basic sin of every Christian tradition to ignore or to minimize the necessity of dying daily with Christ, whether to the self or to the institutional customs and laws that fetter freedom. Originally baptism signaled the death with Christ to the law, together with the intention to die daily with him to every legal system, as evidence of resurrection with him. Ecumenism has restored baptism to its place of continuing importance, reminding us that through the Holy Spirit all believers have daily access to the gift of life that begins when a person dies to self.

It is such participation that can restore saner evaluations of the diverse fruits of the Spirit. Quite inconspicuous virtues can become authentic signs of rebirth: patience, kindness, gentleness, self-control, peace, serenity. Such gifts are, it is true, inconspicuous; but they are rare enough to be welcomed as major miracles. According to the New Testament, it is by such gifts as these that the Holy Spirit seals ordinary men and women for the day of redemption. Not only does ecumenical work alert us to the power of such virtues but it also alerts us to the demonic origins of the opposing vices: laziness, self-pity, fatalism, ambition, suspicion, fear of the future. The usual round of ecclesiastical affairs tempts us to accept these unclean spirits as normal, but the frustrations of ecumenical conversations discloses how demonic they really are. The realization of *koinonia* requires the exorcism of such demons, an exorcism depending less upon hierarchical authority than on the healing powers of the Spirit. In short, the ecumenical movement, along with the New Testament, forces us to recall the essential gifts and fruits: our common baptism, our participation in the death and exaltation of Jesus, the joining of many voices in unison praying, readiness to treat others as better than ourselves, the power of hope to overcome despair, and the hidden presence of Christ among his brothers and sisters. Once we have been alerted to these gifts, we may discern their presence even in the alien atmospheres of a twenty-first-century university.

Four New Testament texts are particularly noteworthy for specific activities of the Spirit that we are all inclined to neglect. These texts are from four authors: Paul, Luke, Mark, and John. First we listen to some familiar sentences from Paul.

> For all who are led by the Spirit of God are children of God. . . . When we cry "Abba! Father!" it is that very Spirit bearing witness with our spirit that we are children of God. . . . The creation waits with eager longing for the revealing of the children of God; for the creation was subjected to futility . . . in hope that the creation itself will be set free from its bondage to decay. . . . The Spirit helps us in our weakness; for we do not know how to pray as we ought, but that very Spirit intercedes with sighs too deep for words. And God, who searches the heart, knows what is the mind of the Spirit. (Rom. 8:14-27)

In Romans 8, the apostle visualizes the Holy Spirit as speaking to God through the prayers of believers. It was by sharing in the sufferings of the present time that Christians were impelled to cry out "Abba! Father!" Among those sufferings was Paul's own futility in trying to heal a divided church. The church from which he was writing (Corinth) and the church to which he was writing (Rome) were bitterly divided, and Paul viewed the restoration of unity in both as his own apostolic responsibility. Paul confesses in prayer his own weakness and ignorance. He did not know how to pray. The Spirit was present not in his wisdom but in his ignorance, not in his successes but in his failures. Notice that it was his own agony, his own ignorance, his own futility, that alerted Paul to the futility of all creation. It was the presence of the Spirit in Paul's own futility that enabled him to believe in God's power to accomplish the good and to fulfill his promise of liberty for all creation. All this was implicit in that simple prayer: "Abba! Father!" (Rom. 8:15-16).

Now let us turn to Luke and to his story of the beginning of the Christian mission. Here the Spirit spoke through the speech of believers, conveying a message from God to a crowd drawn from every nation under heaven. You are familiar with the surrealist stage-setting of Acts 2: An explosive sound from heaven, gale-force winds, and tongues of fire. The Spirit is thus manifest among a company of Galilean pilgrims together in one place, surrounded by many national and religious groups: Libyans, Parthians, Arabs, Romans, Jews, proselytes, and Gentiles—something like a United Nations Assembly or a university campus. The Galileans appear not to have been surprised by the eruption, but all the others were bewildered. Luke takes care to show how this event fit into a longer story, as the sequel to previous episodes: the promises of John the Baptist and Jesus concerning the coming baptism with the Spirit, Joel's promise concerning the day of the Lord, the traditional Jewish festival of thanksgiving for the harvest, and the celebration of the covenant sealed on Mount Sinai. However, even with Luke's help we often miss the character of the Pentecostal miracle itself, without which the story would lose its point. This point comes through clearly when we contrast Pentecost and Babel. At Babel those who spoke the same language suddenly could not understand one another. At Pentecost, there were many languages, used by many races and nationalities, each cherishing its own uniqueness, yet all could understand the unprecedented announcement spoken by these strange Galileans. Three times Luke stresses the same point: "Each one heard [the Galileans] speaking in the native language of each." Speaking about what? About "God's deeds of power." The miracle took place when a foreign language became a mother tongue. It was a miracle of hearing as well as of speaking.

The Gospel of Mark describes another strange work of that same Spirit. In this case it enables human witnesses to speak effectively to their human enemies in a courtroom, where power appears to lie in the hands of the enemies. Listen to this text:

> As for yourselves, beware; for they will hand you over to councils; and you will be beaten in synagogues; and you will stand before governors and kings because of me, as a testimony to them. . . . When they bring you to

trial and hand you over, do not worry beforehand about what you are to say; but say whatever is given you at that hour, for it is not you who speak, but the Holy Spirit. (Mark 13:9-11)

Christianity appeared in the world as a subversive movement. It attracted the deadly hostility of every establishmentarian institution. The story of Jesus reflected that redemption and martyrdom had become inseparable. His followers also discovered that to carry the cross was the only way to carry the gospel into the heart of the enemy camp. They preserved the difficult truth that it was when they were on trial as defendants that the voice of the Spirit could be heard by their accusers. On such occasions that voice was blended with the voice of the defendants as they accepted for Christ's sake whatever penalty might be inflicted. The Spirit not only allayed their fear but assured them that their witness would be effective in forcing adversaries to say yes or no to the gospel. But this work of the Spirit as attorney for the defense was aimed at more than acquittal for the defendant and more than conversion of single (or particular) opponents. Aimed at the rejection by the world, the Spirit opened the way for the reconciliation of the world. That is why Mark believed that this work of the Spirit must continue until all nations would hear the testimony of the martyrs. When disciples were "hated by all because of [Jesus'] name" (Mark 13:13), their stories became fused with the Passion story of the Messiah, a fusion that illustrated the truth that "the testimony of Jesus is the spirit of prophecy" (Rev. 19:10).

Is there any place in the world where Christians can today hear this Spirit speaking to them in trials in court? We dare not say no. Is there any place where this Spirit is speaking through the voice of criminal defendants, put on trial by the religious establishment? Again we dare not say no. Should we say no, we would confess that this gospel is no longer being preached to this nation by this Spirit. A message that no longer arouses enmity in the world no longer exhibits the power to reconcile the world. Where there are no political prisoners, this work of the Spirit cannot proceed.

In the fourth text, this one from the prophet John in the Apocalypse, the Holy Spirit serves as a medium of two-way communication between Jesus and his church. It is the means by which the coming Lord speaks to the waiting church as he sends his angel. This angel identifies himself as "a fellow servant with you and your comrades the prophets, and with those who keep the words of this book" (Rev. 22:9). His message is an invitation to a wedding supper to be celebrated by the Lamb with his

Bride. As the invitation has an RSVP attached, the Holy Spirit returns with the church's response to the sender. Both letter and response are engraved in antiphonal liturgies familiar to the churches in Asia:

> "See, I am coming soon. . . . I am . . . the first and the last. . . ." "It is I, Jesus, who sent my angel to you with this testimony for the churches. . . ." The Spirit and the bride say, "Come." And let everyone who hears, say "Come." And let everyone who is thirsty come. . . . The one who testifies to these things says, "Surely I am coming soon." Amen. Come, Lord Jesus! (Rev. 22:12-20)

This vision, so expressive of the inner dynamics of Christian worship, is part of a very complex fabric of emotions and loyalties. The one who comes to the waiting church introduces himself as the beginning and the end; through his relation to the Creator he is related to all creation; he thus provides the most inclusive brackets within which to set the immediate conversation. His coming to his servants is the dawn of a new day (the bright and morning star), and this day is both Day One and the Day of the Lord. His invitation as delivered by the Spirit offers the churches the promise of full participation in primal and final reality. Authentic worship takes place when the churches hear this Spirit say, "Come." In uttering this one word several speakers take part: the Spirit, the Bride, the coming Lord, the waiting church, the angel, and the prophet. This is more than a committee meeting where everyone talks; it is a cloverleaf intersection of busy highways. Each participant both says, "Come," and acts (comes). The Spirit is at work at the point where these voices and these movements converge. Its presence marks the transcendence of time, insofar as time separates one generation from others and the beginning from the end. Its presence marks the fulfillment of time, insofar as time is the laboratory where God creates and redeems all things.

In most of our ideas about ecumenism we have been too much obsessed by the ecumenism of space, the unity of all the churches that now exist throughout the world. We should be more impressed with the ecumenism of time (a phrase of Georges Florovsky)—the unity of all the churches in successive centuries and epochs. Through ecumenical work we become better acquainted with our living ancestors and our living descendants. It is the gift of the Holy Spirit that creates and sustains this unity. I believe that all of our separated communions have been deficient in that we have not allowed the Spirit to accomplish this strange work of uniting us with churches in other generations.

I have now reminded you of four neglected activities of the Holy Spirit: (1) the miracle of weakness—in prayers of God's people, addressed to God, prompted by their ignorance, weakness, and frustration; (2) the miracle of listening—in enabling many nations, with diverse languages, to hear the gospel in their own mother-tongue; (3) the miracle of witnessing—in speaking through criminal defendants to hostile juries in such a way as to confront God's enemies with his mercies; and (4) the miracle of worshiping—in issuing invitations to the wedding feast and in answering those invitations through antiphonal voices and movements. These are a tiny sample of New Testament resources, a tiny sample of the gifts and fruits of the Spirit.

— 17 —
The Liberation
(Galatians)

The Epistle to the Galatians has often been called Christ's Emancipation Declaration, announcing, "Slaves, you are free!" The same letter could as accurately be called Christ's Death Sentence, announcing, "You must die!" In fact, this death and this freedom were for the apostle quite inseparable. Yet we must ask, "How can this be?" We must begin with a careful analysis of the verse in which Paul speaks of *three* crucifixions as being, in fact, only *one*: "May I never boast of anything except the cross of our Lord Jesus Christ, by which the world has been crucified to me, and I to the world" (Gal. 6:14). Of these three, perhaps we find least intelligible the crucifixion of the world. To understand that crucifixion, as well as the connections among the three, we must explore the structure of the sentence as a whole.

Paul's affirmation concerns the ground and object of his boasting. There are two alternatives to glorying in the cross: a person can boast either in the world or in the self. Yet to Paul those alternatives have been ruled out, inasmuch as both of them have been crucified. Of the three related crucifixions, the latter two are seen as secondary to the first. The tense of the verb is the perfect: though occurring in the past, presumably at the time of Christ's death, that past action still determines the present situation. The voice of the verb is passive: the two entities (the *kosmos*, and I) have been acted upon. Neither the world nor the self has initiated its own crucifixion. The two parallel clauses suggest that there is a subtle interaction between the two derived crucifixions: the *kosmos* has been crucified to Paul, and Paul has been crucified to the *kosmos*. We infer that these two events are in some sense simultaneous and interdependent, yet they are not identical. Neither death can be telescoped into the other, yet neither is fully intelligible alone. We also infer that, although Paul was speaking for himself, he believed that the same assertion should apply to every believer. He believed also that it did not as yet apply to some of his readers. It may be that those readers had expressed their faith in Christ's cross but had not yet recognized the two derived crucifixions. Refusal to do so had cast doubt on the authenticity of their faith. The function of this sentence of Paul's, therefore, is one of persuasion: he reinforces his rebuke of the recipients and summarizes his appeal for a change. He wants his Galatian converts to move toward an unreserved acceptance of the crucifixion of their world.

The surrounding paragraph is quite decisive in setting the boundaries of meaning, and readers must allow their former conceptions of the term world to be modified by those boundaries.

> It is those who want to make a good showing in the flesh that try to compel you to be circumcized—only that they may not be persecuted for the cross of Christ. Even the circumcised do not themselves obey the law, but they want you to be circumcised so that they may boast about your flesh. May I never boast of anything except the cross of our Lord Jesus Christ, by which the world has been crucified to me, and I to the world. For neither circumcision nor uncircumcision is anything; but a new creation is everything! As for those who will follow this rule—peace be upon them, and mercy, and upon the Israel of God. (Gal. 6:12-16)

Galatians 6:15 provides both synonymous and antithetical parallels to Galatians 6:14. Here it is made clear that the crucifixion of the world is an event that marks the total devaluation of both circumcision and uncircumcision. *Kosmos* is a realm where people set a high value on those distinctions. It is with the destruction of those distinctions that the new creation emerges. Where *kosmos* ends, a new creation begins. The two are mutually exclusive realities.

Galatians 6:16 provides still another antithesis, one between two communities. One community walks by the rule as expressed in Galatians 6:15; the other does not. The community that so walks is the Israel of God; the other presumably is not. It is this Israel, governed by this rule, that is implicitly identified with the new creation and set against the world that has been crucified.

The character of the *kosmos* is further reflected in Galatians 6:12, 13.

The people to whom the world has not yet been crucified are those for whom circumcision retains its earlier significance. This is why such persons insist on performing or receiving circumcision. Here appears a third alternative to glorying in the cross of Jesus: these adversaries glory "in the flesh." Paul traces this glorying to two specific desires: the desire to obey the law and the desire to avoid persecution "for the cross of Christ." Thus we find in the paragraph a composite profile of the *kosmos* that had been crucified to Paul. Positively, it is constituted by reliance on circumcision, on the flesh, on the law, and on the covenant community that is bound by those standards. Negatively, this *kosmos* is constituted by its opposition to the new creation, its avoidance of persecution for the sake of Christ, and its rejection of "the Israel of God" that walks by the new rule. When we allow this context to define *kosmos* there is nothing inherently enigmatic about Paul's use of the term. What makes the sentence puzzling is our own habit of using the term *world* to refer to other entities.

The unit of thought here is neither the clause nor the sentence, but the entire paragraph of Galatians 6:12-16, and this paragraph constitutes a powerful epitome of the entire letter. In his rebuke to his Galatian converts Paul maintains the same basic point of reference. It was by this *kosmos*, so defined, that Christ had himself been crucified; accordingly Paul located in the cross of Jesus the crucifixion of this *kosmos*. Only by recognizing the triple crucifixion could a person be freed from bondage to the law. When a person was crucified with Christ, he died to the law, with its system of blessings and curses. Simultaneously that law died to him (Gal. 2:19). If Israel could have been saved through the law, Christ would have died to no purpose (Gal. 2:21). To refuse to recognize that this *kosmos* had been crucified meant that bondage to it was as yet unbroken. In Paul's view the Judaizers, in avoiding the scandal of the cross, had shifted to another gospel entirely. The gospel of Christ liberates only those who accept the reality of this world's crucifixion.

We have noted that in Galatians 6:15 Paul stressed the enmity between the *kosmos*, where circumcision retains its importance, and the new creation, where it does not. The same sharp antithesis underlies his definition of sonship to Abraham in Galatians 3:6-29 and the two lines of descent in Galatians 4:21-31. One lineage comes from a slave woman, the other from a free. Coinciding with these two lineages are two mountains, two covenants, two Jerusalems. Thus Paul traces back to Abraham the antithesis between *kosmos* and new creation. From the first, the children of the flesh have persecuted the children of the Spirit. This ancestral hostility justifies the command to cast out the slave and her son, especially since in the new creation the boundary between Jew and Gentile has been obliterated (Gal. 3:28). We can safely infer that wherever that boundary becomes obsolete, the sovereignty of that *kosmos* has been terminated. But where Judaizers, in their abhorrence of the works of the flesh, insist on circumcision they illustrate a kind of glorying in the flesh that demonstrates continued bondage to the *kosmos* (Gal. 3:1-6). To them Christ still stands under the curse of the law, while to Paul it is they who are as yet unredeemed from its curse (Gal. 3:13). In fact, the *kosmos* represents the realm that is governed by that system of curses and blessings that had been destroyed in the cross of Christ.

Such a line of argument is fully congruent with the bitter irony that emerges in the discussion of the elemental spirits of the world in Galatians 4:1-11. Those elemental spirits had held them all in bondage and had denied them all the promised freedom of sons. Before faith came to Paul and to his Jewish colleagues, they had confused these no-gods with God. This confusion had taken the form of observing the sacred calendar of festivals and holy days. We infer that the *kosmos* of Galatians 6:14 is coterminous with the effective sovereignty of these spirits. To recognize the gift of sonship in Christ was to recognize the crucifixion of that sovereignty. To return to the weak and beggarly elements was to cut themselves off from Christ, that is, from the new creation. Powers that had been worshiped as gods had been demoted to impotent beggars. The Israel that supposed itself to be the people of God had become branded as servants of the flesh and of the elemental spirits. The mark of sonship to Abraham, circumcision (Gen. 17:9-14), had become instead a sign of hostility to God. In fact, Paul's reference to bearing the wounds of Jesus (Gal. 6:17) may have been intended as an ironic antithesis to the good showing which his opponents wished to make "in the flesh" by circumcision, thereby avoiding the persecution that had come to Paul (Gal. 6:12). This same apostle, however, identified himself as one who, before faith had come, had stood with the Judaizers in the same bondage (Gal. 4:3). Then he had been as far from hating this *kosmos* as he had been from hating himself as a son of Abraham. It is only when we give proper weight to this revolution in his own religious world and its sacred language that we can fathom what Paul was driving at in his reference to the triple crucifixion. When we allow the syntax and context to guide our perception of Paul's meanings, the enigma is resolved, at least in part.

We may well remain puzzled, however, in deciding how much weight to attach to Paul's use of language. For one thing, in the assertion that the world has been crucified, the verb is quite plainly a metaphor. What had happened to the world is both like and unlike what had happened to Christ. It had *in some sense* been killed (even though it had not been executed as a criminal), but in what sense? How seriously must such a metaphor be taken? Many readers, on recognizing the presence of a figure of speech, immediately downgrade its value. Is this the proper procedure in this case? The issue reactivates furious, unresolved debates over the respective merits of literal and analogical language, debates cutting across the academic boundaries between linguistics, aesthetics, natural sciences, philosophy, and theology. I stand among those who stress that all language is analogical in character and that all theological language is figurative to a special degree since its ultimate reference is to God. I believe that in contexts like Galatians, literal meanings are less valuable indicators of truth than are the metaphorical. However, I have no wish to debate those issues here, but simply to observe features in Galatians 6:14 that enhance the "specific gravity" of this metaphor.

In this case, the whole force of the argument rests upon the actuality of the crucifixion of Jesus, a fact accepted by apostle and adversaries alike. Paul considered the world's crucifixion to be a necessary implication, a divinely willed consequence, of that undoubted event. The statement may be metaphorical, but the event was historical. Moreover, each reader must reckon with an autobiographical happening to which the author was simply giving witness. Paul was appealing to his own story, in which this radical change had taken place. He was not playing with trivial figures of speech in describing his own crucifixion to the world, and he was no more playful in describing the world's crucifixion to himself. The experience was so overwhelming that he was impelled to use figurative language to do it justice. The truth at stake was the truth of a particular story. Furthermore, this was not Paul's story alone. His thought revolved around an event that had become the center of many stories—stories of Jesus, of himself, of the world, of every reader of the Epistle. With the fusion of these various stories around a common center came a fusion of horizons. Paul's logic was controlled by the truth implicit in this story of Jesus, a story that provided a common retrospect and a common prospect for the other stories. The God of Jesus and of Abraham had acted within the story of Jesus to redefine the center and horizons of the other stories. Finally, we must credit Paul with enough forensic ability to choose arguments that would carry weight with his opponents. Had they been able to refute his case on account of its metaphorical character, Paul's case for the crucifixion of the world would have been fatally flawed. What determined their response was not his use of figural rather than literal language, but the whole range of substantive issues he raised: for example, the covenant with Abraham, the boundaries of Israel, the jurisdiction of the Torah. Was it true that *this* world had been crucified to them?

It may be, however, the ironic character of Paul's language that baffles the exegete more than the figural. It is entirely clear that the whole letter constitutes a highly rhetorical rebuke to its recipients. In it we witness a quite savage explosion of sarcasm. To penetrate his adversaries' defenses, the apostle relies upon a strongly ironic *argumentum ad hominem*. As we have seen, this irony was present in the choice of the word *kosmos*, a word used pejoratively by the Judaizers, but an expletive that Paul turned into a boomerang, so fashioned that it would curve back and strike them. Paul meant one thing by *kosmos*; his enemies another. Can we adopt either of those meanings as normative, with an intrinsic content independent of that ancient battle? We find here a linguistic parallel to William Blake's wry comment: "Both read the Bible day and night, but thou reads't black where I read white."

There is more here, however, than sarcasm and irony; Paul's objective was agreement. He wished to win over his audience to his own understanding of the situation. He wanted them to see that their world had, in actual fact, been crucified to them, and this insight entailed a basic acceptance of his assertion concerning *kosmos*. This reality was as ordered as the system of traditions, customs, and laws that had become enshrined in the Torah. This mode of ordering social behavior had persisted over many centuries and through many cultural changes. *Kosmos* was as cohesive as the ethnic group that accepted the sovereignty of Yahweh, as pervasive as the distinction between Jew and Gentile, as elemental as the observance of sacred geographies and calendars, as universal as the desire for internal and external securities, and as deeply rooted as divisions between sexes and classes. Wherever people accepted the importance of such divisions, there could be discerned the presence of this *kosmos*. It existed at the point where the elemental spirits claimed sovereignty and where that sovereignty was accepted. This *kosmos* was grounded in primordial religious traditions, structured by perennial religious needs, articulated in elaborate liturgies and fealties. The language, to be sure, was metaphorical in form and invidious in use, but the entity referred to was wholly substantial, not only in Paul's mind but also in the behavior of his readers. The very vigor of his attack and of their probable defense justifies our contention that this *kosmos* constituted their true habitat. In fact, one may well wonder whether any word other than *kosmos* would have conveyed more adequately both the irony and the actualities involved.

The conclusion is inescapable: to Paul the reality of the three crucifixions was essential to the gospel and to the existence of the Israel of God. It was only because of them that the apostle could declare: "For freedom Christ has set us free" (Gal. 5:1). Galatians has rightly been called a genuine emancipation proclamation, because the triple crucifixion liberates from all forms of racism, classism, and sexism (Gal. 3:28). Thus it is that one of the greatest—and most enigmatic—of the Messiah's gifts, a triple crucifixion, results in true liberty.

—— 18 ——
The Promise
(John)

Among the Messiah's gifts to the churches were his promises. Among the greatest of these promises is a saying of Jesus that has long hypnotized my imagination. In this tiny capsule a direct command is supported by the briefest of promises: "Ask and you will receive" (John 16:24). The command is so unqualified, the promise so inclusive, that any reader with an atom of skeptical inclination is bound to respond with disbelief. How is it that a teacher, any teacher, could be induced to sponsor such a fantasy? Was he aware of the odds against its acceptance? In making this promise was he entirely sane?

Although a similar saying appears in the other Gospels (Matthew 7:7; Mark 11:24; Luke 11:9), the teacher's wisdom is perhaps most at stake in the Fourth Gospel where, within the space of three chapters, the promise recurs no less than four times (John 14:12-15; 15:5-8, 16-18; 16:22-27). In these chapters the statement is not easily detached, but is woven so tightly into the fabric of thought as to threaten everything if the truth of this saying should be rejected.

Those who are acquainted with ancient literature, biblical and non-biblical alike, will recognize that a similar promise appears in many widely scattered writings. Numerous fables encourage children to believe in the miraculous fulfillment of an impossible dream. Every culture has a Cinderella legend that nourishes the hope that ugliness will be transformed into beauty, or rags into riches. At the end of the rainbow there can be found a pot of gold. Such legends invite, of course, aphorisms that express an opposite cynicism: "If wishes were horses, beggars might ride."

Yet the incredible legends live on as poignant tributes to the stubborn-
ness of human optimism. In these legends the power of rulers is gauged
by their ability to keep such promises; their generosity is measured by
their readiness to do so. An example is King Herod's promise to an expert
dancer who had pleased him (Mark 6:14-29).

We may suppose that the author of the Fourth Gospel was fully aware
of the widespread currency of this teaching and of its rootage in universal human hungers. He must also have recognized the futility of many of
the dreams it had nourished. Why then did he rely on it so fully? This is
the objective before us: to grasp the contribution of this teaching and to
assess its ontological weight by examining the structure of his thought.
We have divided the project into four stages. Because all primary ver-
sions of the saying appear within the farewell discourses, we will analyze
that *literary setting* to learn the evangelist's intentions. Because the teaching is lodged within an extensive constellation of idioms and images, we
will explore its interrelations with those *conceptual patterns* as a whole.
Because the evangelist was a church leader, concerned to discharge
duties toward a specific Christian audience, we will try to recapture a picture of the *social situation* that audience faced. Because an ultimate truth
is involved, we will assess the *ontological implications* of the teaching.

LITERARY SETTING

There is little doubt that John intended these five chapters (13–17) to
form a unit and to serve as a major pivot in his narrative. They mark the
point of transition from Jesus' ministry to his Passion. He has completed
his public work to and among "the Jews" and now engages in intimate
conversations around the table with his "friends." At this table he clearly
acts as their host. Later Christian readers could hardly read these chapters without hearing overtones of the eucharistic and baptismal liturgies.
In that day, Jewish Christians as surely recalled the full range of their
memories of the Passover preparations. The evangelist himself probably
had in mind the scriptural traditions of Moses' farewell to the twelve
tribes immediately before his death (Deut. 29–33). So the time and place
of this occasion evoked vast horizons of meaning for the evangelist and
his readers.

I have spoken of this place as if it could be located easily on the usual
map: the Holy Land, Judea, Jerusalem, and the Upper Room. That is

quite true. For John and his readers, however, another kind of map was even more important, a map of theological geography. This map marked the place where Jesus departed from the world and returned to the Father, in contrast to the disciples who remained "in the world." The promises were given by one who had come from God and was going to God, a prophet who could therefore speak simultaneously from both vantage points. The disciples also were related to both spaces, but in a different way: "You cannot follow me [there] now, but you will follow afterward" (John 13:36). This literary setting made it clear that the promise "whatever you ask . . ." was issued by a prophet who was at home in both places. Its plenitude ("whatever") emanated from the conjunction of these two spatial magnitudes. Addressed to disciples in the world by a leader who was leaving that world for the Father's house, the promise continued to bind them to him, so that henceforth their habitat would also include both places. Though they would ask "in the world," they would receive from the "Father."

But what is most important here is not a visualization of two maps but the way of thinking that perceives two places, one visible and the other invisible. Both of these places represent ways of expressing important relationships: Jesus' relation to God, to "the world," and to his disciples. One set of relationships is obtained in the world; another is obtained in the presence of God. All of these relationships, even that to the world, are person-to-person and not person-to-things. And all are ways of describing movements of coming and going, movements from origin to goal, movements that are oriented toward God, in "his house," which is seen as both primal and final reality.

In John's thought, different times as well as different spaces are involved. To be sure, there is a spatial coordinate in the saying: "I came from the Father and have come into the world. . . . I am leaving the world and am going to the Father" (John 16:28), but the different spaces are linked to two or three successive time zones. "A little while . . . a little while . . . a little while" (John 16:17-19).

John pictures the chief elements of the disciples' lack of understanding in the time before Jesus' glorification, when their incapacity took many forms. They did not, and in fact could not, understand his action in washing their feet (John 13:7); they were unable to understand his remarks about where he was going (John 13:33) or about his role as the way, the truth, and the life (John 14:5). Their involvement in both space and time was indicated by their scattering at the onset of crisis (John 16:32).

The next time frame was inaugurated by Jesus' glorification, because after that event the same men were able to believe his statement, "I am he" (John 13:19; 14:29). Their sorrow was then replaced by joy, turmoil by peace, fear by courage. Seeing Jesus, they were enabled to see and to know the Father, and to recognize the way to his truth and life (John 14:1-7). The Father and the Son had come to them in order to make their home with them (John 14:3). Their memories could now recall what he had taught them and what they had at first failed to understand.

The glorification of Jesus also inaugurated the period in which his disciples would fulfill their vocation as his messengers (John 13:20). They would continue to do his works (John 14:12), to produce fruit as branches of the vine (15:1-2), to give their witness *in* the world *to* that world. It was in that time that they would wash one another's feet (John 13:14-15) and obey his commandment to love one another (13:34-35). They would then live as those who had been cleansed by his *logos* (John 15:3), and would come to share in his knowledge of the Father (14:28) and in his joy (15:11).

The command to ask was assigned to this very time frame and was designed to provide the help that they would need during that period. Having been sent on assignment, on the mission that Jesus had begun, they would be wholly dependent on help that would be received from God, his Son, and the Paraclete. The teaching articulated that dependence.

Still another time frame should be mentioned—the time when they would complete their mission. The conversation clearly anticipated the time when Peter would fulfill his pledge to lay down his life for Jesus (John 13:37; 21:18). An hour would come when they would take the same way to the Father that Jesus had taken (John 13:36), the hour when their enemies would fully exploit their power (John 16:3). When disciples were marytred his promise would reach its intended goal: "I will take you to myself." "Where I am, there you may be" (John 14:3). That would be the hour when the command to ask anything in his name would become especially relevant (John 16:23-26).

To modern historians the confusion of these time frames in a single conversation creates huge difficulties, for they consider their task one of separating that initial event from the anachronistic distortions due to later developments. Actually, the human memory, whether individual or communal, consists at any given moment of a fusion of consecutive time frames into a single cumulative retrospect. Although hindsight often distorts the mirror, it also can give true insights into the meanings of earlier events. However, whether we prefer the perspective of the historian or that of the evangelist, we cannot deny that this particular command/promise was in fact oriented toward the vocation of the disciples during the period after Jesus' death. In his role as prophet Jesus here inaugurated the disciples' later work as his prophetic spokesmen, relaying their knowledge of the Father and the Son to their community and to the world.

CONCEPTUAL PATTERNS

The teaching with which we are concerned always appears within a complex constellation of motifs. To recover its affiliations to those motifs we should examine closely the following passages, recognizing that in separating them from their larger contexts we disrupt longer trains of thought.

Context 1

The one who believes in me will also do the works that I do and, in fact, will do greater works than these, because I am going to the Father. I will do whatever you ask in my name, so that the Father may be glorified in the Son. If in my name you ask me for anything, I will do it. If you love me, you will keep my commandments. (John 14:12-15)

Context 2

Whoever does not abide in me is thrown away like a branch and withers. . . . If you abide in me, and my words abide in you, ask for whatever you wish, and it will be done for you. My Father is glorified by this, that you bear much fruit and become my disciples. (John 15:6-8)

Context 3

You did not choose me but I chose you. And I appointed you to go and bear fruit, fruit that will last, so that the Father will give you whatever you ask him in my name. I am giving you these commands so that you may love one another. If the world hates you, be aware that it hated me before it hated you. (John 15:16-18)

Context 4

So you have pain now; but I will see you again, and your hearts will rejoice, and no one will take your joy from you. On that day you will ask nothing of me. . . . If you ask anything of the Father in my name, he will give it to you. Until now you have not asked for anything in my name. Ask and you will receive, so that your joy may be complete.

I have said these things to you in figures of speech. The hour is coming when I will no longer speak to you in figures, but will tell you plainly of the Father. On that day you will ask in my name. I do not say to you that I will ask the Father on your behalf; for the Father himself loves you, because you have loved me and have believed that I came from God. (John 16:22-27)

In every case the audience is the initial group of disciples (Judas excepted). In every case the time frame anticipated by the teaching is the period after Jesus' death and before their own. In that period, the act of asking will be qualified by at least five factors.

First, such action will be taken in the name of Jesus (Contexts 1, 3, 4). The frequency of this phrase, as well as its strategic placement, indicates the importance of this factor to John. The name of Jesus carries the authority and power of God, which Jesus conveys to the disciples. Wherever this name is used, there he will be present with his ability to perform the works of God.

Second, obedience to this command is closely affiliated with the works that they will do in his name (Context 1). These works appear to be synonymous with the fruit that they will bear as branches of the vine (Context 2, 3). Both works and fruit are typical Johannine images that presuppose direct continuity between Jesus' assignment and their assignment. In fact their works are seen to be his own works, which have been empowered by the event of his going to the Father (Context 1). These works become a form of asking, and asking becomes a form of working. The two actions have the same degree of credibility, authenticity, and reliability. Each action discloses a degree of separation—disciples from master—as well as a degree of interdependence since he will be present in their works (Context 3).

A third coordinate of asking is believing; in fact they are almost equivalent terms: to believe is to ask, and vice versa. This affiliation conditions the force of both terms: to the term believing it conveys a strong sense of trusting Jesus to do what he has promised; to the term asking it conveys a strong sense of personal response to the direct appeal of one who has been sent to them from God. Asking and believing reflect the fact that disciples have now entered the same realm, the same psychic space, where they are enclosed by the same communal boundaries and have begun to share the same field of force (Contexts 1, 2, 3).

Fourth, the character of this conceptual space is also indicated by the affiliation of asking and loving. Loving the master takes many forms: keeping his commandments, holding firm to his logos (John 14:15), doing his works, bearing his fruit, and asking in his name. By the same token, this love entails hatred by the world, for after his death the world would hate them as it had hated him before his death. Just as Jesus' love is coextensive with his sovereignty, so the world's hatred would be coextensive with the sovereignty of the prince of this world.

Fifth, the character of these boundaries to Jesus' command is perhaps best indicated by the term *abiding.* Their asking and their Lord's promising take place within the same space. The Greek verb *(menein)* is used some thirty-three times in the Gospel of John, and in many contexts it refers to an important reciprocal relationship. They abide in him; he abides in them. The bond between this Lord and "his own" embraces the other affiliations we have mentioned: the name, the works and fruit ("fruit that lasts"), the believing, the loving, and ultimately the asking.

Thus far we have focused attention upon the concepts affiliated with John's idea of asking; we now turn to similar affiliations with his idea of the promise: "I will do it." The first affiliation is that of glory and glorification, as reflected in the words "that the Father may be glorified in the Son" (Contexts 1, 2). A basic criterion of this glory had, of course, been made real in the Son's Passion (John 13:1-2; 17:15). It is highly significant that this same glory was to be realized in the works of the disciples, inasmuch as their "greater works" would in fact become works done by the ascended Son. Here the evangelist took care to link the promise of fulfilled requests not to the gratification of the disciples, but to the glorification of the Father. In biblical thought, of course, this concept of glory carried major ontological implications, far surpassing psychic experience or social prestige. It represented nothing less than the basic purpose of God in his work of creation.

The idea of fulfillment was also closely affiliated with the idea of sending. In his prayer in John 17, Jesus' confidence that his own requests would be granted was based on the truth that God had sent him for this very purpose. None of those persons whom God had given him would be lost. The success of his work validated God's commissioning. So, too, the fruit of his disciples' work, which constituted the inner substance of their asking, would validate their commissioning. The chain of askings and the chain of fulfillments were thus inseparable from the chain of sendings, clear evidence of God's involvement in their existence.

Similar evidence was provided by those gifts that constituted God's granting of their requests. The gift of peace was one example of this; so, too, was the gift of joy (Context 4). The gift of love, in particular, illustrated the tight integration of the evangelist's conceptions of asking and receiving. Asking was an action expressive of the community's love for God; fulfilling the request was an action expressive of God's love for this community (Contexts 1, 3, 4). Moreover, these two actions could not be disjoined.

SOCIAL SITUATION

What specific challenges were facing John and his readers during the time when the Gospel was being written? We are now especially concerned with the mission of these charismatics in the world after the death of the bearer of revelation. Their assignments from him demand the full acceptance of homelessness and the surrender of family ties, along with the abandonment of possessions. "Servants are not greater than their master" (John 15:20).

These more general pictures take on a harsh immediacy when we look closely at two statements that are strategically located near the center of the farewell discourse. First of all, consider this statement: "I have said these things to you to keep you from stumbling" (John 16:1). We can be confident that "these things" refers to the surrounding conversation as a whole. We can be equally confident that the statement envisions the anticipated period after Jesus' death when these followers would be particularly vulnerable to "stumbling" as a consequence of their work in his name. When they faced death for their faith, Jesus' disciples would be tempted to fall away and surrender their share in Jesus' victory over the world.

That such death was a lively prospect is proved by the second statement. "They will put you out of the synagogues. Indeed, an hour is coming when those who kill you will think that by doing so they are offering worship to God" (John 16:2). No statement in the Gospel is more valuable in defining the orientation of the evangelist as he edited these discourses.

By implication the pronoun "they" stands against its antithesis, "we." *They* are members of the synagogues who have enough popular support and enough authority to exclude these wandering charismatics from their membership—an action stemming from popularity, prestige, scriptural legitimacy, and the aura of tradition belonging to *them*.

That they will "put you out" tells us that these charismatics have been insiders, attempting to carry out a mission in, through, and to their neighbors in the synagogues. However, they have now become, in a real sense, orphaned from their native religious habitat. That they will be put out of "the synagogues" tells us that this penalty will be painful because those excluded had been at home in the synagogues, had received their training there, had invested their loyalties there, and had accepted God's covenants with Israel there. Exclusion would represent deep personal anguish as well as severe strain to their new faith and vocation. John's reference to "the hour," because these same discourses spoke so frequently of Jesus' hour, linked the completion of the disciples' task to Jesus' completion of his own task at his hour. That the disciples are now defined as martyrs ("whoever kills you") demonstrates the radical antithesis between these two groups of insiders: those willing to kill and those willing to be killed. The conceptual boundary between the two groups was even greater than any institutional boundary. To fall away would reestablish the bond with the majority group; to remain faithful to Jesus would be to recognize the external breach as permanent. Finally, their equation of killing with "offering worship to God" shows that the boundary between "us" and "them" is grounded in contradictory conceptions of what the God of Israel demands of Israel. To accept *their* conception would induce a person to fall away. To defend *our* conception is to hold fast to Jesus' *logos*.

We should be capable of genuine empathy with the leaders of the synagogue who hated Jesus' disciples. John himself stresses their loyalty to God and their willingness to make sacrifices in his service. Every Sabbath found them worshiping the God of Israel; every festival found them rejoicing in the traditions inherited from the fathers. Devoted to Moses and the Torah, they awaited the fulfillment of God's promises to Abraham. It was in good faith and in response to a good conscience that they took such vigorous action against these ostensible enemies of God's people.

Our empathy with this majority position of the synagogues is desirable for reasons other than that of maintaining scholarly neutrality. It is needed before we can fully appreciate the position of the minority.

Empathy with the opponents of Jesus' movement allows us to sense how attractive the option of "stumbling" would be. When we realize how attractive this option was we can assess the strength of the inner, communal cohesion that could prevent loyal Jews from choosing that option. In fact we need an empathy with both sides to comprehend the intensity of feeling that permeates the farewell discourse and especially the prayer of Jesus. The new boundary separating insiders from outsiders would have cut through many families and turned many close friends into bitter enemies. The intensity of this personal conflict was indicated in the identification of their ultimate enemy as "the ruler of this world."

Therein lay an ironic use of the term *world*, since in this context it referred to a devoted religious community for whom separation from the pagan and corrupt *world* had been a major motive. At the same time, this identification assigned ultimate guilt not to the hostile kinfolk and friends themselves but to the "father of lies" who had deceived them. John used the farewell of Jesus as an appropriate occasion for showing that Jesus' ultimate enemy (John 14:30) remained the ultimate enemy of his disciples after his death (John 16:11; 17:15).

ONTOLOGICAL IMPLICATIONS

In the verses at the beginning of John 16 there is still another statement that formulates the issues in the briefest possible way. Speaking of those who would kill his followers as a way of making an offering to God, Jesus said: "They will do this because they have not known the Father or me" (John 16:3; also 16:21). Here John forces us to visualize two opposing groups, a group of murderers and a group of martyrs. Not all members of the majority would have fully approved the murders; not all members of the minority would have readily accepted martyrdom. Even so, the existence of the extremes discloses what was at stake in the conflict. Moreover, the issue could not be resolved in terms of a simple human judgment concerning which set of prejudices was in fact right. By their actions both murderers and martyrs were obeying what they presumed to be divine orders. Their actions demonstrated the incompatibility of two theologies, in spite of the fact that both groups were Jews, pledged to obey the God of Israel. Each group thought of itself as chosen to be children of that God, and each group thought of its enemies (fellow Jews) as children of the devil. The greater the loyalty, the more acute the mutual hostility became. In a civil war like this no third party could serve as mediator, for the point at issue was the divine will, and neither side would entrust to a third party the right to reveal that will or to define the proper mode of obedience. And because both sides were convinced that the God of Abraham was the God of all creation, the theological issue was nothing less than the ultimate ontological issue: which God was the Creator of all things?

So, too, the situation of martyrdom adds ontological resonance to the concept of works. We have seen how all asking had been correlated with the idea of working. The basic Johannine definition of works, whether those of God or of Jesus, focused upon the action of giving life to the dead (John 5:21). It had in fact been this action on the part of Jesus that had prompted "the Jews" to seek to kill Jesus (John 5:18). Jesus promised those who followed him on the way of martyrdom that they would do greater works. By raising the question of the efficacy of this promise, the death of those martyrs became in fact a mode of asking in Jesus' name. Their request would contain petitions not only for their own resurrection but also for forgiveness and life for their opponents. Thus the command/promise of the martyred Jesus served to set the continuing works of his followers within the context of ultimate horizons.

If we now return to one of our initial questions we may discern some possible answers. Why should so fantastic and incredible a promise have become so central a feature in Johannine thought? The high degree of incredibility is an honest recognition of the paradoxical contrast between the humiliation and weakness implicit in martyrdom and the glory and power that this Father conferred on the martyrs. The incredibility of this command/promise was used to show the relation between one ontic space and another. One space was the realm of light, that primal light that on the very first day of creation had disclosed, in response to God's word, the opposing realm of darkness (Gen. 1:1-5; John 1:1-5).

Finally, the religious civil war in which Jesus' followers were engaged helps to explain the ontological dimensions in the concepts of reciprocal love, glorification, and abiding. All of these concepts are reciprocal in that the same actions spring from activity shared by God and the band of servants. In this gift, the asking and the doing are one.

The Thanksgiving
(The New Testament)[1]

Why should an essay about Søren Kierkegaard be included in a book on biblical theology and in part 4 on the Messiah's gifts and the churches' gratitude? Merely this: there exists a profound correlation between Kierkegaard's understanding of gratitude and the gratitude of the New Testament writers for the Messiah's gifts—a gratitude that is in itself a gift. Readers who are familiar with the language of scripture will discover in what follows abundant evidence of that correlation in the frequency with which Kierkegaard thought as well as wrote in that language. I admit, of course, that Søren Kierkegaard's key terms—synthesis, temporal, eternal—are the coin of the philosophical classroom rather than of the early church. A definition, roughly equivalent but more in tune with biblical music, is this: gratitude is the place where, through gifts of grace and peace, God the Father and Jesus the Son create a new heaven and a new earth for the grateful. With this chapter we make a pivot in this final section of the book, turning from the Messiah's gifts to the churches' responses in gratitude—in thanksgiving, mission, and song.

The centennial of Søren Kierkegaard's death (d. 1855) brings into conjunction two things that are incommensurable. On the one hand, it evokes our personal and corporate gratitude for this man, a gratitude that is nonetheless real for all its intangible subjectivity. On the other hand, it marks an exact measurement of temporal succession, which is nonetheless significant for all its impersonal objectivity. Apart from our indebtedness it would not occur to us to number the years. Apart from chronological transience we would not be reminded of time-transcending indebtedness.

This conjunction of two incommensurable and yet inseparable factors has reminded me that we stand at some distance from the thought of Søren Kierkegaard himself. The contour of his thanksgiving is quite different from ours, as is his appraisal of the significance of temporal succession and measurement. It may therefore be worth our energy to explore together his understanding of gratitude and its relation to time. The justification of such an inquiry depends primarily, of course, on whether thanksgiving was in fact of decisive importance to Kierkegaard himself. That it was is a firm conviction of mine.

Another conviction is that the interpretation of Søren Kierkegaard has suffered from a neglect of such categories as gratitude. Often the historian of ideas goes astray most radically when he ignores what was actually the inner passion of a particular thinker. And this is what has usually happened in studies of Kierkegaard. Nothing is more constitutive of Kierkegaard's self-awareness than his thankfulness, yet few things are treated so seldom in books about him. His thought was in constant motion away from and back toward this magnetic pole. The very center of his thought was the awareness of God-relatedness as constitutive of the self. And to him no activity was more creative or revealing of the self than gratitude. I am convinced that a more discerning appraisal of this act leads to an enhanced appreciation of Kierkegaard's mind and spirit.

Let us begin by paying heed to his own testimony:

> I have had more joy in the relation of obedience to God than in thoughts that I produced. . . . My relationship to God is a reflection-relationship, is inwardness in reflection, so that even in prayer my *forte* is thanksgiving.[2]

Why should Kierkegaard have had more joy in his relation to God than in anything else? Surely because to him life itself is constituted by God-relatedness. Existence as a person is impossible apart from this relationship. Nothing is more native to true selfhood, therefore, than prayer. If life is God-relatedness, then nothing creates and sustains life more directly than prayer, and in nothing is life more fully embodied than in prayer. The person who reflects about this life until relationship to God becomes "a reflection-relationship" will naturally move in the direction of giving thanks.

To Kierkegaard, therefore, thanksgiving was not the minimal act, the introductory step, the glib opening of a conversation that immediately gives place to more pressing concerns of petition, confession, absolution, or intercession. It was the end as much as the beginning, the saturating medium of petitions and confessions, the deepest fountain of forgiveness and intercession. As in his praying, so too in his living and thinking, the external, visible actions were but the outward side of this inward relationship to God, a relationship dominated by gratitude.

But some will protest: have you forgotten the constant tension, the bitter controversy, the unremitting melancholy in his story? Are these the marks of a man whose consciousness was oriented inwardly by gratitude? The apparent incongruity here may stem from differing ideas of what thanksgiving really is. To Kierkegaard giving thanks is not an easy response of the heart, but one of its most difficult movements. Prayer springs not from an unreflective self but from the self concentrated in intense reflection and double-reflection. To be empowered to give thanks at all times and for every circumstance is a seal of redemption that lies on both sides of strenuous effort and profound suffering. The enemies of gratitude are most implacable, devious, and deceptive; and these enemies already hold a beachhead in our own minds. The ingratitude of Adam can be named and exorcised only by the gratitude of Christ. Only by the strength that is made perfect in weakness can a person become victor in a subtle struggle with Satan wherein the ultimate decisiveness of victory is completely hidden by the unobtrusive silence and the misleading triviality of the battlefield. In short, the *telos* and consummation of God's entire "training in Christianity" is nothing less than the full release of praise to God for his inexhaustible bounty.

It is easy for us to treat gratitude as a response of person to person, which only for the religious person is gradually extended to include God as its object. This makes it all too natural for us to treat thankfulness as relatively nonessential in defining our selfhood. But for Kierkegaard thanksgiving is authentic only when it expresses our total being, our God-relatedness. God is never the third party in an act of giving thanks.[3] From God alone comes every good and perfect gift. From him come *nothing* but good and perfect gifts. It is quite impossible to grasp in any paragraph the wealth of Kierkegaard's discourses on this theme. This wealth lies nearest to the surface, perhaps, in his expositions of the Bible, whether he is dealing with Job[4] or with James,[5] whether he is meditating on the apostle Paul[6] or the disciple Judas,[7] whether he is analyzing the sin of Adam[8] or the obedience of Christ.[9]

The overwhelming and inexhaustible wealth of God's gifts surely lies behind the choice of a motto for *Point of View:*

What shall I say? My words alone
Do not express my duty.
O God, how great thy wisdom is,
Thy goodness, might and beauty. (Brorson)

To Kierkegaard, however, God does much more than place us in his debt and then wait for us to return thanks. God is the subject as well as the object of thanksgiving. It is God who is active in the movement of the grateful heart. God's Spirit is vocal in the *Abba*, in inexpressible, deep yearning, and in the whole process of reflective inwardness. Gratitude articulates simultaneously our nothingness and the sufficiency of God, who is at work in us to create something out of nothing. To give thanks is an expression of inwardness, and inwardness is "the determinant of the eternal in man."[10] "If every man does not essentially participate in the absolute, then the whole game's up."[11]

This participation in the absolute, however, preserves the qualitative distinction between the thankful self and God. Kierkegaard recognized that the apostle's rhetorical questions must be answered in the negative:

Who has known the mind of the Lord?
Or who has been his counselor?
Or who has given a gift to him, to receive a gift in return?
(Rom. 11:34-35)[12]

On the other hand, Kierkegaard realized that although we cannot repay God's gift, we can respond to God's gift of himself in his gift. We can stand in fear and trembling, in trust and surrender, in repentance and reverence. These responses to God are forms of gratitude, forms in which the God who is active in the giving of thanks is the same God as the God to whom thanks are given.

We can never act, even in the giving of thanks, without dependence on God who has given us not only the gifts but also the power to thank God. This is why Kierkegaard found a childish delight in offering his whole work as a spy in gratitude to God. He handed his entire authorship back to God "with more diffidence than a child when it gives as a present to the parents an object which the parents had presented to the child." He was diffident, but he was joyful because he knew that God would not be so cruel as to take the gift back and to say, "This is [my] property."[13] Our thanks are genuine only if we make an "honest effort . . . to do something by way of compensation, without shunning any sacrifice

232

or labour in the service of truth."[14] To be thankful is to be faithful, but this faithfulness will always fuse together an inward seriousness that glorifies God with an inward testing that destroys any self-importance.[15] The more earnest our response, the more must we appropriate humor to protect the God-relationship.

This welding of earnestness and humor is imperative if the grateful are to avoid the twin traps of absolutizing the relative and of relativizing the absolute. Genuine gratitude relates a person simultaneously to the absolute and the relative, to the universal and the particular, to God and those met on the street. Without seriousness *and* humor, gratitude easily becomes the occasion for getting lost either in the infinite or in the finite. These were very real dangers for Kierkegaard, dangers that made genuine gratitude one true antidote to "the sickness unto death." He overcame despair by an activity of thankful faith, in which every particular gift was the expression of the one incalculable gift, every discrete happenstance was related to divine governance, and the relationship to every person was a particular instance of the relationship of both persons to God.

Although Kierkegaard never allows us to forget that gratitude is God-relationship, neither does he forget that this relationship embraces all of our other relationships. In teaching us to be grateful God employs not only the lilies of the field but also the cup of water and the neighbor. And there was one neighbor for whom Kierkegaard was especially grateful: "that individual whom with joy and gratitude I call my reader."[16] We recall that Kierkegaard addressed many of his discourses to this individual. We recall, too, that his Danish public found these discourses neither witty, clever, nor of great theological or philosophical significance. They took with great excitement what he held out with his left hand, but scorned his right. We must concede that in New York as much as in Copenhagen, in 1955 as much as in 1855, these discourses in his right hand are still virtually ignored. Yet Kierkegaard's word remains true. He is grateful for anyone who takes gratefully what he holds out with his right hand. Søren Kierkegaard insisted that this *reader* contributes more than the *author*. Now I am sure that among us there should be at least one who qualifies as "that single individual." This individual would say: "No, the author contributes more than I do. I am indebted to him." Both of these statements, of course, can be true at once—in fact, both are always true where gratitude works its miracle of abundance. Each person is convinced that the other's contribution is the greater. Thanksgiving celebrates a relationship that destroys *quid pro quo* logic and creates a qualitative increment of debt in some sort of infinite proportion to the reality of gratitude. By thanksgiving for one another, we participate in the infinite beneficence of God and in the mysterious process by which the prodigal Father imparts everything to us who have nothing.

Gratitude, then, is a miraculous event wherein God's abundance becomes available for all, and human cups run over in glorifying God. This event demonstrates how intrinsic is the interplay of subjective and objective factors. The act of thanksgiving is genuine only to the degree that it is fully subjective, only when it is the act of the real self, at the very roots of its selfhood. Any retreat from subjectivity is as destructive to gratitude as it is to the self. Only as it is my deepest embodiment of deepest indebtedness is it gratitude at all.

But the more fully subjective I become in recognizing this debt, the more fully I recognize that it is a debt owed to Another. Thanksgiving at its deepest level turns the most reflective self outward toward its source and its sustaining power. The pervasive joy of the grateful heart is joy over another's amazing grace and unwearied faithfulness. The subjective act breaks the bonds of self-centeredness and frees the self to obey the first commandment. Both the reflection and the double-reflection become inherently dialectical, so long as they spring from gratitude and produce gratitude. It is before God that *an* individual becomes *the* individual, and *the* individual before God is most fully human, most fully realizes the divine image, most fully appropriates the self's human vocation and destiny, when the individual gives thanks to God.

It is my conviction that we are in the habit of undervaluing the onto-logical weight of this gratitude. We assume that the self has the option of giving or refusing to give thanks, and that regardless of the option chosen the self remains the same person. This choice has little to do with existence, with the issue: to be or not to be. But Kierkegaard recognized a genuine ontological reality in gratitude. A self does not exist and then become thankful. Rather, in and through thankfulness the self is born. In gratitude, the self's God-relationship gives birth to a self-awareness and a neighbor-awareness that together constitute the self.

Between the self and God there is at once an infinite qualitative distinction and an unbreakable bond. The prayer of gratitude appropriates and preserves both the relationship and the distinction. The acknowledgment of total indebtedness is a simultaneous recognition of dependence and distinction. The grateful self discovers that the synthesis of relationship and distinction is the source not of confusion and of disorientation but of order and reorientation, the very substance of selfhood. Gratitude discovers that the relation to the God who is qualitatively different is a relation that constitutes the self as a self. Prayer discloses the spirit as the bond that unites the temporal and the eternal in the self, because the prayer of thanksgiving is the act of this spirit.[17]

Existence is bifrontal. To be as bifrontal as existence requires an existing spirit. Always giving thanks to God means that a person is becoming this existing infinite spirit. Reflective prayer is the supreme activity of "the subjective existing thinker."[18]

An alternate way of stating this is to recall Kierkegaard's definition of the self as a synthesis of the temporal and the eternal. By his gifts to us God participates in temporal things. The gifts are temporal, but God gives himself wholly in all of his gifts. The incarnation and the atonement constitute the measure in which God is present in all of his gifts. Between each of his temporal gifts and his eternal life there is an infinite qualitative difference and yet an unbreakable, intimate relationship. God's creative works glorify God as their Creator. None of these works is more fully qualified to glorify God than is the creature made in God's own image. A person, shaped in God's image, "becomes a self" by the gratitude expressed in praise and obedience. Gratitude signals the fusion in the spirit of infinite poverty and infinite riches. The cry of thanks is the birth-cry of a person who is created out of nothing, who becomes conscious of mysterious, miraculous existence as a synthesis of the temporal and the eternal. The act of acknowledging dependence on God is the initial act of self-recognition.

By its intrinsic nature, therefore, the act of thanksgiving defeats various tendencies in the self to escape its rootage in either the eternal or the temporal.[19] On the one hand lies the tendency to treat the temporal as insignificant and to desire "in time to be merely eternal." But if a cup of cold water is a divine gift, if a moment of suffering yields an eternal weight of glory, then it is sinful for us to make ourselves temporally as light as possible so that the weight of our eternal selves may be heavier. This is a movement away from gratitude, away from selfhood, and toward a fantastic existence.[20] Gratitude makes it impossible to equate the temporal with the sinful, for everything temporal becomes good when it is received with thankfulness.[21] In a similar fashion the act of gratitude destroys all despairing views of time as the infinitely vanishing succession of present moments into the oblivion of the past.

On the other hand, the grateful heart will reject every temptation to escape the eternal by obsession with the temporal. It will not tolerate a worldliness that defines selfhood wholly by temporal categories or limits one's horizons to temporal process. Nor will it accept the removal of the eternal to an abstract, distant boundary that impinges at no point on daily decisions or on the progress of universal history. Thanksgiving celebrates the presence of the eternal within the confines of the temporal.[22] It relates one immediately to the eternal.[23] It articulates the truth that there is more joy in heaven over one individual who relates the self inwardly to God than over universal history that is related only externally to the eternal.[24] Thus is one freed from enchantment either with the temporal or with the eternal.

Although gratitude thus prevents any destruction of the synthesis, it does not permit one to determine the precise boundary between the separate elements. The act of thanksgiving so unites the temporal and the eternal in us that only God is in a position to determine the points where they meet. When the self tries to dissolve the synthesis it destroys the self. The self then seeks to form a conception of God in its own likeness rather than allowing God to reform the self in God's likeness. This is why the self can never trust its own ability to separate good gifts from bad, or infinite indebtedness from immediate debts. The measure of gratitude is whether we thank God at all times and for everything. To be thankful in these terms requires a teleological suspension of our finite understanding. This, at least, was Kierkegaard's experience: "In my God-relationship I have to learn to give up my finite understanding, and therewith the custom of discrimination which is natural to me, that I may be able with divine madness to give thanks always."[25]

This madness, however, is a *divine* madness, because it is a mark of our willingness to live in the only element that provides the proper air for our lungs. It marks the transition of the self into "the true liberation from finitude." This liberation is so amazing that the freed heart will forget its desire to dissolve the synthesis. Because the synthesis is realized through the giving of thanks, it will be preserved better by respecting the dialectical boundaries of earnestness and humor than by curious efforts of the speculative mind to assign to the two elements in the synthesis a quantitative weight.

The truth of this may become more apparent if we think for a moment of the links between thanksgiving and love. Both love and gratitude are finite expressions of an infinite indebtedness. Both are expressions of the self as a synthesis. Neither can be etherialized into the eternal or smothered in the temporal. Both recognize that "God has the first priority" and that "everything which a man owns is pledged as security for this claim."[26] To both, "the pure heart is first and last a bound heart . . . bound inimitably to God."[27] The infinitely bound heart is the infinitely free heart. It is bound and free to give itself away. Whoever loves is in debt to the beloved. By loving, the lover comes into the relation of infinite debt.[28] Christianity begins with what everyone must become—the free indebted lover. Love grounds our selfhood in God's eternal *telos*. Listen to the parable:

> When a fisherman has caught a fish and wishes to keep it alive, what must he do? He must at once place it in water. . . . Why? . . . Because water is the natural element of fish. . . . The natural element of love is infinity, inexhaustible, immeasurable. If therefore you wish to preserve your love then you must take care that by the aid of infinite indebtedness, ensnared by liberty and life, it remains in its element.[29]

Gratitude, love, and freedom . . . these have an ontological density as constituting the very being of those who participate in the eternal history. Where the self remains in this native element of indebtedness, liberty, and love, the teleological suspension of the historical takes place. The historical restricts life to the life span, restricts love to one's immediate neighbors, restricts freedom and human gratitude to temporal categories alone. But when by thanksgiving and love the heart is bound to God, it shares in an "eternal history" that does not end with the grave. The span of earthly love constitutes only "a very little section within that eternal history."[30] The debt binds the debtor into a teleological history that includes the temporal and simultaneously transcends it. One measure of the teleological suspension of the historical is the transformation in meaning of the past, the present, and the future. Let us consider the *tense* that was so central in Kierkegaard's own experience: the future. To Kierkegaard, the future is the mode by which the eternal has chosen to have dealings with the temporal.[31]

Apart from its relation to the eternal, the future does not really exist. Yet this nonexistent future confronts the self as the realm of the possible, the inscrutable, the manifold, and the indeterminate. This future generates anxiety and dread. This dread, in turn, creates a false self, a self that considers itself dependent upon the contingent. Obsessed by the future, the self restlessly seeks "to force or to coax from the mystery its explanation" but in vain.[32] It becomes more and more enslaved to the temporal, less and less capable of gratitude to the eternal for the temporal. The self moves farther and farther away from itself, that is, from the synthesis of the eternal and the temporal.

But when in faith the self accepts itself as God's creature, the future is overcome. This victory over the future is the source of freedom and love. It is celebrated by the act of giving thanks. The recognition of total gratitude transforms the self and the self's relation to the future. The coming days remain crammed with manifold possibilities, but these contingencies are subordinated to the reality of God's promise. Expectation of the future becomes the point where the eternal meets the self in redemptive creation. The self is reconstituted and liberated. Its preoccupation with the future is replaced by the freedom of gratitude. Thankful to God for God's future, the self becomes itself in the present act of obedience and love.

By disclosing a new future, the activity of thanksgiving discloses as well a new present and a new past. Having conquered the future, the grateful self comes to understand how that vanishing atom of time—the present—can become as well an atom of eternity, and how the past is preserved, not in the present but in the eternal.

Perhaps the best example of how thanksgiving sublimates past, present, and future into the eternal is offered by Kierkegaard himself. Every day, according to the *Point of View*, he "ascertained and convinced [himself] anew that a God exists." Every day was repeated, "my prayer of thanksgiving for the indescribable things He has done for me, so infinitely much more than ever I could have expected." By his grateful prayer he voiced his amazement "at God, at His love and at what a man's impotence is capable of with His aid." Søren Kierkegaard had no fear that eternity might be tiresome, "since it is exactly the situation I need so as to have nothing else to do but to give thanks."[33]

— 20 —
The Mission
(Romans)

As we noted in the previous chapter, the gratitude of the churches for the gifts of the Messiah was generative of the churches' thanksgiving. Another response of the church in gratitude included from the very beginning an embrace of the Messiah's own mission into the world. It is the task of this chapter to explore that response of the church in mission, or the coalescence of biblical theology and missiology.

One aim of missiology is a more adequate understanding of the apostolic task of the church. One aim of exegetical theology is a more adequate understanding of a biblical writer. When, therefore, the exegete deals with the apostle Paul, and when missiology accepts Paul's apostolic work as normative for the continuing mission of the church, then these two aims coalesce. This coalescence reaches its maximum when we seek to expound the Epistle to the Romans, for here the mind of the apostle with reference to his own mission is most clearly disclosed. It may therefore be of value to both missiology and exegetical theology if we select for scrutiny several passages in which the apostle indicates a strong connection between his sense of obligation and gratitude, on the one hand, and his motivation as an apostle on the other. Romans 1:14 is an example: "I am a debtor both to Greeks and to barbarians, both to the wise and to the foolish." It was because of this obligation that Paul was eager to preach the gospel in Rome.

My attention was drawn to this verse and its implications for missiology when a missionary who had recently returned from China asked a series of provocative questions about Romans 1:14. "Why did Paul consider himself a debtor to people whom he had never seen? What had they done for him to place him in their debt? When was the debt incurred? How could it be paid?"

In ordinary speech, a sense of debt presupposes (1) a gift from one person to another and (2) knowledge and appreciation of both the gift and the giver. In this case, it is clear that neither did Paul know his creditors nor had they given him anything. All commentators are surely right in tracing the source of the gift to Jesus Christ, and in stressing the fact that it was this gift that produced in Paul a compelling sense of apostolic responsibility for the Gentiles. The question remains whether we can press beyond this sense of responsibility *for* the Gentiles to the sense of indebtedness *to* them.

For Paul a debt to Christ was immediately transmuted into a debt to those whom Christ wished to bring to salvation through them. This principle was in fact central to Paul's thought. Obligation to him who died produces obligation to those for whom he died. This very "law" applies with special force to the particularity of Paul's call as an apostle. God's intention in bringing Paul to faith in Christ had been to send him as a "minister of Christ Jesus to the Gentiles" (Rom. 15:16). To the extent that Paul was indebted to God for this call, to that very extent he was indebted to those Gentiles for whose sake God had called him. And the same logic applies to every person who is called to any form of service (*diakonia*). That person is placed under a vast obligation to those whom God intends, through that *diakonia*, to draw within the realm of grace. Thus faith in Christ inevitably creates a mutuality of indebtedness. It impels the faithful, in love for others, to seek to elicit and to strengthen faith in them. Only faith of this quality is apostolic. Such faith recognizes that the believer is as deeply indebted to unbelievers as to Christ, as deeply indebted to the foolish as to the wise. Here is a debt of whose genuineness there can be no doubt. Yet this debt depends not in the least upon the tangible contributions of the creditors to the debtors, but wholly upon the gift of God in Christ. It may then be said that, as Paul sees it, Christ makes everyone a debtor to all those for whom Christ died. God in Christ thereby creates a fabric of mutual interdependence that defies the usual method of computing obligations in proportion to tangible, direct contributions.

This new interdependence is not two-sided but triangular. For example, Paul teaches that Gentiles are indebted to the Jews because Christ became a servant to the circumcised for the sake of the Gentiles (Rom. 15:7-12). So, too, Paul magnifies his ministry to the Gentiles for the sake of the Jews (Rom. 11:13-14). This triangular logic also lies back of his injunction to the "strong in faith" (who were predominantly Gentile) that they should honor their obligation to the "weak in faith" (who were predominantly Jewish, Rom. 14:1-12). This obligation was incurred when Christ chose not to please himself but to accept as his own the reproaches that in all justice should fall on others (Rom. 15:1-3). In Christ, therefore, each man becomes a debtor to everyone.

This is relevant to Paul's conviction that the Gentile Christians owed a debt to "the poor among the saints in Jerusalem" (Rom. 15:26). It is altogether too simple to explain this debt, as is usually done, by *quid pro quo* reasoning. Such reasoning can be expressed thus: "Gentile Christians owed the Jerusalem Church for the initial gift of the gospel. They should seek to repay this spiritual debt with material support." Such an explanation assumes too much. Had these "poor saints" really been instrumental in evangelizing believers in Macedonia and Achaia? Had they been the ones to commission Paul and to support his campaigns? Nothing of this sort is necessary to Paul's thought. What is necessary is the reality of mutual indebtedness to Christ that is voiced in 2 Corinthians 8:5. Christ had become a servant of the circumcised in order that the Gentiles might "rejoice . . . with his people" (Rom. 15:10). The same grace that had obligated Paul to the barbarians and the foolish had made the "strong in faith" debtors to the weak whom they despised (Rom. 14:1-4), and had made all Gentile believers debtors to the saints in Jerusalem (Rom. 15:27). This common debt gives to believers a common mission, whether the debt be honored by welcoming all to table fellowship, by sharing in a philanthropic contribution, or by supporting the missionary campaign to Spain.

This understanding of debt underlies Romans 8:12. Here, to be sure, only one line of an antithetical couplet appears: "We are debtors, not to the flesh." But the context almost shouts the second line: "We are debtors to the Spirit." The Spirit of Christ dwells in believers, sealing them as Christ's own possession. This Spirit is alive and life-giving, being in fact the Spirit of him who raised Jesus from the dead (Rom. 8:9-11). As debtors to this Spirit, believers walk by it, putting to death the deeds of the body and suffering with Christ. The debt determines the whole mode of living and working. When one walks according to the flesh, existence is an embodiment of a debt to the flesh (Rom. 8:12). But if the ultimate debt is to the Spirit, the whole direction and content of existence is transformed. The whole of Romans 8 may be construed as a description of the magnitude of debt to "the Spirit of life in Christ Jesus." So certain of this is Paul that he detects at once the ultimate form of apostasy in any doctrine or practice that implies that God could or should be indebted to us (Rom. 4:4; 11:35). Paul's concept of debt, therefore, has tremendous relevance to the character of missionary obligation: a negative relevance in disclosing the form of false motives; a positive relevance in accenting the power of the true motive.

One further observation should be made about this concept of debt. To Paul the acknowledgment of indebtedness is immediately translated into the sense of gratitude. This is not so for many people and for many debts. We often respond with repugnance to the image of ourselves as debtors, just as we instinctively dislike the image of ourselves as slaves. Most debts represent a burden of obligation that inhibits our independence. They exert a constraint that makes us more grateful when a debt has been repaid than when it was first extended. Yes, in human terms, indebtedness often diminishes gratitude. But the debt of which Paul speaks is very different. In this case, recognition of debt is synonymous with giving thanks. As we turn to his conception of thanksgiving, therefore, we remain in the same circle of relationships. The Epistle to the Romans appears to say little about thanksgiving, much less than do Paul's other letters. And in the two passages with which we deal, the presence of thanksgiving is often overlooked. Attention centers on other concepts, perhaps because we assume that anyone can readily grasp what Paul means by giving thanks. A closer study, however, reveals both how central and how subtle is Paul's thought.

Let us look, for example, at Romans 1:18-24. What is to the apostle the deepest, most stubborn root of sin, the root from which all sinning springs? What leaves all without excuse? How do we all become fools whose "minds were darkened"? What is it that brings God's wrath against all ungodliness? Why does God give us over to the lusts of our hearts? How do we suppress the truth? The answer to all these questions is the same. And until we understand that answer it appears to be both anticlimactic and inadequate: "they did not honor him as God or give thanks to him" (Rom. 1:21). It is quite usual to associate ingratitude with a breach of courtesy or simply a lack of good taste. By contrast Paul associates it with its worst fruits, and by implication views it as worse than all those fruits.

This passage, however, does more than accent the dire results of ingratitude. It makes giving thanks to God virtually equivalent to honoring God as God. To give thanks is to glorify God, and to do all things to his glory (1 Cor. 10:30-31). This presupposes that all things come from God and are intended to move toward God. It is because we are indebted to God for all things that we should give thanks at all times and for everything. These are the basic assumptions lying behind Paul's words, but their basic thrust is to make clear the fateful and inevitable results of thanklessness: futile thinking, deceived minds, diseased relationships, enslavement to self, and the resulting malice and covetousness.

It is in another passage (Rom. 14:1-2) that we find intimations of the positive power of gratitude. Here again the modern reader easily misses the radical implications, probably because for modern Gentile Christianity the dietary commands of the Torah have lost their crucial significance. In Paul's day, observance of those commands had long been regarded as a clear mark of the people of God. It was then a very controversial thing to contend that the act of giving thanks for food had the power to make all foods clean. To Paul this act exerted an even greater power. It destroyed the barrier between Jews and Gentiles, a barrier that was otherwise insuperable. One gives thanks and eats; another gives thanks and refrains from eating. Their common act of giving thanks not only took precedence over their diverse behavior; it also established a covenant fellowship that transcended deeply imbedded and scripturally supported walls of social, economic, and religious division. The key question becomes not "shall I defy the Torah by eating proscribed foods or by treating all days alike?" but simply "do I give thanks to God for this food or this day?" Here Paul had in mind much more than the routine verbal use of a table grace; he was speaking of a pervasive attitude toward every dawn and evening that every day contains. To give thanks is "to live to the Lord," accepting from his hand all food and all circumstances. The question of whether we are thankful takes decisive precedence even over the question of whether we live or die. The ground of Christian gratitude is that "we are the Lord's." Whatever we do, he remains the Lord, and whether or not we acknowledge his possession of us by giving thanks, the fact remains that all things come from him (1 Cor. 3:21-23).

Viewed in these terms gratitude is inseparable from faith. In the light of Romans 1:21 and Romans 14 we could emend 14:23 to read: "Whatever does not proceed from gratitude is sin." Like faith, gratitude is genuine only as a relation between yourself and God (Rom. 14:22). It is genuine only if all are "fully convinced in their own minds" (Rom. 14:5). It respects the fact that God has welcomed those whom we feel bound, even on religious grounds, to despise (Rom. 14:3). It is wholly contradicted by any action that causes "the ruin of one for whom Christ died" (Rom. 14:15). Thus can all Christian duties be subsumed under the demand to honor God as God by giving thanks. The unity of the church can be seen as embodied in the activity of glorifying God with one voice (Rom. 15:5). And the mission of the church can be described as the method by which we, through enabling others to "glorify God for his mercy" (Rom. 15:9), participate in the multiplication of thanksgiving to the glory of God (2 Cor. 4:15).

Thus far we have limited our exposition chiefly to Romans. Veteran students of Paul's Epistles will be aware that even greater use of thankfulness is made in other letters, and that these other letters support and enlarge the argument we have advanced. In 1 Thessalonians 5:12-22, the giving of thanks is shown to penetrate the widest range of Christian duties. In Philippians 4:4-7 it is basic to the joy, confidence and peace that belong to those who are "in the Lord." In 1 Corinthians 10:23–11:1 it is the link between liberty and love, which enables the apostle to affirm, without contradiction, that his liberty can never be determined by another's scruples and that he tries to please all in everything. In 2 Corinthians 4, thanksgiving is both the source and the result of the process of "being given up to death for Jesus' sake, so that the life of Jesus may be made visible" (2 Cor. 4:11).

But we must return to Romans and bring this chapter to a close by reiterating two observations. In the first place, the apostle's sense of debt and his sense of gratitude are not only perfectly compatible but virtually identical. It is not an accident that his assertion of indebtedness to Greeks and barbarians comes within his opening thanksgiving (Rom. 1:8-17). Nor is it a coincidence that his treatment of bitter controversy in Romans 14 should bring into conjunction the activity of thanksgiving and the actuality of mutual indebtedness. In both passages the grateful acknowledgment of debt to Christ is channeled through the honoring of the debt to the wise and the foolish, the weak and the strong.

In the second place, it is clear that, to Paul, one's status as a debtor and thanker is immediately and totally translated into missionary motivation. The mode and motive of giving thanks can be nothing else but a participation in Christ's ministry to the world. And Christ gave to this ministry such a form that indebtedness to him can be honored only by indebtedness to those who do not as yet give thanks to God. As an apostle, Paul may have received obligations that could be fulfilled only by his uniquely apostolic work and not by all believers. If so, as an apostle he was charged with persuading all disciples to recognize their own obligation to extend grace "to more and more people" (2 Cor. 4:15). His debt was no greater than theirs. Their obligation to serve Christ by serving others was no less inclusive, no less demanding, than his. *Missionary* motivation, consequently, is not intrinsically different from the motivation expected of all slaves of Christ. Nor can the missionary task be segregated and assigned to a selected few within the church. If there is a difference between the church and the world, it is a difference between those who do and those who do not honor God as God, and this very difference should make those who do give thanks recognize that they are deeply and permanently in debt to the others. And if we are converted from life on one side of the line to life on the other, the change will be most authentically indicated by the emergence of a radically new indebtedness and thankfulness. For we, too, are debtors "both to Greeks and to barbarians, both to the wise and to the foolish." Were our gratitude to God to take the form of recognizing our debt to the world, we would have to draw afresh the boundary between church and world. And every shift in that boundary would force a revision in all of our thinking concerning missions.

21

The Hymn
(Philippians)

T

One of the most astute aphorisms to have come from the pen of Amos N. Wilder is this:

> Before the message there must be the vision, before the sermon the hymn, before the prose the poem.[1]

That aphorism applies point by point to the prose and the sermon of Paul's letter to the Philippians. At the core of this letter one finds a literary construction that is certainly poetic, probably hymnic, and possibly the fruit of prophetic vision. I refer, of course, to Philippians 2:6-11. Along with thanksgiving and mission, the hymn represents the response in gratitude of the churches to the gifts of the Messiah—a hymn that is both itself a gift and a response to God's gifts. In this concluding chapter I wish to sketch the possible influences of that hymn on the perspectives and structure of the letter as a whole. Among those influences I will include the possible results of the singing of that hymn in the fledgling Christian community.

PRELIMINARY THESES

The first thesis is that the poetic construction in Philippians 2:6-11 may be viewed as an early Christian hymn.[2] A second and less widely recognized thesis is that throughout the ancient Mediterranean world the creation of such hymns, with their striking coincidence of vision, poetry, and song, characterized the gift of prophecy. An excellent example of such coincidence is furnished by the Apocalypse of John. Here one needs only to glance at the Passion chorales in Revelation 5, those songs, set within the context of a heavenly vision, that celebrate in poetic rhythms the worthiness of the slain Lamb.

A third thesis is that the native habitat for these prophetic hymns was the liturgical gatherings of early Christian congregations. In Corinth, for instance, the apostle urged every member, on coming to meeting, to bring along a hymn (1 Cor. 14:26), even though the singing of those songs often produced bedlam. Of course, those Christians did not have the benefit of modern service books, so their songs must have reflected a spontaneity and flexibility evoked by the emergencies and excitements of the moment. There must have been a great variety of "psalms, hymns, and spiritual songs" in the Gentile churches. The author of Colossians and Ephesians was confident that "the word of Christ" could be heard through such singing and that "the peace of Christ" could invade the church through its music (Col. 3:15-17; Eph. 5:15-20). In such singing, the voices of several singers were fused—the voices of God, Christ, and the Spirit, along with the voices of the congregation.

A fourth thesis is that when these poetic strophes are viewed as a hymn, that hymn must be viewed as originating earlier than the letter in which it is now found. It is unlikely that the author of the letter should have created so carefully balanced a poem simply for the purpose of inserting it within a prosaic dialogue dealing with other matters. Hymns are usually composed for communal use in worship and not for a teacher bent on making polemical points or enforcing moral imperatives. Those very stylistic features that mark this structure as hymnic presuppose an origin prior to the writing of the letter.

A brief detour is needed now before specifying a fifth thesis. The question of how the hymn was used in this letter can be separated from the question of its authorship. As scholars know, the matter of authorship is vigorously debated. The origin of the hymn has been assigned to a Jewish-Christian church, to a Hellenistic-Christian church, and even to a non-Christian Gnostic cult. However that may be, I am concerned with only one moment in the hymn's history—the moment when Paul was writing this letter. The only extant version of the hymn is found here, and it appears here only because Paul found it useful for his own purposes.

But can we now say anything about its origin before it was embodied in this letter? I think we can, and this is my fifth thesis. The hymn was used in a Christian congregation where every tongue was engaged in confessing "that Jesus Christ is Lord, to the glory of God the Father." But can this context be made even more specific? Only by conjecture, but in some situations conjectures are better than silence. In which Pauline church had it been used? Presumably Paul had been present, if not as author, at least as one of the singers. Two congregations offer the best options. One option is the small community where Paul was writing, comprising "the friends who are with me," including such trusted workers as Timothy and Epaphroditus, and "the saints . . . of the emperor's house" (Phil. 4:21, 22). In this case, the singing had been quite recent, and the libretto was fresh in Paul's mind. The words would have received emotional force from his imprisonment experience, whether in Rome, Caesarea, or, as I think is more likely, Ephesus.

The second option would be the community of "the saints . . . in Philippi" to whom Paul was writing. They had shared in Paul's suffering, first in Philippi itself (Phil. 1:29, 30) and more recently, through Epaphroditus, in the prison from which Paul was writing. In this case, perhaps some months had elapsed since the apostle and converts had sung it together. But there had been frequent interchange between them, and the period would have been short enough for the words to be remembered by both the apostle and his church. If this option is taken seriously, it would help to account for Paul's placing of the hymn at the very center of his letter. It is not irrelevant to recall that it was the singing of such a hymn at midnight that had triggered an earthquake in the Philippian jail (Acts 16:25-26).

Because a hymn fulfills distinctive functions, the interpretation should respect those functions. This is the final thesis. This Passion chorale, like many other early hymns, had a confessional component. It voiced a prophetic disclosure ("Therefore God also highly exalted") and a communal response ("confess that Jesus Christ is Lord"). This creedal role was clearly vital; yet, interpreters should not mistake the hymn for carefully formulated doctrine or for a test of faith. The hymn has often been distorted by an overemphasis on dogmatic substance; music is not the place to look for theological precision. So, too, early Christian hymns often fulfilled historical functions by epitomizing the story of Jesus, giving an overview of his vocation as a slave of God, from its invisible beginnings to its invisible ending. Yet, it would be a mistake to interpret the song as if it were historical in the same sense as the account in Acts of Paul's journey to Rome.

In similar fashion the hymn was designed to exert moral pressure on the singers. One can hardly read the urgent appeals in the preceding and succeeding paragraphs and deny the presence of this function. Yet, interpreters should not construe the moral injunctions in quite the same way as they view a list of commandments. The hymn was much more than a bland suggestion that because Jesus had been humble his followers must become humble. The hymn functioned in such a way as to shape the "mind" of the congregation and to clarify its sense of vocation. Emerging from deep levels of communal experience, the song articulated in both verbal and musical terms a rich cargo of nonverbal affections and emotions. It elicited memories that were relevant to meeting current dilemmas and dangers. The hymn assumes that the story of Jesus is prototypical of the story of the Messiah's family. By singing it the congregation affirmed a hidden conjunction between God's exaltation of Jesus and God's design for all things. Interpreters must seek to do justice to its multiple motifs: confessional, historical, moral, liturgical, and existential. Like all authentic music, the hymn encouraged participation at a level beyond the reach of analysis, where the "mind" of Philippian saints was being shaped.

2:6	Though he was in the form of God,
	[he] did not regard equality with God
	as something to be exploited,
2:7	but emptied himself,
	taking the form of a slave,
	being born in human likeness.
	And being found in human form,
2:8	he humbled himself
	and became obedient to the point of death—
	even death on a cross.
2:9	Therefore God also highly exalted him
	and gave him the name
	that is above every name,
2:10	so that at the name of Jesus
	every knee should bend,
	in heaven and on earth and under the earth,
2:11	and every tongue should confess
	that Jesus Christ is Lord,
	to the glory of God the Father.

THE HYMN AND THE AUTOBIOGRAPHY

The singing of the hymn concentrated attention on the action of two subjects: first Christ and then God. The hymn first pictured the downward movement of Christ through two stages—his becoming a slave and then his obedience in death on the cross. It then celebrated the action of God, first in exalting Christ and then in securing all creation's subjection to him. The hymn preserved a basic symmetry between a beginning that referred to equality with God, a center that pivots on God's own "therefore," and an ending in the glory of God. Only after it is recognized as a *theo*logical hymn should this be called a *christo*logical one.

Now we must ask where lie the correlations with the story of the apostle. First of all, Jesus' action in taking the form of a slave corresponds to Paul's view of himself as a slave of Christ (Phil. 1:1). In his salutation, Paul stressed this role by omitting the usual reference to himself as an apostle. In this instance he refused to advance any claim to authority except as such a slave. Furthermore, Paul's movement downward passed through two stages. In the first he had divested himself of all advantages that had accrued to him in earlier life: "confidence in the flesh . . . a Hebrew born of Hebrews . . . as to zeal, a persecutor . . . as to righteousness under the law, blameless" (Phil. 3:4-6). When he had become a slave he had counted all such gains as loss. There was, of course, a distinction between the *status quo ante* of the two slaves. For Jesus this was the "form of God"; for Paul it was "a righteousness of my own that comes from the law" (Phil. 3:9). But there remained a significant correlation of direction, a downward movement from the highest conceivable status toward total voluntary deprivation, a self-humbling (Phil. 2:8; 3:21) in which all former privileges and securities had been voluntarily surrendered in obedience to God.

The correlation extended to a second stage, where the two descriptions were virtually identical—that is, each slave carried obedience so far as to die. The second slave speaks unambiguously of his own death: "I want to know Christ . . . and the sharing of his sufferings by becoming like him in his death" (Phil. 3:10). Paul's death takes the same form as Jesus' death. At the time of writing there was only one difference: Jesus had already died, Paul had not. Even so, Paul considered it far better for him "to depart and be with Christ" (Phil. 1:23). He urged his readers to rejoice with him when the time should come for his life to be poured out "as a libation over the sacrifice and the offering of your faith" (Phil.

2:17). So for Paul this second stage covered his vocation from the time he had become a slave to the time of his obedience to death. And this stage required continuing divestment of every conceivable advantage. He chose to forget everything that lay behind, including not only his status as a Pharisee but also every accomplishment as an apostle, all the results of the gift of the Spirit. Such renunciation was seen as an intrinsic mark of maturity (Phil. 3:13-15).

It is sometimes argued that the second strophe in the hymn (God's action in exalting his slave) has little linkage to the rest of the letter. That argument, however, runs counter to extensive correlations to the autobiography. It was through this exaltation that God had issued the "heavenly call" to the apostle (Phil. 3:14). It was through knowing the power of the resurrection that Paul would receive whatever strength needed for him to share in Christ's sufferings. And it was through becoming like Jesus in his dying that Paul expected to attain the resurrection (Phil. 3: 10, 11). God's action in exalting Jesus had given this slave both the power to die and the assurance of reunion through death with the other slave.

The correlation extends even beyond such reunion. According to the hymn, the plan of God found its completion in the subjection of all things to Christ. Now it was in that very subjection that Paul expected his own story to end. "He will change the body of our humiliation to be like the body of his glory, by the power which enables him to subject all things to him" (Phil. 3:21, my translation). To share the sufferings of Christ was to share in his subjection and thus to form a single body with him. To gain Christ by dying was to be found in him. Unity in the one body was accomplished when one slave by his sufferings confessed the other slave as Lord, to the glory of the one Father. Nothing could be more congruent with the triumphant conclusion of the hymn.

Paul detected other signs of such subjection. Just as the hymn helped him to face his own death with courage and joy, so also it elicited similar courage and joy among the choir as a whole. Indeed, the singing itself became a way of expressing this courage and joy, a motif not at all rare among early Christian hymns. Paul also detected positive results of his own imprisonment. It had produced positive effects among his captors (Phil. 1:13) as well as among his coworkers, including former members of Caesar's household. He hailed both of these reactions as signs of the advance of the gospel, evidence of God's power to subject all things to the slave Lord. To the extent that the hymn defined the core of the gospel, its singing by slaves and prisoners achieved a role in the strategies by which that gospel spread.

THE HYMN AND THE POLEMIC

As Paul discerned various synonymous parallels between the hymn and his own story, so, too, he discerned various antithetical parallels between the hymn and the stance of his opponents. This letter is marked by an explosion of anger against those adversaries. So we raise the question of whether the hymn exerted any influence on the ways in which Paul visualized that conflict. The antithesis reached its sharpest thrust in the double reference to the cross. In the hymn the nadir of the downward movement was death on the cross as a measure of the Messiah's slavery. In sharp contrast Paul spoke of his adversaries as "enemies of the cross of Christ" (Phil. 3:18), presumably because they still viewed such a death as something to be avoided at all costs.

Paul's expletives (Phil. 3:2-4) would not have been so vitriolic had those enemies not been Christians and apparently leaders within the Philippian church. At the outset the letter plunged its readers into the recognition of strong partisanship and jealousy among rival leaders (Phil. 1:15), all of whom claimed a degree of authority over the fledgling congregation. It is entirely possible that these leaders had sung the hymn with Paul at previous meetings of the church. If so, that would have given Paul a special incentive for citing the hymn in his attack on them. He did not call them enemies of Christ, for, after all, they proclaimed Christ, and the apostle reluctantly accepted that as a commendation (Phil. 1:18). Rather, he called them enemies of the cross, the cross that marked the decisive transition between the two strophes of the hymn, and, indeed, between the two ages.

We have noted the two stages in the descent of Christ and Paul. As Paul saw things, these leaders had failed to share fully in either stage. Unlike Christ, these enemies, on becoming believers, had stopped short of renouncing circumcision and the degree of security and superiority it conferred over others. They had not treated as garbage their earlier achievements of righteousness under the law. They continued to cherish the glory inherent in their former status and required others to seek the same preferments. They did not accept complete self-humiliation as the mark of a slave, nor did they encourage others to begin their discipleship as slaves.

It is not strange, then, that they refused to share in the second stage of the Messiah's descent. In Paul's view, this disqualified them from exercising authority over other believers. Their mind-set was the test; by giving preference to self-interest they failed that test (Phil. 3:19). The apostle considered suffering for Christ a gift from God: "He has graciously granted you the privilege not only of believing in Christ, but of suffering for him as well" (Phil. 1:29). These leaders did not welcome shame as such a gift. But for Paul the hymn signified that a voluntary sharing in suffering marked the boundary between salvation and destruction; enemies of the cross could not escape that destruction (Phil. 3:19).

A case in point was their reaction to Paul's imprisonment. For one thing, Paul's absence gave them a welcome chance to enhance their own authority over the congregation. For another, they exploited the reports of Paul's disgrace as evidence of the superiority of their own wisdom and strategy. To them, his foolhardiness discredited the faith and impeded the work of evangelism, and they urged the church to forgo such dangerous exploits. In response, Paul viewed their arguments as efforts to "increase my suffering in my imprisonment" (Phil. 1:17). In all probability, these leaders had found added ammunition in the fate of Epaphroditus. In an earlier burst of loyalty to Paul, the church had sent this member to help Paul in his troubles, a move by which they accepted complicity in Paul's "guilt." We must remember that the charges against him were serious enough to threaten capital punishment (Phil. 1:20). Sure enough, disaster had almost struck down this emissary from Philippi; he had narrowly escaped death (Phil. 2:30). The reactions in Philippi were so intense that Paul felt it wise to send their deacon home, both to relieve the anxiety of his friends and, perhaps, to thwart Paul's adversaries.

To sum up, then, because these leaders were unwilling to share the body of humiliation, they forfeited any claim to share in the body of glory (Phil. 3:21). As a result they could share neither the courage nor the joy from the kind of obedience the hymn celebrated. They had challenged Paul's authority, and he returned the favor. To Paul, authentic authority stemmed only from sharing in the Messiah's suffering. The suffering that validated Paul's authority invalidated theirs.

This may become clearer if we trace the hymn to one of its scriptural sources, the Genesis stories of creation. From other letters we know that Paul found it congenial to contrast two archetypical figures, the first Adam and the last (Rom. 5:12-21; 1 Cor. 15:45-50). The hymn echoes an awareness of that basic contrast, as demonstrated by at least four correlations.

1. The two Adams had comparable origins: "God created humankind [Adam] in his image" (Gen. 1:27); "He was in the form of God" (Phil. 2:6).
2. Both Adams had been tempted by the desire to be like God, but only one had succumbed to that temptation: "You will be like God, knowing good and evil" (Gen. 3:5); "[He] did not regard equality with God as something to be exploited" (Phil. 2:6).
3. Moved in opposite directions by their responses to temptation, the two Adams had based their actions on different appraisals of death, one accepting it and one rejecting: "You will not die" (Gen. 3:4); "[He] became obedient to the point of death" (Phil. 2:8).
4. Their contrasting actions justified contrasting verdicts from God— destruction and exaltation: "You are dust, and to dust you shall return" (Gen. 3:19); "Therefore God also highly exalted him" (Phil. 2:9).

Again we notice the distinction between the two stages in the Messiah's downward movement. First the becoming like Adam, and then the becoming unlike him.

These subtle correspondences would have been more obvious to Jewish-Christians than to Gentiles, and therefore more relevant to those leaders in Philippi who continued to prize circumcision and the achievement of legal righteousness (Phil. 3:2-6). By recalling to their minds the familiar stories of creation and fall, the hymn would have buttressed Paul's polemic and his warning that their fears of suffering were an omen of their destruction (Phil. 1:28; 3:19). By underscoring the bond between humiliation and glory as God defined them, the hymn clarified the essential contrast between the two Adams. To sing the hymn was to articulate the antithesis between Christ and these enemies of the cross. The antithetical parallelism reinforced the polemic.

THE HYMN AND THE EXHORTATION

Neither the autobiography nor the polemic, however, constituted the central purpose of the letter. That purpose was better revealed by the number and force of the exhortations. More than thirty such imperatives may be counted, a remarkable number for so brief a letter. In them Paul showed an intense concern for the morale, or better still, the "mind," of the saints in Philippi.

Those imperatives were typically absolute and uncompromising. With few exceptions (for example, Phil. 4:2), the exhortations appealed to the entire congregation as a single unit. They presupposed an involvement by the congregation in the same struggle as that of Paul (Phil. 1:30), a struggle entailing immediate risks of imprisonment and possible martyrdom.

The hymn was strategically placed near the center of the longest series of imperatives. From Philippians 1:27 on, the injunctions pointed ahead toward the hymn, every command being designed for those to whom God had given the grace to suffer for Christ's sake. From Philippians 2:12 to at least 3:1, the injunctions were grounded in the hymn, governed by the conjunction "therefore" in 2:12. This literary context thus made explicit what was only implicit within the hymn—that is, to believe in this slave Messiah was to suffer for him (Phil. 1:29). Both in preparing for the hymn and in drawing out its implications, Paul stressed the necessity for readers to choose between his acceptance of such suffering and his adversaries' avoidance of it (Phil. 1:28-30; 2:17-21).

This orientation of the exhortations becomes clear when one analyzes the injunctions that are repeated most frequently. For instance, the recurrent calls for unity provide silent evidence that the adversaries' challenge to Paul's authority had threatened such unity. So, too, the frequent commands to rejoice reflect that the adversaries had been exacerbating the anxieties of the congregation. Paul's many exhortations to the congregation to stand firm in the face of persecution testify to the temptations to be frightened by his opponents. The frequent use of the term "mind" (repeated ten times) makes it clear that the choice between two opposing mind-sets constituted the central issue of the letter.

Now we should look more closely at the correlations between the two strophes of the hymn and the exhortations. Most obvious, perhaps, is the parallelism between the two downward movements; to share in Christ was to share in this movement. Motivation for such movement stemmed from Christ, from love, from the Spirit, and from the fountain of mercies (Phil. 2:1, 2). Saints must give absolute priority to the needs of others, doing nothing from private ambition or self-concern. Their minds must be united to Christ's by a common humbleness (Phil. 2:3, 8).

Like the descent of Christ, theirs had two stages, the second of which still lay in the future (Phil. 2:12-18). They had not yet carried obedience so far as to die. The prospect of death had tended to demoralize them and to make them vulnerable to the arguments of the adversaries. So it had become more and more difficult for them to choose between the two minds. The implications of working out their own salvation (Phil. 2:12) had become more ominous; "fear and trembling" had become inescapable. Even so, confidence that God was at work at the roots of their desiring would enable them as God's children to hold firmly to the word of life as a word of salvation and not destruction.

In the definition of this salvation the letter established a link to the second strophe of the hymn. This link came to the surface near the end of Philippians 3, after the autobiography had shifted from the singular *I* to the plural *we* (Phil. 3:14, 15). The climax of thought was reached in Philippians 3:20, 21, which Lohmeyer recognized as a second hymnic construction.

> Our citizenship is in heaven;
> from there we also expect a Savior: the Lord Jesus Christ.
> He will transform the body of our humiliation
> to be conformed to the body of his glory
> by the power that also enables him
> to subject all things to himself. (my translation)

Solidarity in the single body of humiliation and glory marked the *telos* of the story for both Paul and the Philippians, in full accordance with the *telos* of the hymn in Philippians 2:6-11.

This essay at the outset recognized the creative work of E. Lohmeyer in his identification of Philippians 2:6-11 as a hymn. Many of his successors have acknowledged this debt, and a great debt it has proved to be. But there is also a debt to this scholar for a second discovery, one that is less frequently recognized. Lohmeyer was convinced that the central problem in this letter was the threat of martyrdom to both apostle and church.[3] So convinced was he of this that he made the issue of martyrdom the organizing principle for a detailed outline of the letter. In almost every verse he detected a justification for that outline. It is not necessary to follow his outline or to accept without qualification his word martyrdom, but later scholarship would have profited greatly if it had taken more seriously his emphasis on persecution as a central key to understanding the apostle's thought. To have observed that key would have inhibited the tendencies toward euphemistic perversions that have plagued interpretations of this letter. Paul's commands have been trivialized into moral attributes that are highly honored in conventional middle-class behavior. As a result, the command to rejoice has become virtually meaningless. Nothing so quickly insulates a reader from the steel-tough logic of this appeal sent from an Ephesian jail. Nothing so quickly reduces the range and power of the hymn. Lohmeyer's accent on martyr-dom cuts through such perversities of interpretation.

But is *martyrdom* the best term? It is true that for Paul martyrdom was a direct implication of the *therefore* of Philippians 2:9 and the *wherefore* of Philippians 2:12. It is true that the parallelisms, both synonymous and antithetical, between the hymn and the letter described radical obedi-ence to the martyr Messiah as the litmus test of discipleship. But as Paul interprets the hymn, the accent falls on the opposite reactions to the death of the Messiah. Given God's action in exalting this martyr, can the gospel be advanced by any other strategy than that of the Messiah? Does the prospect of suffering "in the Lord" evoke courage, firmness, and joy; or fear, caution, and dread? Does sharing in "the body of humiliation" define destruction or salvation? Lohmeyer rightly focuses attention on the danger of martyrdom. But Paul focused attention on the opposite reactions to that danger. And the singing of the hymn in Philippi would have encouraged the reactions Paul favored.

ADDENDUM

The following resources by the author are also relevant to those issues in biblical theology addressed in part 4:

"The Preface," in *Kierkegaard and the Bible: An Index* (Princeton Pamphlet #9, Princeton Theological Seminary, 1958), 3-13.

"The Vocation of the Church, Some Exegetical Clues," *Missiology* 5 (1997): 13-37.

"Video and Audio in the Church" in a volume in honor of John W. Snyder, *On Being the Church,* ed. Peter C. Erb (Waterloo, Ontario: Conrad, 1992), 11-26.

GLOSSARY
(specialized terms as they are used in this volume)

Alpha and Omega	the beginning and the end (the first and last letters in the Greek alphabet)
anabasis	a movement upward
anthropology	doctrines in theology dealing with the nature of the human being as created and redeemed by God
apocalypse	a prophetic vision or series of visions disclosing God's present and future struggles with his adversaries in heaven and on earth
Apocalypse, The	Greek title of the book of Revelation, reporting the visions of the prophet John
apostle	one sent from another with authority to deliver a message or mission in the name and with the authority of the sender; a member of the Twelve chosen and sent by Jesus to proclaim the news of God's kingdom
archaism	the survival of a word from the past that has lost its currency in the present
archegos	(Greek) a leader or ruler

archetype	an original pattern or model that shapes or controls all later examples or copies
bibliolatry	worship of the text of the Bible, literally interpreted
catholicity	a view or conviction that is potentially applicable to all humankind, universality
charismatic	a speech or action attributed to the presence and work of the Holy Spirit, at times including speaking in tongues and works of healing—related to the gifts of the Holy Spirit (Greek, *charismata*)
Christology	reflections and doctrines on the nature, person and work of Jesus as the Anointed One or Messiah
christophany	an appearance of Jesus after his exaltation to heaven
cosmology	the philosophical concept of the world, its space and time, its causality and freedoms
determinism	the doctrine that all events, including human beliefs and choices, are determined by laws of nature
ecclesiology	theological reflections and doctrines dealing with the origin, nature, and mission of the church (Greek, *ecclesia*)
ecumenical	the modern movement that seeks to promote the unity of Christian churches around the world
Emmanuel	a sign given to Israel that "God is with us" (Isa. 7:14; 8:4, 8, 10; Matt. 1:23)

epiphany	an appearance of a heavenly being
eschatology	views concerning the end or purpose of human history; as used by apostles and prophets, the disclosure of God's purposes in creation through the death and vindication of Jesus as Messiah
eschaton	(Greek) the end as measured by the fulfillment of God's purposes: "to him are all things" (Rom. 11:36)
Eucharist	Holy Communion or the Lord's Supper, the sacrament commemorating the last supper of Jesus with his disciples
exegesis	an analysis of a biblical text that aims to recover the thought of the original author or authors
existentialism	according to Rudolf Bultmann, the gift of freedom from determinism when, in response to the message of Jesus' death and resurrection, a believer becomes responsible for his own faith; the moment when authentic historicity triumphs over historicism
gnosis	(Greek) knowledge of spiritual world
hermeneutics	the principles and methods used for the interpretation of scripture
hierophany	a manifestation or appearance of the sacred
historicism	in the thought of Rudolf Bultmann, the story of the past viewed as determined by the laws of nature
historicity	viewed by Rudolf Bultmann as the realization of freedom from historicism when by faith in the gospel one shares in the transcendent freedom of God

historiography	the principles and methods of historical scholarship
incarnation	"the Word became flesh and lived among us" (John 1:14)
inclusio	the beginning and end of an unmarked long parenthesis in the literary structure of a biblical book
infinite qualitative distinction	when the distinction between God and his creation is seen to be both qualitative and infinite
kosmos	(Greek) world
Kreuzseligkeit	(German) the blessedness of the Cross
linguisticality	the view of Fuchs and Funk that the moment of faith should be seen as a linguistic event, verbal and not scriptural, grounded in the word of the preacher and not in the biblical event
logos	(Greek) word
Mariolatry	a veneration of the Virgin Mary in terms that are appropriate only for God
Messiah	one anointed by God and sent to reveal his will and save his people; Jesus viewed as fulfilling this role
metaphysics	the department of philosophy that deals with ultimate reality, above and beyond the physical world
militia dei	(Latin) army of God

mythology	a symbolic and imaginative language that expresses a community's views of the whole of reality—natural and supernatural, visible and invisible
ontology	systematic thinking about ultimate *Being* as the source of all things: "From him . . . are all things" (Rom. 11:36)
Paraclete	the person of the Holy Spirit working as advocate and intercessor
paradigm	the pattern of presuppositions, perceptions and procedures that shapes and directs the investigations into any reality
parousia	the coming and/or the presence of the Messiah
Passover	a festival celebrating the deliverance from Egypt of Israel, with new meanings for the church accruing from the Last Supper and the crucifixion of Jesus
Pentecost	A Christian festival commemorating the gift of the Holy Spirit in fulfillment both of prophecies to Israel and the promises of Jesus (Acts 2:1-42)
prevenience	the divine will that precedes the human response of rejection or faith
primordial	the original or elemental form from which all later forms are derived
protological	the original or first instance of a reality
rationalism	the acceptance of human reason as supreme authority in knowledge, belief and conduct, rejecting the possibility of divine revelation

reflection and double-reflection	Kierkegaard distinguished three movements: the unreflective self; the self whose reflection turns entirely inward; the self turned entirely outward in gratitude to its hidden source
relativism	the theory that all human judgments vary according to persons, groups, times and places, in such a degree as to exclude the possibility of objective or final values and truths
revelation	God's disclosure by way of vision or word to those chosen by him concerning his purposes for them and for others through them
Satan	the devil or the evil one; in heaven the ultimate source of opposition to God's authority and on earth the deceiver of God's people and the ruler of demons
secularism	a culture, a society, and a point of view dominated by an atheistic conception of historical process
soteriological	pertaining to salvation
stigmata	marks resembling the wounds of the crucified body of Christ
teleological	theological doctrines dealing with the end (*telos*), viewed either as the end of time or as the fulfillment of God's purposes for his creation
transcendence	the vast invisible realm that is not accessible to human observation or reducible to the categories of thought at our disposal; eternal not temporal, heavenly not earthly, immortal not mortal
typology	systematic analysis of the types of literary images and symbols in scripture

NOTES

1. The Musician Versus the Grammarian

1. Karl Geiringer, *Johann Sebastian Bach: The Culmination of an Era*, in collaboration with Irene Geiringer (New York: Oxford University Press, 1966), 83.

2. Jan Chiapusso, *Bach's World* (Bloomington: Indiana University Press, 1968), 13.

3. Geiringer, *Bach*, 83.

4. Leo Schrade, *Bach: The Conflict Between the Sacred and the Secular* (New York: Merlin, 1946), 114.

5. Hans T. David and Arthur Mendel, eds., *The Bach Reader: A Life of Johann Sebastian Bach in Letters and Documents* (New York: W. W. Norton, 1945), 137-49, 152-58.

6. Chiapusso, *Bach's World*, 266f.

7. Helene Werthemann, *Die Bedeutung der alttestamentlichen Historien in Johann Sebastian Bachs Kantaten* (Tubingen: Mohr, 1959, 31. [My translation.])

8. W. H. Scheide, *J. S. Bach as a Biblical Interpreter*, Pamphlet 8 (Princeton: Princeton Theological Seminary, 1952), 9f.

9. Joseph Sittler, *Essays on Nature and Grace* (Philadelphia: Fortress, 1972), 81.

10. Quoted in ibid., 127-28.

11. See Karl Barth, *Word of God and Word of Man*, trans. Douglas Horton (Grand Rapids: Zondervan, 1935), 60.

12. J. A. Ernesti, *Elementary Principles*, trans. M. Stuart, 4th ed. (Andover, Mass.: Allen, Morill, and Wardwell, 1842), 55f., 83f.

13. Albert Cook Outler, *Who Trusts in God: Musings on the Meaning of Providence* (New York: Oxford, 1968), 6.

2. THE TRANSCENDENCE OF GOD AND HUMAN HISTORICITY

1. A. E. Loen, *Secularization: Science Without God?*, trans. Margaret Kohl (London: SCM, 1967), 10.

2. Thomas S. Kuhn, *The Structure of Scientific Revolutions* (Chicago: University of Chicago Press, 1962).

3. Thomas J. J. Altizer, *The New Apocalypse: The Radical Christian Vision of William Blake* (East Lansing: Michigan State University Press, 1967), xiv.

4. Loen, *Secularization*, 7, 10.

5. Ibid., 92.

6. Rudolf Bultmann, *History and Eschatology* (Edinburgh: University Press, 1957), 78.

7. Cf. ibid., 138.

8. Ibid.

9. Cf. ibid., 96-97.

10. Ibid., 139.

11. Ibid., 154.

12. Cf. H. Ott in Robert W. Funk, *Language, Hermeneutic, and Word of God: The Problem of Language in the New Testament and Contemporary Theology* (New York: Harper & Row, 1966), 110-11 and, also, in Charles W. Kegley, *The Theology of Rudolf Bultmann* (New York: Harper & Row, 1966), 52-57.

13. Funk, *Language, Hermeneutic, and Word of God*, 12.

14. Ernst Fuchs, *Studies of the Historical Jesus*, trans. Andrew Scobie (Naperville, Ill.: A. R. Allenson, 1964), 38-40, 47.

15. Ibid., 43.

16. Cf. Amos N. Wilder, whose *Language of the Gospel* (New York: Harper & Row, 1964), is free of the linguistic reductions I find in Fuchs and Funk.

17. Julian N. Hartt, *A Christian Critique of American Culture* (New York: Harper & Row, 1967), 144.

3. CHRISTIAN ESCHATOLOGY AND HISTORICAL METHODOLOGY

1. Walther Eichrodt, *Biblical Authority for Today* (S.C.M. Press, 1951), 192.

2. Ibid., 183.

3. Ibid., 182.

4. Dorothy Sayers, the most noted mystery writer of the time (and to some readers, even better known for her theological audacity), died in 1957, the year in which this chapter had its origin.

5. Ibid., 179.

6. Though this statement was first made in 1957, theology has not yet in 2002 reached such a consensus.

7. Eichrodt, 273-83.

4. BIBLICAL ONTOLOGY AND ECCLESIOLOGY

1. Patrick C. Rodger and Lukas Vischer, eds., *The Fourth World Conference on Faith and Order* (London: S.C.M. Press, 1964), 43-44.

2. Walter M. Abbott, S.J., ed., *Constitution on the Church: Lumen Gentium. The Documents of Vatican II* (New York: America Press, 1966).

3. The reader should note that this paragraph represents a significant addition to the original publication.

7. THE OFFENSE (MATTHEW)

1. Roberto Salvini, *Michelangelo* (New York: Mayflower, 1981), 130-31.

2. Ibid., 120.

3. William W. How, "O Word of God Incarnate," *The Pilgrim Hymnal* (Boston: Pilgrim, 1958), 252.

9. THE CREATIVE WORD (JOHN)

1. This strain in John's thought has for centuries been used to fan the flames of anti-Semitism, a tragic betrayal of the Jew whose love for his people led to his death. The fact that John traced the violence back to Cain, acting under the instigation of the serpent, shows that his concern was with all such violence, with a universal human guilt. Compare my book *John, The Martyr's Gospel* (New York: Pilgrim Press, 1984), 24-36.

2. This grounding of thought in the Genesis story of creation-and-fall establishes a perspective that transcends later ethnic and religious con-

flicts. Adam, Eve, and Cain were neither Jews nor Gentiles but archetypal representatives of all races and religions. For the more immediate relevance of this passage to the historical situation faced by Jesus, compare my essay, "Writing on the Ground: The Puzzle in John 8:1-11," *Horizons in Biblical Theology* 24 (1991): 23-37.

11. THE FAMILY (HEBREWS)

1. Amos N. Wilder, *Theopoetics* (Philadelphia: Fortress Press, 1976), 71. All nonbiblical quotations in this chapter are from this book.
2. Ibid., 94.
3. Ibid., 6.
4. Ibid., 7.
5. Ibid., 28.
6. Ibid., 75.
7. Ibid., 8.
8. Ibid., 12.
9. Ibid., 11.

13. THE BOND (2 CORINTHIANS)

1. In these paradoxes Paul sought in his own way to translate "the mystery of the cross and its glory in a way that would speak to all," Amos N. Wilder, *Theopoetics* (Philadelphia: Fortress, 1976), 12. By indicating the physical and moral dimensions of the Passion story, Paul also indicated its historical, cosmic, and mythical dimensions as well; compare Wilder, 91-100. Using the principles of synonymous parallelism to analyze these paradoxes in 2 Cor. 6:8-10, we find as congruent to the notion of dying the following: impostors, unknown, punished, sorrowful, poor, and having nothing.

14. THE PEACE (THE NEW TESTAMENT)

1. This chapter is dedicated to the memory of my father, George L. Minear, who graduated from the Boston University School of Theology in 1901.

15. THE HOPE (1 PETER)

1. J. Ellul, *Hope in Time of Abandonment* (New York: Seabury Press, 1973), 10.
2. Ibid., 6.
3. John V. Taylor, *The Go-Between God* (London: SCM Press, 1972), 75.
4. Roland de Pury, *Journal from My Cell* (New York: Harper, 1946), 11.
5. Ibid., 21.
6. Ibid., 23.
7. Ibid., 61.

16. THE SPIRIT
(ROMANS, LUKE, MARK, AND REVELATION)

1. Within the World Council of Churches, this study by the Faith and Order Commission, between 1952 and 1964, broke down many doctrinal rigidities and encouraged greater flexibility in ecclesiological attitudes. So, too, in the shaping of the first two chapters of *Lumen Gentium* at Vatican II, this same variety of images helped to open some of the windows of which Pope John XXII had spoken.

19. THE THANKSGIVING (THE NEW TESTAMENT)

1. A form of this chapter was prepared initially for inclusion in a memorial volume to honor the centennial of Søren Kierkegaard's death and to show gratitude for his sustained and profound understandings of the biblical text. At the time I had been engaged in preparing an index of Kierkegaard's references and allusions to the Bible, work that gave me a profound respect for his exegetical insight. His gratitude was grounded in and shaped by his daily encounters with the biblical witness.
2. *The Point of View for My Work as an Author*, trans. W. Lowrie (Oxford, 1939), 68f.
3. *Concluding Unscientific Postscript*, trans. D. F. Swenson and W. Lowrie (Princeton, 1941), 61.

4. *Repetition* trans. W. Lowrie (Princeton, 1941), 110ff.; *Edifying Discourses*, trans. D. F. and L. M. Swenson (Augsburg, 1943-46), II:7ff.

5. *Edifying Discourses*, I:35ff.; II:27, 45ff.; *For Self-Examination and Judge for Yourselves*, trans. W. Lowrie (Oxford, 1941), 228ff.

6. *Edifying Discourses*, I:139ff.; III:95ff.; *The Gospel of Suffering*, trans. D. F. and L. M. Swenson (Augsburg, 1948), 125ff.

7. *Christian Discourses*, trans. W. Lowrie (Oxford, 1939), II:284ff.

8. *Edifying Discourses*, II:27ff.; *Gospel of Suffering*, 59; *Concept of Dread*, trans. W. Lowrie (Princeton, 1944), 81.

9. *Gospel of Suffering*, 44ff.; *Christian Discourses*, 228ff.

10. *Concept of Dread*, 134.

11. Ibid., 102.

12. Compare *Concluding Unscientific Postscript*, 124f.; *Journals*, trans. A. Dru (Oxford, 1938), 369.

13. *Point of View*, 88-90 note.

14. Ibid., 7, 8.

15. *Concluding Unscientific Postscript*, 124f.

16. *Edifying Discourses*, I:5.

17. *Concluding Unscientific Postscript*, 145.

18. Ibid., 75, 83.

19. Ibid., 239.

20. Ibid., 54.

21. *Edifying Discourses*, I:47; 1 Tim. 4:4.

22. *Concept of Dread*, 135.

23. Ibid., 102.

24. *Concluding Unscientific Postscript*, 116.

25. Ibid., 159.

26. *Works of Love*, trans. D. F. and L. M. Swenson (Princeton, 1946), 121.

27. Ibid., 120.

28. Ibid., 143.

29. Ibid., 146.

30. Ibid., 121.

31. *Concept of Dread*, 80; *Concluding Unscientific Postscript*, 271.

32. *Edifying Discourses*, 18.

33. *Point of View*, 66, 67.

21. THE HYMN (PHILIPPIANS)

1. *Theopoetics* (Philadelphia: Fortress, 1976), 1. See chapter 11 of this book for additional examples of the significance of Wilder's observations.

2. E. Lohmeyer, *Der Brief an der Philipper* (Gottingen: Vandenhoeck & Ruprecht, 1953), 90-99.

3. Ibid., 4-8.

SUBJECT INDEX

INDEX OF SELECTED SCRIPTURE REFERENCES